THE SIX-MONTH FIX

ADVENTURES IN RESCUING FAILING COMPANIES

Gary Sutton

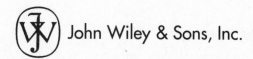 John Wiley & Sons, Inc.

Published by John Wiley & Sons, Inc., New York.
Published simultaneously in Canada.

This publication is designed to provide accurate and authoritative information in regard to the subject matter covered. It is sold with the understanding that the publisher is not engaged in rendering professional services. If professional advice or other expert assistance is required, the services of a competent professional person should be sought.

Library of Congress Cataloging-in-Publication Data:

Sutton, Gary.
    The six-month fix : adventures in rescuing failing companies / Gary Sutton.
      p. cm.
    Includes bibliographical references and index.
    ISBN 0-471-03626-9 (cloth : alk. paper)
      1. Corporate turnarounds.   2. Corporate reorganizations.   3. Business failures.
  I. Title: 6 month fix.   II. Title.

HD58.8 .S884 2001
658.4'063—dc21   2001024900

Printed in the United States of America

10 9 8 7 6 5 4 3 2

CONTENTS

INTRODUCTION

If you're the CEO of a struggling business, let's hope we never meet.

I'm a turnaround guy. When I arrive, you leave, and profits return. This book shows how we can avoid that unpleasantness.

You're probably smarter than me, undoubtedly know your industry better, and may be a superior leader. But I've fixed more businesses. I don't cling to unrealistic hopes or hesitate to change things. Any fresh set of eyes, not just mine, will simply do the rational and obvious things, getting results before those nasty creditors padlock your doors.

We outsiders, having seen it all before, free of your emotional baggage, find the fixes and do them with comfort and confidence. The process would nauseate you. This faltering child was yours. We discipline and save the kid. You and I, together, might celebrate this youth's graduation much later. But for now, stand aside.

To check my thin veneer of credibility, flip to Chapter 68. This gives audited or publicly reported performances on every single CEO, founder, or chairman's job I assumed from 1980 until *The Six-Month Fix* rolled off the presses in 2002. You'll see garbage hauling, satellite communications, forms marketing, retail advertising, aerospace manufacturing, printing, a private college, burglar alarm sales, plus a data storage business. It's nowhere near a perfect record, but every investor saw either losses vanish quickly or profits jump above their industry norms. A few basked in outrageous cash returns. Some was luck. Some wasn't. I'm not sure which was which, but the same basic tactics somehow worked every time.

Being the CEO du jour in eight different industries gave me an unusual perspective. Yup, I'm a mile wide and an inch deep. You think your business is unique from all others and most folks say that. You're all wrong. Sorry. The tactics described here work in all nonregulated businesses. How to use this book depends on who you are.

1. If you're a director, shareholder, or executive of a company that's losing money at a rate that'll bankrupt you within the year, please, do not read the whole book. You don't have that kind of time, pal. Go straight to the turnaround chapters titled in **boldface.** These tell how to stop the bleeding. Follow them and within six months your losses will be gone, your cash stabilized, and employees shall smile once again. Really. If you're the CEO, however, you'll have been "made available to industry" in this process and should be doing other things. But your stock will rebound, so chin up.

2. If you're breaking even, or making modest money but losing ground to competitors, skip the turnaround chapters and go straight to the chapters headlined with *italics*. These 52 management lessons read easy. Each ends with three action steps. Commit your management to executing one chapter a week. No more, no less. At the end of twelve months your company will coin money and great things will be within your grasp. But my fears are greatest for you break-even people, even more than for those hemorrhaging cash. The impending doom that motivates losers is absent from your comfy, mediocre existence. Crank it up a notch.

3. If you're making sinful and growing profits, good show! (I'm thrilled you bought the book, but why?) You can enjoy this more than the other readers. Try a dollop or two of the secret sauces when you have time, and if you feel like it. Your reward is that you get to read straight through, starting at the beginning and shuffling straight through to the end. The turnaround chapters, which are in boldface titles and longer, are mixed with the profit-boosting sections, which are italicized and shorter. This gives you changes of pace as you go. Hey, I cater to winners.

Stopping losses and boosting profits, by the way, are day and night, hot and cold, yin and yang. Think of turnarounds as **blacksmith work,** throwing off sparks, energy surrounded by clanging noises while the turnaround manager flails away, reshaping some stressed iron. Think of boosting profits as *watchmaker tasks,* with quiet discipline, thought, and small, careful moves by a professional manager. Both shape the metal, but these two moments demand different mentalities, speed, and leadership.

Saving your business requires bringing in an outsider, often a turnaround professional. Some are birds who work for creditors while others are fish who toil for shareholders. Even battle-scarred professionals remain strangely unconscious of this distinction, but these folks, unaware of the difference themselves, think and act uniquely without knowing, and share few objectives. You'll learn the difference here. The turnaround sections also tell how to identify frauds.

Oh yes, there are frauds aplenty. Anytime a board or owners are paralyzed by steep losses, the one-trick ponies and unemployed CEOs come a-calling, soon followed by those firms who specialize in bailing out the seven-piece-suit lenders from their nervousness, getting that debt remortgaged to tougher guys while the quivering client corpse gasps for air, stripped of any prayer for equity recovery within the current ice age. You'll learn how they maneuver you into this.

Another trap, common as a cold, is that even the top turnaround managers are wholly incapable of leading a business after it's fixed. These Cinderellas stay too long at the dance, and get ugly after midnight. Chapter 17 peeks at those embarrassments.

Don't think about this turnaround stuff for a second if you're above break-even.

What you need then are the building blocks that enhance profits. Most turnarounds fail after they rebound. They celebrate prematurely and forget to shift into the next gear. That's why the 52 profit-enhancing chapters are included. They'll guide you after the fix, and lift your company to new heights.

This part, rebuilding profits, takes a full year easily. The turnaround itself happens in six months.

If that sounds too fast to be true, you are part of the problem. There's no reason to dally. It'll be traumatic and requires two management makeovers, but converting a loser into a winner is worth some turbulence.

Winning beats losing. Duh. Watching your employees sniff a breeze of success feels better than burying everybody under six feet of losses, food for worms, sucking stale air in a corporate coffin, dazed and glassy-eyed. Okay, okay, a single failure might not destroy all careers forever, but it takes years to recover reputation, self-esteem, and lifestyle. And that's not all. Customers suffer, shareholders get hurt, bankers gobble too many Tums; since you pay less tax, you don't even cover your fair share of road repairs, school costs, or the military protection we all enjoy, you parasite.

Losses are malignant. Let's stop 'em.

FIRST STOP THE BLEEDING

W e're not talking brain surgery.

Getting a loser to break even should take six months or less. It's gut-wrenching. The turnaround happens best, and probably *only* happens, under somebody new. The outsider's detachment saves time and grief.

You must stop the bleeding before anything else. Management can't manage until the business is self-sufficient. Investors, bankers, and creditors assume the right to help management when an outfit is losing money, and that kind of help doesn't.

Oh, and please, don't try to sell your way out of losses. Knock down your costs first.

We never control revenues or margins, do we? Sure, we try, but our customers have more than a small effect on sales and markups. We can always squeeze our costs further down. Unless yours is that rare business where added sales create no added expense, or that bizarre situation where bringing in new business raises average prices, then don't pretend more sales will solve your core problem.

Forget, for now, the grand plan, your cure-all product, that huge new order from the attractive but unknown client. Just stop the negative cash flow. Work with what you've got. Then you can begin to think rationally about the next move, and you'll do it smarter and on your own schedule . . . after you're breaking even. And you'll analyze that next risk more carefully, since finally there's a real business to lose. That bolder thought may not look as promising when you've gotten off your money-losing belly and are finally kneeling at break-even.

It takes two things to stop your losses. Two. Dos. Zwei. Futatsu. Let's read the actual annual report from a 1995 turnaround, and you may detect those two moves.

September 11, 1995

Dear Knight Protective Shareholders:

Here's the last annual report. Your low expectations and my dumb luck made this year a winner, and it seemed timely to sell. So we did.

Knight netted over $2 million from operations, peddled the monitoring contracts to Protection One, sold the trademarks, a patent, and leasehold improvements to an AT&T distributor, then licensed both the industry's leading manufacturer and marketer with another two new patents for an added $12 million.

After taxes and smelling salts you received checks with many zeros and commas. Here's a second one. This is probably the end, but depending on some late bills, you might get another. That'll cover a burger and fries. No Cokes. Sorry.

A trifle of this bounty fell my way, but now déjà vu repeats itself all over again once more, and next year this CEO hopes to work for food somewhere new. Anywhere. Please.

Hence the immodest report.

In the unlikely event I've failed to cure your insomnia with my biased view of Knight's history, may I now?

This alarm company lost $3.5 million in 1989, $8 million in the prior few years, and possessed just enough cash for six more payrolls when I became CEO in 1990, provided no silly payments were made, such as rent or utilities.

I did not face excessive competition for the job.

Our California economy conspired to make any recovery tougher, while average system prices plunged from $3,200 to $1,800, enhancing this insurmountable opportunity. Our chicken-hearted auditors declined to certify Knight as an ongoing concern the year I joined, while American General and Home Finance refused all new credit applications that were Knight-related.

Employee turnover hit 380% in 1989, three distributors sued Knight for fraud, the AARP commissioned independent tests which ranked our company's best products among the industry's worst; but as the highest priced, your company showed at least one kind of leadership. Knight's two largest shareholders, a Midwestern public pension fund and a Rocky Mountain partnership, added distractions by suing each other and threatening me between 1990 and 1994, spending $4 million in legal fees.

Their dispute? Who controlled Knight. Did each claim it? Nope. Both argued that the other side owned this sparkling gem.

There's more.

In my first Knight board meeting, the other directors seemed eccentric. Yeah, even to me. Perhaps it was the shouting match that developed between my new boss, the chairman, and myself. Perhaps it was the resolution he passed forbidding my say-so over any board expenses. Perhaps I displayed insufficient respect for this chairman's background as a former congressman, his billion-dollar public pension fund, the respected Republican governor who certified his books, and the prominent Democratic mayor who presided over his board of trustees through the eighties.

Naah! Scratch that. A trained chimp could hardly overlook this guy's flaws. His bipartisan support is everything we've come to expect from either flavor of politics.

So I made a pitch. The pension fund gave me their proxies and I fired the board, including their own chairman. Delicate surgery, that was.

One year later, this former chairman misplaced $67 million of the taxpayers' money. His upper body absorbed four 38-caliber slugs two weeks before the first public whitewashing was scheduled. Another ex-director now makes little rocks from big ones, courtesy of the Colorado penitentiary, the third was just indicted by the SEC, while a fourth filed for bankruptcy. World class board, eh?

No kidding. I couldn't make up this stuff.

How did it affect Knight's employees? I'm delighted to report we discovered entrepreneurs in our group. The northern California installers, for example, displayed this by burglarizing customers. The Orange County office boosted margins with cocaine sales. The recurring revenue after an initial snort apparently was more predictable than monthly monitoring fees from burglar alarms. Oh, and our two top vice presidents had set up a dummy corporation that, interestingly, had become the fastest-growing vendor to Knight, in spite of stratospheric prices. Once this vendor's ownership was suspected, we merely placed some huge orders with the bogus outfit, received the goods, and stiffed them on the payment. Funny. The perpetrators never quite worked up the courage to attempt collecting. Justice outside the system can be quite a kick. Anyway, from all this, Knight Protective did boil down to a hard core of solid employees and we restructured for a positive cash flow in my first half-year.

It's easier to think when you've stopped bleeding.

Previous annual reports documented parts of this, and brashly anticipated record profits which our employees exceeded. Knight Protective always had a semi-unique method of monitoring, called two-way voice. It offered legitimate benefits. Management dumped all distractions, concentrated on two-way voice, and, as happens each and every time, things got better. Profits and new customers followed.

"What did you do?" one shocked shareholder asked.

"Less," I answered.

This is not nuclear science. We did little more than uncover one positive within this bag full of tragedies, focused on that, and spun off the rest. You have been complimentary, but it's all so simple that I should be indicted for fraud.

You invested at different times and prices, experiencing varying returns, but the public reports from the pension fund show their $130,000 in 1991 Knight stock returned over $6 million in cash last year alone. Not shabby.

Happy ending. But it wasn't always a barrel of laughs. In a desperate and, some say, failed attempt to maintain sanity, I helped start another business through these five years. It is totally disrelated to Knight. No surprise there. Some shareholders don't know about this second job I held. Others asked, so for broader disclosure, here's that story.

This other business, which I cofounded in 1989, is developing a satellite-based telecom network that will bring service to sparsely populated areas of the globe. Among the humble requirements, the project needs to:

1. hoist 840 satellites into low earth orbits,

2. get worldwide approvals from Albanians, Mongols, Buddhists, Muslims, etc., even (gulp) the French, to enter their airspace and beam into their countries,

3. negotiate launches at a fraction of current costs,

4. prove, finance, and develop theoretical breakthroughs in phased-array antennas,

5. develop new gallium-arsenide chip technology, and

6. make high-speed packet switching work with voice signals.

Piece of cake, huh? Oh, by the way, this project also requires a mere $9 billion more to get going. That's "billion" with a "b" . . . "$9" followed by so many zeros it looks like a bowl of Cheerios . . . big bucks. After spending that, the investors may find out if Teledesic, as it is named, can come close to working.

My deranged friend, a venture capitalist who conceived this modest proposal, and I might have faced investor reactions more suitable at the Improv, had it not been for one thing: This proposed network reaches an unserved market, and can do it with costs per minute and variable bandwidths that none of the other so-called information superhighways approach. (Any of you out there know what an information superhighway is? Me neither.)

So he and I put together a list of 100 possible investors, each with billion-dollar pockets, oversized glands, and potential lapses of judgment. We screwed up our courage. Sketched it. Made some slides. Did a spreadsheet. Showed it to the first three.

"Yes," "Yes," and "Yes," they said. We were prepared for anything but that.

In this Lewis Carroll scene, we actually declined one investment, accepting just enough for feasibility studies and started.

Through the years that followed, some leading aerospace, telephone, and financial types started shaking their heads. Some even shook them up and down. Not many. Another sent a check. This saga was so unique that pages 215 to 219 in *Tight Ships Don't Sink* chronicle it. When Simon & Schuster published, I didn't have a clue if big-time financiers would ever bite on Teledesic or not. Please order copies through your bookstore. My last royalty check caused no unsolvable tax problems. Costs you $15.95. A hardback edition, with the Teledesic story updated and a Knight Protective chapter added, comes out next month. It is retitled *Profit Secrets from a No-Nonsense CEO* and sets you back $21.95. Hey, a guy's got to eat.

Anyway, Craig McCaw invested. Bill Gates followed his lead in 1994. Teledesic received a firestorm of publicity when the press learned about their involvement. The October 10, 1994, supplement to *Forbes, ASAP*, devoted ten pages comparing Teledesic with Motorola's Iridium, GM/Hughes's Spaceway, and Qualcomm Globalstar. Some George Gilder quotes:

"Motorola should join Teledesic now, not later."

"Globalstar is the easy current winner, but Teledesic can add phone to broadband computer services. Over time, Teledesic will outperform Globalstar. Iridium is too expensive and too narrowband. Spaceway is maturing. Big winner for the next decade is Teledesic."

"Teledesic's impact on the world may rival McCaw's and Gates's contribution in software and cellular."

Well, that quickens my breath, but there are no slam-dunks in high tech. The Teledesic game rapidly ascended, or degenerated, depending on your tastes, into a multimillion-dollar-per-year lobbying effort and the moment passed for the original round pegs like myself, so I stepped aside, seconds before being nudged, while more socially graceful and colorfully suspendered talent was recruited, leaving me to cling to this vision as a minor, minor shareholder.

Sad? Nope. Normal. And it could be worse. For example, I might be sipping Chardonnay right now with some bureaucrat in Washington, but this management makeover saves both that slack-jawed zombie and myself from those irritations.

So last summer I moved into the dormitory at Christ Church, Oxford, and studied Roman history. Veni, vidi, vino and Guinness. Now I hit the streets again, seeking a new scam. Enough self-promotion. On to the close.

Do you know:

1. an absentee owner of a troubled business,
2. a venture capitalist with a less than perfect portfolio,
3. an investment banker,
4. a CPA firm partner, or an
5. outside director who sits on several boards?

If so, would you pass this report on to them?

They may be entertained. Possibly they'll even call. It could end up with my tutoring one of their "F" students into a barely passing grade.

Relax. You need not feel any implied endorsement. If your contact responds, before we even meet, I'll mail them clippings and annual reports that prove my ability to fool auditors, media, and Wall Streeters. One prospectus shows the largest printer in the West enjoyed a 30% average annual profit growth from 1980 to 1986 while I was CEO. A closer look reveals it was a lumpy 30% due to leverage. In 1986 to 1988 Price Waterhouse verified that their PC accessories client snapped around to industry record profits from a decade of losses and was acquired at a lofty price by an industry leader while I ran it. Ernst & Young admits that their aerospace client rebounded from steep losses in 1988 and 1989, while I was chairman, and was acquired. Since then, it's been all Teledesic and Knight Protective.

Should one of your contacts be so panicked that we negotiate seriously, I may also hand them copies of:

1. interviews with every director or shareholder I've worked for between 1964 and 1989, done by a search firm on behalf of an overzealous Midwestern fund a few years ago, and

2. two separate psychological profiles on me, done for LBO investors in the eighties.

That should subvert their due diligence, or I don't know what it takes. Some love these second opinions. Besides, it gets you off the hook. I will not consult. I assume complete control, take a modest salary plus 20% of the profit improvement. $10 million is the revenue minimum. Bigger yet is better and easier.

No happy, healthy deals please: only wobbling startups or well-established losers.

Thanks for your support at Knight. I'm relieved that it worked so well for us. Okay, okay, I'm amazed. Flabbergasted even.

Gary Sutton

Those investors averaged a 53× cash return on their shares during my five years. My personal bank account wasn't damaged either. And it wasn't so consuming that I couldn't write a couple books and start Teledesic, which blossomed into a $3 billion valuation in the ten years after scratching it on an airport napkin.

Some ask if Knight Protective was really this bad. No, it was worse, but I was afraid to divulge some of the truly scary stuff. And that's why the opportunity interested me. It's tough to step into a totally upside-down situation without showing dramatic improvements, since almost anything you do will make things better. And management rarely does only one dumb thing. Where there's a single stupid practice, be ready to discover many more. So you'll make lots of improvements.

This is why a shrewd turnaround practitioner seeks terrible situations. Expectations are gone and the outside interference is minimal. Owners and creditors are terrified, and step away in delight when you're dumb enough to grab the wheel, which makes fast change possible.

At Knight, we did the two classic things. First we found the margin. In this case it was all in the monitoring. Second, we shut down or sold everything that had little to do with the margin-generating part of the business, regardless of effect on revenues. This is not brain surgery.

In this case, manufacturing, marketing, and installation divisions were chopped. In a "minor adjustment to payroll," Knight went from 230 employees to 40 in my first quarter. The normal arguments, that the profitable part of the business couldn't survive without the losers to support it, were made by voices shrill enough to clear sinuses in each contiguous zip code, but, as is often the case, those fears proved false. (A lot of folks get comfortable in a money-losing company, and fear any change. You must splash cold water in their faces. Show the bank account and trend lines to those in denial. With them, estimate the date all paychecks stop.)

Hold it right there. If you're thinking that this layoff was awful, eliminating that many jobs, then you are truly clueless.

The shareholder that was a pension fund, for just one example, had 5,000 retirees, blue-collar workers who one way or another lived on $20 less per month for their lifetime of work, while this disaster had its grasping hand clawing into their pockets and the taxpayers'. Most of the fired employees were a long way from models of citizenship. And the customers were getting systems installed that were embarrassingly deficient and dangerous. In every way, this layoff was positive, if momentarily unpleasant.

The turnaround took five months. The business couldn't sell for four more years, because the two largest shareholders were suing each other and there was no way to peddle the stock until that spitting contest ended. I hung around as a caretaker.

Finding the margin is easy sometimes. In the case of Knight, the accounting was good enough that it was self-evident. The only question, and a serious one, was whether this business could continue by monitoring other accounts without generating its own.

Monitoring other accounts is much lower margin, since that only gets wholesale pricing, not retail. But the competition was less, way less, the skills more specialized, and it helped that we didn't compete anymore with our only sources for new monitoring accounts, other alarm installers. So it worked.

In a different troubled business, a few years earlier, the margin was hidden. Checks To-Go made and sold two products. One was software-compatible forms, mostly checks, but some invoices, envelopes, and so forth that were laid out to match the particular format of different softwares like Peachtree, Intuit, and Great Plains. The second business was custom forms, made to fit unique needs of customers. All sales were by phone.

The markup on custom forms was 100%. Costs to produce them, mostly purchased outside, were simply doubled. This looked wonderful.

The markup on software-compatible forms was 40%. Standard forms were purchased with magnetic codes and users' imprinting done internally.

But the software-compatible-forms business faced only four competitors nationwide: RapidForms, NEBS, Moore, and Deluxe Check. Our point of difference was color at no extra charge, a minor point, but since it brought in more business, we got better and better at it. Most of the market was happy with black and white, by the way, but we didn't want most of the market. Plus the trend, as always in every business, was toward more color.

Custom forms, on the other hand, faced 99 competitors in the San Diego Yellow Pages alone. And the returns of custom forms, with changes and free replacement required, hit about 10% compared to less than 1% with the software-compatible forms.

Then a simple walk around the floor, sensing how much artists' time this custom work seemed to actually require, plus listening to the customer service talking about them versus the software-compatible forms made it pretty clear that the accounting records didn't really show where the profits came from. There was too much overhead and return expense being generated by the custom work.

But I made a sickening mistake.

Fearful of the effect that simply shutting down the custom work would have on revenues, and being quite tight on cash, we simply began to price our way out of it. Every month for an entire year we raised quotes on the custom work by seven percent. Month after month, prices chunked up, seven percent every month, twenty-one percent per quarter, eighty-four percent within the year. We drove most customers away, began to make some serious money on what was left, and had half as much custom business in a year, but a horrendously profitable half. The most complaints had come from the customers who disappeared as their prices first edged up, so the remaining were easy to deal with. (There's a universal truth right there, by the way: Get rid of those cheap whiners.)

But custom forms were now a declining part of our business, so this move of pricing our way out, while cute, probably cost us time and distraction compared to simply shutting it down. Cutting your tail off an inch at a time causes more pain in total. And it distracts from the bigger growth opportunity.

In a turnaround right after Checks To-Go, and immediately preceding Knight Protective, Smiley Industries straightened out quickly by doing the same. All margin came from a particular type of work, described in Chapter 13. In that recovery, which was idiot-simple, identifying the best type of work for the business got the employees and reps moving smarter, and profits returned overnight. No cost-cutting was required, the business just fell into its natural strengths and was acquired. All we did was define what we did best. And raised prices, which got easy when we stopped doing the me-too kind of work.

Henry Ford is often ridiculed for selling his cars "in any color as long as it's black." These storytellers totally miss a greater truth. Yeah, Hank was insensitive to customers' superficial requests. But Mr. Ford created the mass market for the cars by understanding their deeper need, low cost, so he shipped one color. He merely stuck with it too long. By driving costs down no matter what, he delivered what the market truly wanted in the beginning: transportation that cost less per mile than feeding a horse. And no tidying up after it.

Find the margin. Cut all other costs.

We live in increasing specialized times, and death is fast for those who "round out" their offerings with stuff that can be gotten elsewhere for less.

IBM can't compete in personal computers. Yeah, they sell a lot, rank in the top five, have elegant features from time to time, but IBM loses money on every last one they ship. Why do they keep it up? Maybe somebody likes seeing their stock drop, I can't figure it. Montgomery Ward got killed by Costco from below and the boutiques like the Limited from above, while Sears, being bigger, has been among the walking dead for decades. Ditto Kmart. And before you suggest that Wal-Mart has triumphed, which is correct, remember they built a business by putting stores in towns with populations under 100,000, a true niche approach.

Specialize. Do it where the margin lives. Stop everything else.

There's every probability in the world, if you're the CEO who guided the company into this mess, that you cannot emotionally fix it. It's likely that the employees, who understand it's your fault, won't follow your advice with much enthusiasm if you try the turnaround. And it's rare that the board will grant you that privilege.

This is why an outside turnaround manager gets the task. If you're wondering how to find this person, hold that thought; it'll be answered in Chapter 65.

If you're the soldier approached to fix the business, your first chore is to make sure that the shareholders are, in fact, ready to make radical changes. If not, don't touch the deal. They haven't felt enough pain yet to recognize the truth.

As the outsider, you have unfair advantages. You have no emotional baggage tied to a new product dream or a historically interesting but economically irrelevant service. You can ask dumb questions without looking dumb. One or two of those dumb questions will turn out to be brilliant.

Contrary to what most expect, you'll find you're handed loyalty from employees. Other executives have to work for that devotion, but these folks understand that you represent their last chance, and that you didn't create the problem. They knew the business was wobbling off course before the board or the owners understood it. If your demeanor is to the point, without being rude, they'll guide you immediately toward some major problems. They won't all be correct, but some will be solid, and few will hold back if you listen hard. If you've really quizzed them, and they lose their jobs anyway, it's less painful for them, since you both tried.

Here's what you do the first morning. You've already gotten the owner's opinions. Interview the CEO, wherever he is, then the CFO, VP Ops, VP Marketing, and VP Engineering. Ask each individually what the problem is and what the solution is. Try this the first morning, give each about an hour, one at a time. Don't hit them cold with the questions. This is a scary time, and catching them by surprise only gives you a measure of how articulate they might be, which doesn't have much to do with anything. Give them a day to think about it. Let them know that this is what you must hear. Those who hold back or waffle on answers are part of your problem.

It's okay if they point the finger elsewhere; in many cases this will reveal a truth. But get them to be specific about that problem and give them a chance to say where their own area is not doing well, and ask what they hope to do to make that better.

Spend that first afternoon on customer calls, and stress to marketing that you just want to chat briefly with a random selection of customers, but include a couple biggies, possibly including a good one they've failed to hook. Introduce yourself to customers as a person who's considered investing some time with the company, and you need to know what this client sees as the outfit's biggest strength and largest failing. At the end of that afternoon, you may have a decent picture of what's wrong and who the major competitors are. If there's no consistent response, well, that's why you make the big bucks, and the fix is going to be less obvious. Or if all complaints are price, then you failed to open the customers up for any honest comments. Nobody wants to pay more. Price is always important but is never everything.

Get back with top management that night, as a group, and toss out what you heard for reactions. See which comments they buy. If there's no consensus, thrash away again the next morning, and if nothing emerges then the decision is all in your lap. That's not all bad.

Also spend an hour the next morning going through the checkbook. If practical, sign a stack yourself. That'll get you energized and angry. Since every signature shortens your company's life, you'll discover some pretty silly things that never show up on the income statement. You'll find yourself acting on them.

This can be a trap. There are those who thrill and swagger at making small decisions. Your role is to do neither, but to make a rapid series of small ones quickly, only to set a tone, sending ripples by example through the outfit that are clearer than any mandates or policy statements. Don't make a big deal out of this, just start rattling them off, let them speak for themselves, and rush back to the bigger and tougher actions.

"Shouldn't we have a booth at that trade show?"

"No, but let's spend a couple days there and have breakfast meetings with potential clients X and Y."

"But won't people notice we don't have a booth?"

"The world doesn't care that much about us anymore, we can't afford it, and if we walk the aisles we'll make more contacts without being tied to a spot on the floor."

Another manager grabs your sleeve: "Can we meet to discuss the development schedule of next year's widget?"

"Of course, how about 8:30 P.M.? And can we agree to freeze the schedule before we finish tonight? That way we won't waste time redoing it next week or next month."

A secretary pages you: "We have a commercial rate in Detroit at the Ritz Carlton. Is that okay?"

"No. Book me at the Holiday Inn that's closest to the client." Then fire that secretary and book your next rooms through a travel agent instructed to always find the lowest fares, or book yourself online. Give her good severance, it wasn't her fault, it was mismanagement and unnecessary overhead. And so on. Don't get bogged down in these decisions, but make them quick to rebuild a rational atmosphere. Don't do anything that jeopardizes quality, unless quality doesn't matter. There are a few very rare businesses where "polishing the cannonball" doesn't make sense. Try to keep the most promising new development going, the company will need that one day soon, but stop spending on the fuzzy ones.

Now that you've signed a batch of checks, start interviewing employees at random. Talk with at least a dozen. Do a few in groups. These folks will point out several problems that the board and owners aren't aware of, and half of these will matter.

Your personal demeanor is critical. You must get straight to the point without terrifying people.

You can spread panic if it appears that you're counting paper clips and figuring out ways to copy documents on both sides of the page to save paper costs. Yet you will fail to spread any cost-cutting attitude if you do not, instinctively and with lightning speed, make many of these minor cuts every day without ever mentioning them. Just do them every time they pop up and don't tell anybody. The word will spread fast. And if you're talking publicly about the bigger issues, that maintains morale and displays a larger leadership.

"Jane, why do you think Amalgamated Widgets is losing money?"

Listen. Push her for details in areas that sound valid.

Ask other employees, "What would you do if you owned the business?"; make it clear to each that your entire personal incentive is to help the company survive, that you suffer financially if it doesn't, and that it will vaporize unless something big changes fast. Show them cash positions and loss rates to prove it.

Now that you're halfway conversant, call one or two trade editors. Your approach should be the same; you're an executive considering investing serious time in this company, and you'd be thrilled if this publisher or editor can confide a few observations to you. Ask lots of questions, these folks spend their lives listening and enjoy having the talk go in the other direction for once. They also happen to be in love with their largest advertisers, so factor back their praise for those spenders, but also remember somehow those competitors did succeed in order to develop those big budgets. Send them a personal thank-you note and a small gift that shows you were listening and heard something about their personal interests.

These editors are not without their own kind of ego. They deal daily with the industry CEOs, several who fawn over them, and the media is painfully aware that their paychecks display a digit or two less than these industry titans. They've adjusted to that fact, resent it only a little, and you should be able to work with them. This is just the way it is in every business. They can be irritating but they have some perspectives you need.

Always cater to anyone who buys ink by the barrel. They'll be whispering about how you're doing to the industry, long before the results show.

In weeks, not months, not even a single month, you should know what the major shift will be. You should have shared financial information with everybody inside, so they all get it and will understand and support the change. In fact, they'll be anticipating and ready for almost any switch.

Talk directly with all who are laid off, and give them as generous a severance package as the company can afford. Personally intervene with those who are undeserving victims, and have management make personal calls and write letters to get them placed elsewhere. If they can avoid missing a paycheck, and possibly gain a raise or a shorter commute, you've elevated the company through the process of a layoff. Go for that. It's amazing what a personal letter to fifty nearby CEOs will do, expressing your embarrassment at the layoff and personally endorsing this particular candidate for an interview.

This activity doesn't help the company directly. It just makes you feel better. When you feel better, the company does better. Despite what your lawyer and human resources department will urge, be preferential, and don't do this for those who were marginal performers. That's fraudulent. Helping them degrades the boost you give the worthy departees.

Paint the picture for the surviving employees around the remaining service or product, and where you all hope it can go. It's not inappropriate to show some enthusiasm, in spite of somber times.

Before planning the cutback, take ten minutes for a test. Write down the names of all the companies you've seen that failed because they didn't have enough overhead. My bet is that your list is a close match to my zero.

This is also the prime moment to fix your balance sheet. You've just restructured. A few folks were laid off. Your competitors are gleefully spreading the word, warning customers that you're tumbling over the edge. That's their job. Your trade editor friends may temper these rumors, but the noise will be loud for several days. You'll get several calls.

Most of our world thinks companies are healthy before a layoff, and our same world believes they are dying after the layoff. Usually the opposite is true. The company was sick before the layoff and is healthy afterward. Here's how you turn that misperception to your advantage.

First of all, don't spend much time fighting it, you can't win that battle yet, just reassure key customers when they call.

But somewhere among your creditors, leaseholders, or debtors are some who act way more nervous than the others. They may be sincere, it may simply be that their organization has a new policy to upgrade quality and reduce exposure, or an individual may just be one of those miscast lenders with the wrong DNA for the loan business, trembling through life.

That person will call. Explain the situation. Tell why you made the change and what you hope to achieve and when. Try to sell this to Wobbly Willy. Then wait for WW to call back (he will in days) and express your hopes then for signs of positive cash soon, along with the still unsolved problems.

You see, you can be totally honest, because it just won't matter. This person isn't buying your hopes for a second. He's mortified. When he calls back in thirty days, update him. Then offer to pay him off early, explaining that you haven't yet done this for anybody, but he will have to settle for twenty cents on the dollar, plus some warrants.

Send him a check for this amount, with a letter encouraging him not to cash it, explaining again that you fully expect the business to recover and to pay the balance due in full, and that if your plan works, he'll be making a mistake by cashing the check.

You do this, by the way, only when you're convinced your plan will work. You'll believe in the turnaround plan before anybody, so this is the moment to cash in on that.

Mark the check "Void if endorsement altered." Mark the backside "Negotiated as payment in full of outstanding debt." Call the creditor a day or two after they receive the check, and repeat your encouragement that they should absolutely not cash that check, since you believe they will ultimately be paid in full. Then tell them that "I'm a little nervous about having made this special offer, and will stop payment on that check in one week." Then call early in the morning of the seventh day to remind them that the offer expires in a few hours and that the check will have a stop put against it. Confirm this by e-mail.

At Knight Protective, the first creditor cashed the check. We offered twenty-five cents on the dollar and no warrants. After the first creditor accepted, we called all the others with the same offer, explaining one creditor negotiated this deal with us, so making the same offer to them merely eliminates any claims of favoritism. We urged all not to cash their checks, and gave them a week. Most took the deal. The balance sheet went from positive to negative in that month. Cash stayed tighter for longer, but got much better soon. It's a rare creditor who can stare at that check for a week without endorsing.

Time it for early in their quarter, when optimism reigns. Every company starts fighting write-downs as they approach reality in the last weeks of their quarter. With private companies this is more of a monthly phenomenon.

Now fix the business. You've got a tighter focus. Your balance sheet is patched up. You'll be amazed at how much better everyone performs, having a more singular mission, and the business gets better and better with fewer distractions.

Keep that focus. Remind everyone what the mission is. Do it in speeches, newsletters, and ads. Work hard on the ten words or less that describe exactly what it is that you do better than anyone. Don't let a single dollar or hour go against anything that doesn't drive the business in that direction.

And watch the cash sputter at first, then trickle up, sputter, spurt up, sputter, and finally gush into your account. Notice your banker stops by for lunch. See how your parking lot fills earlier and stays clogged later.

Now you need a new leader. Again. You began the search for this permanent CEO in the second or third month of the turnaround.

Let's assume you're the turnaround manager, and you took the assignment. Those superrational skills you possess, the icy water in your veins that guide a successful recovery, are usually strangers to the inspirational skills that accelerate a company into the next stage. That's why we change CEOs again. We'll give famous proof of this in Chapter 17.

A common question when looking for a CEO is, "Do you use a recruiter, advertising, or your Rolodex?"

The answer is "Yes." This step is too important to leave to a single source. Little else matters. Most turnarounds fail after they've succeeded. That's the bigger battle.

Use a recruiter but manage them. Extra tips come in Chapter 16. Don't hire any of the large recruiting firms. When they boast, by showing off the long list of clients they already know in your industry, that's simply proof that they cannot recruit from the most logical companies without a conflict. If they say they will anyway, you've just learned that they'll feel free to pirate your company after they get to know it, and sense who your stars are.

This is why large recruiters are merely a guarantee of mediocre performance. Get a small practitioner. Go to The Directory of Executive

Recruiters. Your library has a copy, or call 603-585-6544, write them at One Kennedy Place, Route 12 South, Fitzwilliam, NH 03447, or email bookstore@kennedyinfo.com. Find several in your area. Stick with those who specialize in your industry. As smaller shops, this means they'll have a few conflicts but not nearly as many as the bigger body factories.

Agree on the number of calls to be made weekly and discuss what the feedback is every seven days. You should get a log and see that 150 relevant new phone calls were made during the first few weeks. You should spot-check these for credibility and, more importantly, let the search firm know you'll be doing this in advance. Pay only one-third of the fee per month, and don't make the second or third payments if they're not delivering.

You need to review the telephone interview notes for a dozen, and quiz the interviewer where the comments seem interesting.

Setting up the process like this is more important than interviewing and looking at presentations to find the perfect recruiter, a person that doesn't exist, by the way. They'll all interview and present well; that's the heart of their business. It's knowing the precise effort level that determines the success rate and protects you in case they land three unexpected other assignments the day after they sign up for your search. (When that happens, you never hear about it. You just end up scratching your head 90 days later, wondering what went wrong, irritated that you've spent big money and have no viable candidates. This happens to 40% of all searches. Programming the effort ahead of time improves your chances.)

Prepare a selling document that the recruiter can email or mail. Work hard on this, using the text from your want ad to start, but filling in with history and market details to give candidates total comfort.

Don't try to hire a vice president from the largest company in your industry. That person hasn't had real profit-and-loss responsibility, but has merely proven her political skills by rising high. That person has her salary set in relationship to her department size and budget, so her entire motivation has been to hire more and spend more to get paid better. Bad training. They'll immediately increase staff, need a new IT system, and enlarge the HR department.

Too many people understand that the best salesperson won't always make the best sales manager, but fail to understand this holds even more true for a VP becoming a CEO. VPs are political and have peers. CEOs work alone, and are measured by results. (Converting Controllers to CFOs is just as tough. The skills are the same but the personality is different, and even the Mayo Clinic isn't performing personality transplants just yet. Controllers set budgets, squeeze dollars, and control. CFOs sell forecasts. One sells the outside world. The other squeezes internally.)

Bigger company experience fails. Lee Iacocca did a masterful turn-around of Chrysler, less by the shabby K-Cars and more by his charisma and the fact there were enough voting employees and vendors to force a government bailout. Later Mr. Iacocca floundered, trying to resurrect Koo Koo Roo, a chicken restaurant chain. He enjoyed having fewer staff to bully and not enough employees to get any political help, so he quietly exited.

And don't hire a superstar from a company 10% your size; that person won't let the staff do anything and will die trying to handle every chore alone. Size matters. Find a track record within a similarly sized company.

Open up the industries you'll search in. If you are Cessna aircraft, and have a CEO candidate from Merck drug and another CEO candidate from Chris-Craft boats, you've got an interesting choice.

The boat person understands marketing a leisure product to upscale individuals, from a factory with welding equipment, jigs, and dies. Hey, that's just like a small plane business. But the Merck candidate understands the FDA, and might handle the FAA more effectively. Hey, working through the FAA is critical to a plane maker. Think through that stuff, and expand your list of companies to recruit from.

Somebody from GE might adapt well, despite size. GE creates smaller profit-and-loss centers and truly manages against those numbers, eliminating marginal performers. Somebody from IBM won't work out. They create processes, and reward the most nondisruptive disciples of procedure.

After recruiting several CEOs, I began to wonder if there were any predictable patterns.

There are.

To find these secrets, I surveyed 1000 directors who sit on six or more boards. This was intended to get a perspective from those with the greatest personal exposure to a variety of CEOs. My letter asked them to think of the best and worst CEO they'd ever worked with. The questionnaire asked that they not name them, just answer a few questions about each; 280 responded.

By encouraging them to speak about the best and worst CEO specifically, the survey attempted to rid the directors of their personal biases and find out what career backgrounds worked best and worst. If I had asked what experience worked best, they'd just spew out their own prejudices. This approach, hopefully, guided their responses closer to the truth.

The single most important key for success was prior profit-and-loss experience. Without that, the disaster rate jumped. With it, success was far more probable. The CEO spot is no place for on-the-job training. And be careful, every candidate claims some profit responsibility in their current position. Most of them even believe it. But unless their compensation is primarily based on profits, they do not have that responsibility.

Career paths weren't as effective as predictors, but they showed certain trends. Engineers with prior profit-and-loss experience were about as good as it got, with financial and operational types close behind. Marketing followed, and legal and scientists were on the bottom. As a wheezing, balding, marketing guy, and a research and development retread, a couple of the worst places for breeding CEOs, I can report that without being accused of bias.

Their answers also showed that coming from a similar-sized company counted much more than coming from the same industry. Coming from a customer or vendor, however, was good, while coming from a direct competitor was bad. Maybe there's a character measure in that. Perhaps they just knew the candidates better, ahead of time, when they came from a customer or vendor.

If I ever do another survey, getting similar growth rates might also be key, since the attitudes in a fast-growing outfit vary so radically from a slower business.

Now the search firm will lecture that they do the best work because they find executives who are employed and not looking to change, unlike advertising. And a search firm should be used. But that doesn't preclude some advertising. The argument for search is that you should want somebody who is happy in their current job. This, however, also suggests that the person can also be recruited away from you later, even if you fill them with bliss. And they're certain to cost more. Not being content with one's current position is no black eye. It may be a sign of intelligence. So both advertise and use a search firm. However, be ready for a disturbing pile of nonqualified resumes from advertising.

When looking for marketing talent at Teledesic, I used a three-column, two-inch ad in the Southern California edition of the *Wall Street Journal*. It ran twice. The price was about $1,200 and generated two Safeway bags full of resumes, mostly junk but a few gems.

Part of the process is simply being prepared to wade through these stacks, setting aside time to telephone-screen a couple dozen and personally interview eight to ten. Identify the company, situation, and salary range. This doubles response and gives a more qualified group. (Instead of 98% inappropriate, it'll drop to only 96% inappropriate.) So you have to answer all, increasing the chore, but you get twice as many good ones.

Never let the HR department write or place the ad. That's why most ads fail. Personnel people are more worried about putting in phrases about EOE and Affirmative Action, never even thinking deep enough to realize those programs contradict each other, and cannot generate any excitement with their careful words.

Use the regional edition of the *Wall Street Journal* plus several appropriate trade publications. Appropriate means "Boating Business Monthly" and "Pharmaceutical Executive" if you're filling Cessna's CEO slot, as well as "Aviation Weekly."

The reason for a regional ad is that our country is large enough now that wherever you are, you can find all the talent you need within your own time zone. Instead of running one national ad, and getting several cross-country prospects, comb your region more tightly. Inevitably, there will be trips and travel and real estate questions in the process, and soon that will dominate the process. By not reaching so far geographically, you end up with the same number of qualified interviews but half the hassle. And hassle, with its frustration, is the danger to this process. You do not want to get antsy.

Yeah, I know, what about the perfect candidate who's several time zones away? Well, trust me, response doesn't drop for an ad until you've run it three times in a row. And the reality is that there's time and expense to this process, and keeping it efficient by talking mostly to nearby folks means you talk to a few more with less time and expense wasted. And you'll be excited at the beginning of this process but weary near the end, creating a dangerous situation. Conserve your energy so you don't settle for mediocrity.

Be specific in the ad. You'll screen away nonqualifieds and get more that fit. Say something like:

CEO
Small Aircraft Maker

Widget planes makes one of the safest and most economical light planes in the business. The company stumbled two years ago, and is just emerging as a recovered business, with new cash in the bank and happy lenders. Better yet, the next-generation model looks like it just might startle our industry with some unheard-of performance and unique value. But we need a CEO who can grasp that and mobilize the troops for a head-turning launch.

I'm the interim CEO and it's time I move on.

We intend to make the stock package a life-altering incentive, with a livable salary, for the executive who escalates this progress. If you have several years of profit-and-loss experience, and the plane business interests you, could you drop me a personal note? I'll get a packet back to you, and suspect you'll find the details interesting. This contact, of course, is strictly between you and me.

There are some exciting possibilities. I'd love to hear your reactions. My board does insist on several years of profit-and-loss experience, and we'd like to see that most of your past compensation was incentive-based.

Sincerely,
Mr. Turnaround or Director
phone number, address, and email

Don't let the recruiter become involved in this part. Recruiters favor their own finds, and won't sell as hard to candidates that the ads dig up. Let them know you're doing this parallel effort, but keep them out of it, making this a competitive function to their solicitations.

Now, here's how you get that ad to really perform. Make 200 copies after it runs. Enlarge them 100% for drama. Send copies to every contact you now have in the industry, with a note asking if anybody comes to mind. (They'll consider this more real after seeing the ad, and you'll get noticeably more response.) Send copies to vendors and customers. Offer everybody a trip for two to London or Hong Kong for one week, all expenses paid, if they uncover a candidate who's hired. Also hit several dozen appropriate folks from your personal Rolodex. Ask everyone to pass the ad along to the single most qualified CEO they can think of, whether they presume that person is looking for a change or not. Remind them that most executives hide their restless moods.

Send it to your shareholders and directors and ask them to come up with one or two names each. Do this last. This group, which should be your most supportive, won't be yet; they're wrongly hoping you'll stay, but as they hear about some great resumes coming in, they'll remember the strategy and start to pitch in.

Doing this will generate more leads than the ad itself. Your contacts take it more seriously when it's set in type. You'll describe the opportunity better after writing the ad. They'll start to think seriously about the position. You've done some of the work for them, put the selling words in their mouths, so they can deliver the message. And they will. Ironically, this is the most important function of the ad: mobilizing your contacts and honing the message.

Do not restrict the recruiter geographically. They typically call someone who ends up referring them to someone else who's a great fit, and requiring those candidates to come from a specified area is counterproductive. With the ads, it's merely a choice that must be made, so regional space is better than national.

Now, about the package: Don't get woozy and assume you have to pay twice the industry average to capture a star. Overpaying gets you candidates who got lucky once and are just insightful enough to fear they can't do it again, and show this by seeking big pay and low incentive. The income tax bite vs. favorable capital gains on a stock option illuminates this, so counter with more incentive but don't push too hard. Just fade away quickly from those who show no eagerness to bet on themselves. They should know. There will be some slick ones who are very articulate at the reasons for hesitating, and they'll agonize in front of you about the family, the great position they're leaving, and so on, and you shouldn't even fall into the trap of discussing. They've bared their soul, and it lacks confidence.

This is no longer your decision, however, since the board must pick your replacement. For board support, it's important they make the pick and set the pay. The board will be a little giddy at this stage, so prep them with these attitudes, lest your recovery efforts slip away fast under a new leader with a fat salary and skinny incentives.

Once hired, introduce the new leader to the employees and disappear. Don't lurk. If invited to stay on the board, do so only under the condition that you won't attend meetings for six months. The new CEO needs to make some decisions and changes to things you've done without looking over his/her shoulder for your approval. This is a new leader. Let's pray that this new hire won't agree with every change you made. The new person needs to live and die by their own acts.

You, as the turnaround manager, came into the mess with huge advantages. You weren't emotionally attached to the business. The employees rallied to you as their last hope, especially when you talked frankly with them and coughed up the bad news as quickly as you raised new hopes. You had the privilege of being able to ask dumb questions. You're not as beaten down as the incumbent was. A fresh set of eyes has all these advantages.

But the next step, building a new business, takes a year and different skills. Don't overstay.

Why six months for the turnaround? And why a year to rebuild a solid profit base? Well, I hope you're suggesting neither should take that long. That's a healthy attitude. It's those who suggest a slower approach, more deliberate, who are part of the problem. There are plenty of emotional reasons for trying to move slower with a turnaround, but few of them hold water. They all come back to a fear of facing the inevitable. When things are getting worse, they rarely get better spontaneously. Bad trends accelerate. All by themselves.

Both parts of the turnaround are rallying moments for all, and cannot be maintained as an attitude without turning into self-deception, if given too much time. Time is your enemy.

If the current losses suggest bankruptcy within the year, and you're on the board, bring in a turnaround manager on a six-month contract. Pay more incentive than salary. That manager will instinctively find where the margin exists and dump everything but the most promising of the promising new product developments, and even that'll be trimmed back. Stay out of the turnaround manager's way. Start looking for the longer-term CEO in the second or third month of the turnaround, and be as involved as you choose to be with that search.

CHAPTER 2

TURNAROUND SCAMS AND SCREWUPS

C elluland was a hot franchise in 1986, but it blew up on the launchpad. The first thirty units installed cell phones in cars. It flattered me that two of the major investors, disappointed by growing losses, asked me to look at it.

I spent a few hours at the company, then called a couple cellular service vendors.

I gave them a report the next day that went something like this: "You've got three huge problems. First, the concept is flawed. Most of your investment goes to finance these beautiful installation bays. Cell phones sell to people who are very busy or who at least think they're very busy, and the first thing you do is to require this busy customer to book an appointment, costing them a half day, to get this time-saving cellular service installed. Drop the installation bays. Use trucks that go to the customer's office parking lot or airport, so they don't lose a minute. This also slashes your capital expenditures.

"Second, right now you're getting paid $300 by the service provider for each subscriber you install. They plan to drop that payment next year. Your numbers are terrible now and headed for worse. Your CEO apparently is unaware of this change coming.

"Third, you gotta worry about handhelds replacing installed phones someday, as the battery technology and signals get stronger.

"Offsetting these problems is the fact that cellular is growing 100% per year, and that makes many solutions possible. (Nobody knows how to turn around a market. Here you don't need to.)

"I'm willing to step in, two days a week, for $5,000 per month and 5%

of the equity. The real task is to switch your leases over to another use, get some installing trucks rolling, and figure out some enhanced services before the cellular payments stop or handhelds begin to catch on. It may be windshield replacements, detailing, or oil changes in parking lots."

Well, they declined my hasty offer. At least I think they did. Seventeen years later I'm awaiting their response. Doesn't look promising.

What I didn't realize was that there was yet another problem, one that I've seen twice since. This business started franchising after the first outlet became an instant success. It had a great location in an Autoport Mall. In fact, the location was so good that the revenues couldn't be duplicated in any of the next dozen outlets.

Franchising is more about real estate than the business. If it's the right corner, burgers, mufflers, or flowers will sell.

My advice was too abrupt, too radical, and too fast for the beleaguered investors to accept. They hired Grisanti, Galef & Goldress, which then and for decades before was the most respected turnaround firm in business. The firm spent six days monthly at Celluland, charged $30,000 per month, and Celluland disappeared in two years.

That's not a criticism. I saw the problem but didn't provide any specific, happy answers. It does show that when companies are in trouble, they'll pay a bunch for handholding. This case also shows I should have spent more time and given a more creative and detailed solution if I was serious. And it proves you can't win them all.

Many established turnaround firms loftily suggest that if they take equity kickers instead of flat fees, they are in a conflict of interest. That's only true if all they care about are the creditors, and we'll show how you can stumble into that situation in a minute.

Flat fees for turnarounds, with small incentives, is as rational as a sales force on high salary with low commissions. Don't do it. Most of these turnaround outfits won't give out their track records, explaining that client confidentiality is something you'll respect them for maintaining. There's one other reason. That's this nagging fact that most of their patients died. Their fat fees become part of the problem, instead of part of the solution.

Now, back to the creditors vs. equity holders—here's how one of the largest lenders in the country does it to their stumbling clients.

They meet with the client to review the default and get a sense of what can be done.

"By the way, Jim," the account manager says, "have you ever thought about getting a consultant's opinion on what to do next? We, of course, have heard about a few that have handled situations similar to yours."

Awkward silence.

"You know," Jim replies, "maybe I should."

"Great," the lender replies, "let me make some calls and send you a few names." About thirty minutes after the creditor leaves, a FedEx letter goes from the account manager to client Jim.

> Dear Jim:
> As you requested, here are three consultants we've heard about in your area. We, of course, can't endorse any and leave the decision to you about which, if any, you hire.

Blah, blah, blah. Now the deal may be that the lender already knows #1 and #3 are busy, possibly on other assignments for the lender, but #2 has an open calendar and is eager to keep getting the lender's referrals.

Turnaround Expert #2 is then hired by Jim. He charges in, after a couple days demands that Jim stop all new product development (bad), begins shipping some marginal product (bad), cuts costs (good), and starts some sales and leasebacks of company buildings and equipment (bad).

In the process, enough cash is freed to pay down the lender. So they do. Now the other leaseholders control the company.

Turnaround Expert #2 has done so many deals that Jim, his directors and company management were impressed. The guy's been there. He's seen it all. What Jim and the managers overlooked was that Turnaround Expert #2 is experienced because he's one of the lender's favorite boys, getting them off the hook before a wobbling business expires. So the lender just keeps feeding him deals, scraping the sludge from their portfolio, and sending Turnaround Expert #2 a case of fine wine every Christmas to keep the deals flowing. Turnaround Expert #2 doesn't work on any equity incentives, by the way. Those poor folks, the shareholders, don't fare so well. And after all, they picked Turnaround Expert #2, not the creditor . . . so there's no liability when they file for bankruptcy. That's the whole trick.

Jim and company management have slipped from worse to worse yet, having mortgaged their future.

This isn't a half-bad career for Turnaround Expert #2, by the way, since he'll always have deals coming. Much of the trick in making a living at turnarounds is finding them. (Some shameless self-promoters even write books. Like this. Besides being one of the few turnaround guides in print, and the only readable and practical one, this book does attract and screen possible situations, without lunching myself to death or grinding through the speakers' circuits.)

Working for the creditors produces a steady deal flow, but trains the practitioner to go for the shorter of short-term solutions, at risk to the shareholders. That is not unfair, by the way. Creditors deserve their payments more than anybody. That's why it's called debt. And when the risk grows beyond their appetite, squeezing the delinquent client is their solemn duty.

But as a shareholder, you have a duty to worry less about their problems and try to avoid compromising your future. We're talking about different objectives and it is going to be sticky.

(Sharp-eyed readers should note in Chapter 1 that Knight Protective shareholders got a 53× cash return in my fifth year. Really sharp-eyed readers will further note that in my first year, Knight Protective creditors got a knee-capping. I was hired by the shareholders in that situation.)

A couple other types to watch for are the One-Trick Ponies and the Job Seeker in Disguise. Most individual turnaround experts who don't work with lenders are one or the other. If the candidate has one dramatic victory, but no others, be careful. Dig in to see if that person has philosophies or can describe the most common problems and solutions. See if they know what caused their single success. There is this thing called luck that startles us all from time to time.

"Chainsaw" Al Dunlap had one huge victory at Scott Paper, where he slashed costs but also got very lucky when commodity price trends swung his way. He tripped and fell, big time, on his next assignment as an upcoming section shows.

The Job Seekers in Disguise tend to talk turnarounds, but will readily hint that they might be willing to stay on longer. This is okay. We've all got different desires in life. But it does suggest a bit of insecurity, a fear of relying wholly on their ability to turn around business after business, which pays a bunch better than clinging on afterward, and is a wholly different activity. It's likely you've uncovered another consultant who needs the security of longer-term work. This isn't all bad, it's just that you may not be picking up the intensity needed, and psychotic levels of energy help during the first six months.

Industry specialists are usually quite good. I'm not sure if this is because they are familiar with the industry or if it's just that they were good to begin with, and the word automatically spreads in their industry.

One such friend of mine, John Carrington, will only accept software company turnarounds in Southern California. His 20-20-20 formula is for $20K per month, 20% of your equity, and a location within 20 minutes of his home. He normally gets it, and has some reasonably ecstatic clients. I, on the other hand, possessing a low threshold of boredom, have changed industries every time. This keeps you alert, but means the rewards average less. At least I notice four waterfalls within John's house. His and my careers intertwined in the seventies and we've been friends since, but his home's waterfall count beats mine by roughly four.

So always look closely at an industry expert. They probably already know something about your company and you can easily check on them.

Avoid any firm or individual that promises to find new investors. There's always a catch. When things are tight, it's tempting when anyone lays out that bait. But, ultimately, it never comes without sharp barbs.

I say this, knowing fully that this will be the most ignored comment in the entire book. Cash promises are too seductive an appeal to ignore. Trust me, it won't work.

Miss a commitment and the penalties will be awesome, as a lender or firm of this type must reasonably insist, perhaps not in your first meeting. And they'll suck up your time, since you're eager and they're less so; letting you fidget, always under some prerehearsed reason for delays, making you more and more pliable.

When you're losing money, getting more dollars simply subsidizes and institutionalizes your problem. This new cash rewards bad habits. The function of a business is to create money, not consume it, and the longer you postpone this the harder it gets to fix.

Watch out for these traps. Don't be easy on your business. Make it perform, and mistrust referrals from those with narrow interests in your business. Remember there are always those who promise new money to troubled business, and none are people you want your mom to meet.

CHAPTER 3

OVER AND OVER AND OVER AGAIN, THE SAME MISTAKES

In every floundering company, you hear one of the following comments:

"We're pushing for the X contract, and if we just land that one, a lot should fall to the bottom line."

"Since the old man retired, his kids really modernized this place."

"We were probably ahead of our time."

"Our name is so good that adding these other services should pump up sales."

"We created this industry."

Pushing for revenues in hopes something will "fall to the bottom line" is the single biggest cause of tragedy in American business. Nothing "falls" to the bottom line. There are a whole series of ugly, biting, scratching cost lines between the top and the bottom, each whacking their slice from every number as it tries to tumble down, and little to nothing is left by the time it hits the profit column. This is especially true when you push to get that new business or huge sale. Pushing means diverting resources. It rarely means increasing price. So we're talking extra expense and less margin from the start.

Wanting to get bigger instead of getting better is stupid. Work on becoming better and, guess what, you naturally grow bigger. But pushing for size, by itself, makes you fatter, not bigger, less special and easier to kill. Often you lose the thing that made you viable in the first place.

"Since the old man. . . ." Now, there are exceptions, and Chapter 50 gives one example. But I cannot ignore the fact that my first three turnarounds were all private firms that slipped into deep trouble under the second generation.

This may be peculiar to smaller firms, where a dominant personality might have *been* the company.

In each case, the following generation was better educated and more articulate. They had bigger ideas and ambitions. Most were more pleasant to be around than "the old man." They were more active in trade associations and committed to capital equipment and nicer furnishings quicker. And none of that has anything to do with success.

No entrepreneur should allow his or her children into the business until they've worked outside for fifteen years. Let the world teach them the nasty lessons. If they return to the business, they'll appreciate it more and get some respect they'd otherwise never enjoy. (If they fail outside, keep them way outside or your family will experience a Shakespearean tragedy and self-destruct. Let them run the family foundation and attend lots of black-tie receptions for the crusade against plant abuse and other critical issues. Send them some dividends. Don't deepen their declining self-esteem by putting them inside where they either fall on their face if given responsibility, or, if given no real duties, are snickered at for that.)

You've seen it. Junior walks down the hallway and stops to talk to several supervisors.

"How about those Bears?" Junior asks.

"They're going to have a long season," one supervisor says.

"Yeah," Junior says, "I never got to play ball myself. Dad always wanted me to sweep floors here after school."

"He's a toughie," another supervisor chuckles.

"You got that," Junior replies, "being the boss's son is a mixed blessing."

Junior waves, walks away, smiling and shaking his head. The supervisors smirk at each other. One makes a gagging gesture after Junior turns the corner. They drift back to their offices, make a few personal calls and, after getting another coffee, start to work again, half-speed, for the company they'll never have a chance to lead.

When offspring return to a family business after working outside for fifteen years, two nice things happen. One is that the younger generation has shed radical ideas for practical ones, and received that tuition at some other employer's expense. The second is that the parent has mellowed with time, and has likely mellowed with age so chances for conflict between the generations is lessened.

"We were probably ahead of our time." This excuse somehow seems noble to the speaker. The damage from being early hurts just as much as from being late. And saying you were ahead of your time just isn't knowable. You may have been a century ahead of your time and/or the moment may never come for the super-duper new concept you've developed.

Don't keep pushing that breakthrough. Mothball it. Shore up your existing business, that one you ignored while taking this riskier bet. With time, and restored cash flow from the boring old standard stuff, maybe the world will come around to wanting that new device or service, and if so, you'll certainly detect that moment before competitors. You'll also be in a better position to seize the day. And, perhaps, with time, you'll come to realize that the idea wasn't so much ahead of its time as it was simply dumb. Anybody with spirit will make these errors, remember it with humor, and don't hesitate to try again. I won't suggest you be more cautious next time, I suspect you've already sworn that oath, once burned.

"Our name is so good. . . ." Yeah, but Betty Crocker doesn't wear a miniskirt, you don't buy pacemakers from Mattel, and the proud Boeing name doesn't make me want to buy a car. AT&T put their name on fax paper and burglar alarms after deregulation. Now, AT&T was one trusted name, but are you eager to try their fax paper? Does that enhance my loyalty to Ma Bell? Hardly. It confuses it. And the burglar alarm business did do okay briefly for AT&T, but very briefly, and most folks who responded to their telemarketers were simply confused, and set up for the hard sell.

Your name is never as good as you think it is. And it's rarely stretchable.

If you're the most dependable source for rivets, and add a line of bolts, that probably works . . . provided your customers aren't so big that they have one buyer for rivets and a different buyer for bolts. (That bolt buyer, unbeknownst to you, used to date the rivet buyer's son and the romance ended with some nasty accusations. You'll never hear about that, of course, and you'll never quite understand why you can sell Megacorporation so many rivets and never get a single bolt order.)

Miller Lite was a great extension. Tripled revenues. Alka-Seltzer Plus cannibalized existing sales. Heinz owned the pickle business, and lost it to Vlasic when they expanded into ketchup. You'd think pickles and ketchup went together, but somehow they didn't.

The logic is never as easy as it appears.

"We created this industry." Oh please. You should be embarrassed by that wistful look backward. Why did you lose it? Work on that.

Nobody cares about the story of your founders working in their garage for a year before introducing the first blankety-blank. The market remembers how you eased credit during the downturn of ten years ago. They remember for somewhere between five and ten minutes. When that new competitor offers faster delivery than you, it saddens them, for a moment, when they feel no choice but to drop you. Can you hear it?

"What a great guy old Jonesy was, remember how he shipped when we couldn't pay during the recession? It's tragic he couldn't keep up. How quick can we cancel his POs?"

These companies that talk about creating their industries tend to be very active in trade associations, spend more time with vendors than customers, and have, unfortunately, the most overexperienced management team in the industry. They've got dirty windshields and large rearview mirrors.

The last, and most toxic comment you'll hear in most troubled businesses is silence. That will be the response when you ask each executive to fill in the blank for this sentence: Ours is the only product that ____ (put a meaningful buyer benefit here). Not knowing what you're best at, or can be best at, is death.

Nirvana is finding a company that has this problem, one that has a unique but unrecognized benefit. Those are the deals that you can turn around without trauma. Simply mobilize the company toward their strength and get everybody to ignore the me-too crud that takes away their edge.

Here comes the hard part. If you're a turnaround manager, most of your life will be facing these same situations. It gets repetitious. The fixes are the same. While the outside world views you as a sharp-eyed gunslinger, we're really assembly line workers.

But the part of a turnaround manager that's effective, the no-nonsense, cut-the-meandering, get-right-to-the-point behavior that's necessary also needs a touch of humanity when hearing these same, wrong beliefs over and over.

You've got to waste some precious time hearing them out. You've got to do some head-nodding before you act. Then you've got to explain why you're responding as you are, and do it in a way that draws support and enthusiasm without wasting time. You need the troop's support. Being too abrupt is a temptation. That's why it's tough.

Quickly take the team through the probable costs and margins of that big new order they're chasing. Don't kill it, this is a great attitude, just show them exactly where it must be priced to enhance the business.

If the old man's kids are still around, put them all in the field selling. Respect the comments about their ambitions, just put them where they have to prove it without spending more money for awhile. They'll probably leave after a few months.

Gently but quickly get several key buyers to either support or help you shelve the breakthrough concept that may be ahead of its time. Don't kill it yourself, let customers do that, and get to know them in the process.

Do the same with product extensions, not just based on interviews but trial orders. Find out if your relationship is expandable to those other areas.

Acknowledge that your company created the industry every time it's brought up, and within the same sentence turn it around into a question for the speaker. "How did we lose it?"

More important, way more important, critical beyond belief and toughest of all, make everybody think and argue until you agree what it is that you do better than anybody else. There are no single secrets to turnaround success, but this comes close.

Turn this into a mantra that's repeated under the logo of your letterhead, as a tagline on all emails that go out, in the employee newsletter, and repeated in the voice mail system.

Make it specific. "Best" is meaningless. "The only parts NASA certified" says something. "More value" is meaningless. "Lowest cost to operate in its class" comes closer. "Fastest service" is meaningless. "Delivery next day, guaranteed" says a lot.

It doesn't have to be true, yet, by the way. If this unique benefit is within reach, start preaching now. That'll get you there faster. Quarterbacks don't throw the ball to receivers. They toss the ball to where the receiver will be in a few seconds.

CHAPTER 4

MAKE WHAT SELLS

(Remember, if bankruptcy looks probable within a year, skip these ital-icized chapters and go straight to the next boldfaced section, which is Chapter 17 in this case. C'mon now, you're not ready for this yet.)

Yellow-tipped skis tipped me off. I careened down the mountain at Vail, taking a break from Iowa State with my beer-infested roommate, Willie. We survived to the bottom of the slope on our first day when we saw the tips. They swarmed down the hill, carrying various shapes and sizes of skiers, all faster than we corn-fed mortals on mere wooden slats. We were there for a week of awkwardness on our gothic Midwestern skis, wax required, that must have looked as if they were cut from the bottom of a barrel next to those around us with the yellow-tipped steel skis.

These sunshine points marked Head Vectors. "How can you tell?" I asked Willie, and he pointed, "Look at the yellow underside." The new steel skis had a plastic coating on the bottom and they were visible from the front because the tip curled up two inches from the snow. Thus, the yellow tips.

Howard Head, an inventor in Boulder, developed steel skis because he thought they would sell. After two years of testing, bending, and cracking prototypes on Colorado Ski Patrol volunteers, Howard narrowed down the formula. He figured out what temper, how thick, welded where, and just what shape to cut. Steel, as he ultimately developed it, was lighter, springier, more consistent, quicker than hickory. In 1963, he made them fly, and they blossomed like spring daffodils over the Rocky Mountains. Vectors were his top-of-the-line model, and their signature was the yellow bottom.

The yellow-tipped skis looked faster, and, of course, they were race-proven. When I saw them in action, I lusted for them. I wanted faster, springier, lighter. So did everyone else, and that was proven in the market.

It wasn't a fad market riding a promotional wave or a drop in pricing.

The product was real. It enticed potential customers like Willie and me who went back to the flatlands and sat daydreaming through lectures while fashioning intricate doodles of Head skis complete with a 39-cent yellow pen to shade in the tips. I learned a lot in those lectures. I learned I wanted to ski more than learn, and I reaffirmed in my signature doodle logic that it had to be on Head skis.

Two years later, as soon as I graduated and found a job, I bought Head skis. Everyone did. Other skis stacked like cordwood in stores. Even when woodies were price-slashed and slashed again, Head skis cost four times as much, and dealers couldn't keep them in stock. The factory was back-ordered and expanded and ran their production lines three shifts a day. At one point, with some 20 companies around the world making skis, one of every three dollars spent for skis was for Heads. It was an exhilarating run, but inevitably others learned to make steel skis and Head lost some position.

Head had a trademark look—the black skis with the yellow bottom. Competitors came along with colors and took a little more away. But Head still dominated.

This European outfit, Rossignol, snuck in with an epoxy-composite ski. It made steel look like wood. The new skis were once again faster, lighter, and stronger. Faster, lighter, and stronger won again. The new company did to Head what Head had done to the market earlier. Head stubbornly stuck with steel too long in the same way that many companies stick with tradition, while blind to world changes.

If Head had recognized sooner that steel skis were obsolete, they could have dumped the metal-stamping and cutting equipment and reinvested heavily in epoxy laminates. They might have saved a large portion of their market through brand loyalty and customer trust. They probably could even have made them black with yellow bottoms.

But instead of customer loyalty, Head remained loyal to its process, believing quixotically that time and progress would stop with Head at the peak. If Head had moved forward with the market, they might not always have dominated, but they would certainly have done better than they did. It was an opportunity lost, and few even know that Head makes skis anymore.

What some remember is that Howard Head sold to AMF. They bought his name, not just the company. So when he started a tennis racket company, he called his new racket the Prince, not Head. Can you guess what the Prince was? Right. The first steel racket, oversized.

It's easy to become inward, to get mesmerized by the stuff you do well. It's easy to not notice the world has changed directions, tastes, or desires, but a strong company must always look outward more than inward. Companies that sell what they can make always die, but companies that make what they can sell have the formula for longevity.

Here's how to make your company healthier this week. This can last forever:

1. Start an advisory panel of customers. Get them comfortable so they'll criticize your directions. Listen hard for emerging threats, new concepts that are starting to do well in their minds. Rotate some members on the panel each year to get fresh viewpoints. Gauge their business health as you go; when they are threatened by trends, so are you.

2. Set some criteria that determines when you change. If imports move from 20% to 35%, do you shutter the domestic plant and move offshore? If one major chain switches from wood chair frames to plastic, should that be your signal that it's time to convert the factory? Numerical guides should be in place. You think sharper before getting caught in the downdraft.

3. Never forget that hidden beneath all expressed customer preference is the more true desire, the never-ending appeal of lower price. This means your costs are critical, and this low cost is the sole reason for having any pride in your process. When your costs are below all others, you will win. Every time. When Head Skis sold for quadruple the wooden prices, their costs were still below the competition. This huge margin made some killer marketing possible, plus expansion to seize the market. Rock-bottom cost is the only reason for forever loving your process. Sprinkle several reminders of this, in your own words, through your calendar. Every December 31, remind yourself to reduce costs again the following year. That keeps you focused.

CHAPTER 5

RAISE A FLAG, ANY FLAG

The store manager was stunned by the numbers. His chain, Home Depot, knew about rapid success, but this printout was staggering. He had found a way to add $14 million a year in profitable sales with no risk or investment.

He tapped his pencil on his desk. He picked up a pen and drumrolled the two together. And then he pushed his chair back from his desk and clasped his hands behind his head with the confidence that a soon-to-be-discovered corporate champion deserves.

He sprang from his chair and bounced to the door. He thought about how much fun it was to say "million dollars," so he said it 14 times. He opened the door and before him lay his Home Depot, a link in the 160-unit chain, going to 422 by 1997. At that time, sales were approaching 35 billion bucks a year. And he was contributing, nothing minor either, a $14 million discovery.

He strolled from his office through his Home Depot like a merchant prince in an orange apron. He knew it well. Sure, he learned some from training, but mostly he learned by doing. He marched ahead, scanning. He surveyed the plants, mirrors, drills, sinks, shower heads, drapes, toilets, garden fencing, tools, light fixtures, rugs, sprinkling systems, paintbrushes, saws, mattresses, lawn mowers, doors, and garbage cans. He knew where every item belonged, and he knew many of the sale prices. This was his turf.

He looked at it and he looked past it, ambling toward something at the front of the store. All the while there was confidence, a swagger in his walk.

Three months earlier, this manager had agreed to put a small kiosk near the cash registers. It was a simple test. The kiosk held one thing: Hanes hosiery for women. The Hanes distributor would keep it stocked and the Home Depot would pay in 60 days. The nylons sold for $3 a pair, and Home Depot was invoiced for $2.40. The kiosk took up only four of the 102,000 square feet of his store.

It had been five years since the first Home Depot opened in Atlanta. The idea was to sell everything for the home. With the coliseum-sized store, there was a broader selection than the typical lumberyard offered, and not that much lumber. The concept worked. Product turnover was greater than a lumberyard or hardware store could ever dream, so margins could be reduced while generating megaprofits. The huge selection drew customers. The customers knew that whatever they wanted for their home could be found at Home Depot.

Each Home Depot was carefully located near dense middle- and upper-class residential areas. Each store generated about $34 million in sales. It was incredibly consistent.

Into this atmosphere ventured a persistent Hanes sales rep who hit it off with the store manager, the one now marching to the front of the store. The sales rep convinced the store manager that a Hanes kiosk would fit right in and make lots of money.

It made lots of money. It was easy to put in. The Home Depot did not have to stock the kiosk or keep it orderly. That was the distributor's job. Their delivery person restocked the inventory, dusted it off, and refilled the display at least twice a week. The store manager had to do only one thing: Keep the movable kiosk within 30 feet of both a cash register and the front door.

When the manager reached the front of the store, he scrutinized the action by the kiosk. He studied the nylon packages and then the woman behind the third cash register. Just an hour ago, he had asked her how the Hanes were selling. And now, $14 million.

Here's how he figured it, back in his office. She had said, without batting an eye, "Oh, maybe two dozen, three dozen pair so far today. They sold better yesterday, when the kiosk was next to my register."

That estimate made the manager think that if the more-distant cash registers also sold a few pairs, they were probably moving about 75 pairs of nylons a day. That's almost $235, which makes $85,000 a year. Put that in all 160 stores and there's over $14 million in new business every year. And they were selling so fast they were paid for before the bill came due, thus, zero investment.

The store manager was pumped, but he had a conservative streak so he kept this to himself. He studied it further. He personally audited the cash register tapes to make sure the estimates were correct. For two months he watched, all the while writing and fine-tuning a report. Sales held up. He was destined to be the $14 million hero.

Finally, he sent his report to the area office. And he waited. He knew what they would say. He could taste it.

He was wrong. They killed the idea. They called it "a good little business." And then they laid out their reason.

"You know," they said, "we're afraid it's going to cost us more than it makes us. It doesn't fit in." He was incredulous. They continued. Slowly, he began to see what they meant. The store manager, in all his excitement, had lost one perspective.

"What could happen here," they explained, "is that this may confuse our image. We're the Home Depot. We should have a $10 billion business in a few years and it has been built on one theme. Homeowners come here to buy things for their home and yard. We don't sell bicycles. We don't sell candy. And we don't sell clothes, including panty hose. The truth is, we're afraid a $14 million distraction might confuse our customers and not be worth it. You know, fuzzy direction kills more businesses than competition or dying markets. We know our direction, and it doesn't include panty hose."

(Note to readers: these profit-building stories, with headlines in italics, are revised from my 1993 book *Tight Ships Don't Sink,* published by Simon & Schuster but now out of print. The Home Depot was then such a tale, with 160 stores. In 2001, the years since make those examples look pretty solid. The Home Depot's profits accelerated as a percent through '98, '99, and 2000 with 1,087 stores and 2,300 planned by 2005. Sales in 2001 will surpass $44 billion.)

The example of how to start up a business, Chapter 63, was a struggling idea I cofounded and had spent three years on when that first book came out in 1993. It required updating for *The Six-Month Fix* since Teledesic had four employees and twenty consultants in the old book. Today it's still dicey, but Teledesic sits on $300,000,000 in the bank, has several hundred employers, and recent investors valued it at $3 billion.

That '93 book also predicted mediocrity ahead for IBM, General Motors, and Sears. All three cooperated by fumbling and stumbling.

My point is that this stuff works.

(To sell books by the carload, *The Six-Month Fix* should have a theme and title like *Get Rich in Sixty Seconds without Working,* or *The Eleven Secrets All Millionaires Know.* Politicians, faith healers, and "No Money Down Real Estate" tape-peddlers, folks who understand what sells and who worry less about results, understand this phenomenon well. The first business book to become a bestseller, *Up the Organization,* entertained, with the Avis CEO telling how they became number two. It was a fun read. But

Avis never elbowed Hertz aside. More interesting yet, *In Search of Excellence,* a classic text with great counsel, saw its examples of superbly managed companies collapse in the decade that followed. Not all, but enough.)

The people who ran the Home Depot knew what they were doing. They were clear about what Home Depot was, and they made sure the store manager also understood. But they weren't angry with the manager. Quite the contrary; they applauded his initiative. And then they began to spread the story because it, as well as anything, helped define the Home Depot.

They told other store managers. They told shareholders, and they told the business press, which picked up on the story. A newsletter to employees repeated the fable, again praising the store manager for his initiative but repeating exactly why the Home Depot was successful. The direction was this: "Broadest selection of items anywhere for the home and yard at a fair price."

That's it. That's their flag. They raised it and they stayed with it even under the rocket's red glare of quicker money. Home Depot continues to outgrow the economy. Lowe's is giving them a run now, but is way behind. Lowe's would have experienced a tougher time, probably, if the Home Depot had not momentarily forgotten their mantra, and expanded into designer items with Home Depot's EXPO. Oh well. Consumers recognize Home Depot as the place for selection and value.

Here's how to put your business on a straighter track this year:

1. Survey your customers, employees, and vendors. Figure out where your organization excels, or could. Decide which most-mentioned things have the greatest validity and future.
2. Put all this into several short phrases. See which stick with people. Never claim best quality, price, and service together because all three are incompatible. Pick one. Maybe two. Be specific. "At 60 miles per hour, the loudest noise is the clock," says Rolls Royce. That tells much more than a tired claim like "quality." It says a little more than "quiet." It's specific, so it's memorable. Dominos defines its pizza service as "delivered in 30 minutes." They don't say "better" or "cheaper" or "hotter" or "spicier" or "bigger." They don't even say "quicker." They say "in 30 minutes."
3. Use the phrase in speeches, advertising, and letterheads and on the front door, shipping labels, and brochures. About the time you are sick of it, others just might be starting to grasp it. Never dilute the key phrase by mentioning all the other boring things you also may do. Nobody cares. Talk to your strength.

CHAPTER 6

SPECIALIZE OR DIE

Doug Smith was cursed. He inherited the worst set of blinders imaginable. Doug was rich.

His never-ending source of familial cash kept the kid's company, Software Express of Big Sky, Montana, afloat no matter how badly mismanaged. He needed little perspective because he had a trust fund. And so the company grew outward, into three separate areas, and kept pace by losing money. Finally, after 53 quarters of losses over ten years, Dad and the other trustees grew weary of writing check after check.

The board of Software Express, through a recruiter, asked me to take over as CEO.

It was interesting, but I wasn't interested. I told the recruiter that the Smith family had messed up the business for so long that failure was part of the corporate culture and that it would take drastic redirection to make the company merely break even. And then the danger was that everyone would celebrate mediocrity. "If they want to make money," I said, "they must yield all operating control."

"I don't think they're ready for that," stammered the recruiter. He cited Doug Smith's soulful commitment to the company. I reminded him that it wasn't a company, it was a black hole for cash, a welfare system that discouraged productivity.

Doug Smith was bright, he bristled with energy, and he could program most anything. But when it came to running a business, he never developed any struggle muscles. His instincts never developed since he never had to worry about cash. It was like learning tennis without the net. Meaningless.

He worked hard, was always enthusiastic, and usually had a grand plan du jour. The grand plan never had anything to do with profits. It was often a vision of new revenues, a tangent to avoid dealing with niggling details like cost, profit, and loss.

Oh, and there were prayer meetings daily. Good thing, a miracle would help. But while the Lord works in mysterious ways, one thing the man seems to hardly ever do is provide money for mismanaged businesses. Tough guy, that Lord.

"Let them hire an eager Cub Scout," I said to the recruiter, "let them experience losing another million dollars this summer. Then we'll talk."

The discussions continued back and forth until finally the family trust's lawyer, frustrated, insisted it was time to cede control. So I joined. Doug Smith, the son and 20% owner, stayed and became a pal. His dad, the Chairman, left the building and didn't return. Board meetings would be held if I called them, and I didn't.

It was impossible to dislike this puppy, Doug. But pat his head and he'd wet the carpet every time. His unbridled enthusiasm for everything was magnetic. But it was part of a disjointed attention span with no economic sense or consistency.

He had previously lasted two semesters at Montana State. He was brighter than most and hustled. But he flunked out. He couldn't conform. It had to do with something silly like class attendance.

Doug next worked at McDonald's in Billings, Montana. After six months, they Mcfired him. Then he moved to Big Sky, where the family trust backed him in Software Express. As I checked out the company and talked to Doug, it was obvious there was only one thing Software Express needed: focus. The company was jumping in so many directions without following through on any that it was losing money and offending customers on every front.

After eight weeks, Doug and I talked about this and how we really could make money on any of several areas the company was in. He agreed with zeal.

I put together the new rules. There was to be no investment in any new areas for one year. There was to be a modest investment of money (and more time) into several existing projects. Budgets were to be set and kept. We would tighten the ship.

Doug read my proposal and liked it. The next week, he resigned, saying his talents fit better in a more entrepreneurial environment. It was best that he left. But it was sad, since I feared he would start wallowing in the dissipation of cash again.

One thing Software Express produced was software that calculated mortgage amortizations for realtors and bankers. It could be customized to display tables in three different ways. These packages cost about $10,000 and took a month to customize.

The company's second product was statistical software. It had been developed at Montana State and was then acquired by Software Express for a royalty. This product appealed mainly to academics, and even that demand was shaky. It cost $25,000. It was more precise and less flexible than other systems. Practical users, in quality control departments of manufacturers, showed zero interest in the product. The only people who were interested in it were bureaucratic purists. The Census Bureau and the National Institute of Health both had signed long-term licenses for the software and its revisions.

The third product of Software Express was simple legal software. It sold to small law firms that wanted to computerize word processing. It was a shelf item, no customization required. It sold for $1,500 and displayed in color. It also printed in color.

I called on several buyers of all three products to sense what appealed and what turned off users.

We found two competitors who made nearly identical mortgage software.

We learned that our statistical system was the best. We also learned that it was best by just under one-half of one hair diameter. A thin hair. It also took more work to run, and it cost a lot more than the next best.

And we learned that lawyers thought it was nice that our word processing package was the only one around in color. Not overwhelming, just nice.

We thought about improving the mortgage package over our two competitors. But they had programmers on staff who were undoubtedly thinking ahead of us already. And besides, that market wasn't growing. We tried anyway. We kept improving quality, and we raised prices 5 percent a month for a year. At the end of the year, 20 percent of the customers remained loyal; 80 percent told us to stuff it, and left.

Those that remained were most concerned with quality, which we had improved upon each month. The 20 percent of the business that stayed was profitable, and we sold the mortgage package to a fidgety, retired banker looking for a hobby. He made more money in his next five years running this restructured business out of his den than he enjoyed in the previous 30 years squeezing borrowers from his old granite office.

We thought there would be an ongoing market for the statistical software if we could redesign it to be more user-friendly. ("User-friendly" is one of those computer words that's trying to say "easy." If they ever say "easy" they might be approaching a level of humanity that suggests the PC industry is approaching the truth.) We decided against the redesign after seeing it would take 18 months and $250,000. Instead, we sold it to Scientific Associates, a lower-priced but stronger competitor. Scientific Associates did their own redesign and peddled the package as their Cadillac of statistical software. It worked for them.

We renamed Software Express as Legal Rainbow. We chose to pursue the lawyers' word-processing market because, of the three original products of Software Express, only the legal package offered something of value to the customer that was unique in the market. It wasn't anything fancy that allowed us to stand completely apart. It was simply color. We had it, no one else did. It was our point of difference, our specialty.

Color didn't even serve a rational purpose. And our customers were lawyers . . . people who deal with guilt and innocence, black and white. On first glance, this may seem like the wrong group to fall for color. They still wear a lot of white shirts and black shoes. But it didn't cost any more money. A few lawyers, having analyzed every last reason to pick software, tumbled over the edge for our color, all other differences being pretty subtle. It doesn't hurt with jury presentations, makes the clients feel they're getting more professional help and everything . . . from cars to dress shirts, toothpaste, and skis, and PCs graduate from black and white and gray to color as the markets grow. It's sort of the way Steve Jobs reignited Apple, with mint- and lemon-colored Mac shells, for a brief moment.

Sales tripled in a year. All the employees got better at color graphics because that became all Legal Rainbow did. Eighteen months later, a computer manufacturer bought the business.

I remember Doug Smith from time to time and hope he's gaining the real confidence that only comes from self-sufficiency. His family ego got bruised a bit, but their net worth jumped several million dollars in the year this turnaround required.

(Warning: by the time you finish this book, you'll think I've been CEO of eighteen companies, but you'll only be half-right. Chapter 68 tells you everywhere I've been and what happened. In several of these stories I've changed locations and the industries to avoid embarrassment to people who were good spirits but economically challenged.)

Legal Rainbow succeeded because it specialized. Nobody can be all things to all people. The dumbest words in business are either "full product line," "no job too big or too small," or "one-stop shopping." That proves the company is exceptional at nothing. Since it does more than anybody else, it does it all worse. And since it does more, it has more overhead. The life span for companies with poor service and high overhead is best measured by a stopwatch.

Here are three tactics that will elevate your business this year, about as much as anything you can do. The results will start to crank out in the second half if you start this week:

1. Rank every product and service you sell by its gross margin. Sell off, raise prices, or shut down everything on the bottom half of this list within a year. This takes guts. It always works.
2. Distinguish your distribution from others. If they sell to bankers, you sell to realtors and learn their language. If they sell to Fortune 500s, you sell to mom-and-pop businesses. When others sell direct, cut your overhead and use sales reps. Pick one region to dominate instead of being number two or three everywhere.
3. Chart a separate course with either deeper or shallower volume discounts. If others have fifty product lines, narrow yours to five and do it better. If they offer generous terms, shave your prices and tighten up credit, becoming the prestige line. Zig when they zag.

CHAPTER 7

SCORN BREAK-EVEN

A silver and a brass ring pierced his left nostril. (How do these people blow their noses?) The jeans were oily and torn, his hair snarled in tangles across the shoulders of a leather jacket. "Hey, dudes, the new boss man's here," he said, straightening from a slouch in a squeaking chair. Stuffing spilled from the seat cushion. He dropped a cigarette, snuffed it on the tile with his boot, and extended a hand.

"Welcome to Knight Protective," he sneered.

This was a telemarketer. I signed on as CEO that March of 1990, before meeting any employees. My contract paid poorly for survival, handsomely for a rebound. There were 80 more telemarketers on the payroll, not all as charming as this guy.

Their job? Selling burglar alarms. Getting sales appointments over the phone. Relating to homeowners.

Wait. Relating to homeowners? Nose rings? Hmmm. Well, it got worse before it got worse.

Besides this underwhelming introduction, Knight's checkbook showed that one supplier got most of our business. A little sniffing around proved that two of my top executives owned this vendor, under different names, and their prices were inflated sky-high.

That was fixed easily enough; we just ordered a huge quantity and didn't pay. This supplier's owners (my less-than-honest executives) couldn't reveal themselves by trying very hard to collect, so the culprits quit and our cost of goods sold dropped for a moment.

Losses were running about $80,000 per week. If Knight hadn't capitalized research and depreciated equipment over 10 years, it would have looked worse and been more accurate. Every Knight alarm used two-way voice. This meant that during an alarm, and only during an alarm, an amplified speakerphone turned on in the customer's home. Instead of a simple siren, which we all hear and ignore daily, a voice boomed through. "This is the security center. Can I have your code word?" our dispatchers demanded.

That verified false alarms quickly, without a separate phone call. More importantly, during a break-in, this immediately detected burglars, who knew it and left. Unfortunately, sloppy manufacturing and crappy design meant that installers spent an average of two visits to satisfy our customers.

Knight's financial statements contained another time bomb. Lifetime warranty sales had brought in several million dollars, but this cash had evaporated. Worse yet, these guarantees were sold to the most troublesome customers and installations. That apparently was seen as easier than fixing the problems. Some contracts promised to change batteries for the customer every time they ran down, and some of these systems ate batteries like nickels in a slot machine. No cash, lots of ongoing expense.

Meanwhile, ADT and Brinks entered the market with systems selling for $195. Our average installation cost was $3,400. C'mon, they had no two-way voice. But at 6 percent of our price . . . uh, cough . . . selling that legitimate advantage got tougher. At their prices, ADT and Brinks had hardly any sales expense and could close deals over the phone. Their advertising costs remained, but that was far less than sales commissions. An installer could finish their job in three hours. Our systems took a couple technicians all day to install. Sometimes two.

After spending a few nights riding with the Los Angeles police, seeing how intensely busy they were and beginning to understand that, since 99 percent of all alarms are false, they simply could not afford to respond immediately to alarms, if at all, Knight's advantage seemed stronger. We challenged burglars, demanding the code word, and listened in during an alarm. Knight didn't merely report an alarm. Knight reported verified alarms. Police respond to real alarms. They like to catch bad guys. So this concept worked. Kind of.

But there wasn't enough cash to continue. Marketing expenses shot out of sight when consumer price expectations dropped.

Our monitoring center received fan mail, but our servicemen were despised and demoralized. You didn't need a room-temperature IQ to realize that while we monitored well, everything else we did carried a barnyard odor.

So Knight stopped aggressive selling. Adios, nose rings. Knight stopped making the proprietary system. Knight licensed the top manufacturer with two-way voice and bought reduced quantities from them.

You can't think clearly when you're bleeding. But now, with a positive cash flow, Knight was ready. The industry's marketing costs shot so high that other dealers were strapped for cash, and it became cheaper to buy other dealers' accounts than it had ever been to create accounts by selling new customers ourselves. Nobody in our markets saw this silver lining. Everybody froze, waiting for things to return to normal, but it was over. The world had changed.

So we started buying other accounts. Within four years we owned 14,000, free and clear, and paid off all other debts. We sent several million dollars to our startled shareholders and piled up $2 million in the bank.

Several hundred more dealers across the country began to understand the problem of false alarms and switched to two-way voice. The manufacturer we licensed began to sell modest quantities. This meant royalty checks for Knight. And since Knight was now focused, we discovered and patented new ways to improve monitoring. Other monitoring stations liked this technology and signed licenses.

Then the inevitable happened. Protection One, a fast-growing West Coast alarm company, noticed us in the summer of 1994. It acquired Knight for well over triple our annual sales by November, and two other bidders were close on their heels.

My phone rang the day we distributed the cash. It was a shocked shareholder, who had just received a check for several million dollars. "What in the world did you do?" he asked.

"Less," I replied. And that was all.

Fortunately, we never had enough cash to subsidize the dumber activities. The business had to be fixed immediately.

Was it tough? Not for long. We were in so much trouble there were few choices. Thank God we weren't breaking even. You can languish in that mediocrity forever and retire one day, not living too high, and wonder why it was all so unrewarding. We didn't have that luxury. And it wasn't so strenuous that I didn't have time to write the earlier version of this book, have a life, and cofound Teledesic.

Here's what to do this week if your profits are meager.

1. Take drastic action immediately. You are losing ground to competitors, which means you'll be dead soon, so anything you do will probably help. Doing nothing is extreme risk. Stop selling and start buying, or stop buying and start selling. Raise prices 30 percent, close

a factory, and buy from somebody else. Decide in one day what you'll do. Can't quite do this? Then quit. Don't wait for things to get better. They don't. Don't give yourself time to think about it. You don't get smarter by watching bad things continue.

2. Squeeze in receivables, stretch payables, and find one cost reduction, no matter what size, every week. The amount doesn't matter as much as the habit. This will spread and it does add up. (Never seek funding when you're in trouble. If you don't get the money, which is likely, you've wasted time at a critical moment. If you do get it, the cash subsidizes bad business, making it possible to continue to do bad things. You also give up too much by selling shares cheap or paying high rates when weakened.) You cannot think clearly when cash isn't growing, so just do whatever you must to start a positive flow first. Nothing else counts.

3. Spread the money as it grows. This is the hard part. More cash can make you stupid. So cling to that previous panic. Put a little more back into development, send the shareholders some, and pay down debt a trifle. Any single idea that sucks up all this new bounty is toxic.

CHAPTER 8

SLASH COSTS

There is a business that created itself because of an unending quest to cut costs. It was called Price Club, now Costco, and it is the product of two men with different backgrounds but the same philosophy. Cut costs constantly.

Thirty years before Price Club was founded, Sol Price was an attorney in San Diego. During World War II, many of his clients had to pay bills by giving him their watches, rather than cash. So many clients did this that he started a secondhand jewelry store. Thirty years later that store had evolved into FedMart, a chain of discount variety stores.

In 1975, Price sold the company to a German retailer, Hugo Mann. Price stayed with the company as President, and the Germans flew Hans Schoepflin over to be Executive Vice President. Sol Price fought the German's rigidity, such as the requirement of three signatures on every expense report. Sol rebelled, but it wasn't his company anymore. Sol was fired.

Hans Schoepflin became President of FedMart, and Sol opened a new business called Price Club. Sol also sued FedMart, Mann, and Schoepflin for breach of contract.

Sol leased a warehouse in a commercial area 10 minutes from my home in La Jolla, California, just north of San Diego. "Nobody came," Sol recalls, "After six months we had to decide whether to put some more money in to keep it going."

Price Club eliminated middlemen, salesclerks, and excessive handling. It was a warehouse. Customers helped themselves to huge quantities for incredible discounts. For instance, the panty hose that Home Depot wouldn't touch in Chapter 5 were sold at Price Club for $25 a ten-pack when, and only when, the Price Club got a deal. It worked here; it was win-win.

But, for the first six months, the concept sat dormant. There were few customers and lots of inventory. Sol and a handful of friendly investors were $750,000 into it. At six months, Sol didn't hesitate, he decided risk another $250,000. No more. He still doesn't know why, it was a feeling, something instinctive. Whatever, he was right. Customers finally started trickling in.

Maybe the few customers from the beginning started talking. Maybe word of mouth moves more slowly in balmy Southern California. Maybe the switch from company sales to individuals as members did it. There is no explanation for the delay in success. But there is an explanation for the success: Customers loved to save money.

For a year Sol and Hans never talked, but they met regularly in courtrooms and lawyers' offices. Sol listened intently to every deposition Hans gave in the lawsuit, and over time it became clear they shared a philosophy. About two years after the split, Hans sensed Sol was right and his home-country owners were wrong. This wasn't Germany. This was San Diego. Beards were fine, jeans were okay, and suits and ties were okay once in awhile as long as you looked ill at ease. What wasn't good was always carrying an item no matter what the cost and stocking too many sizes and paying high rent. Hans knew, as Price had said, there should be only one rule: Cut costs. But Hugo Mann wanted to expand.

Hans lost, too; he didn't want to expand FedMart, so he quit. About the same time, the lawsuit was settled.

In the summer of 1978, Sol asked Hans to come work with him. They met for coffee and discussed the vision of reducing distribution costs. That system required low-rent warehouses, all-palletized racks, and forklift direct-loading of merchandise from the truck onto the sales floor.

They kept talking. They both believed deep discounting had a healthy future. Sol Price was depression-scarred and cost-conscious. Hans Schoepflin was a CPA by trade; he saw every cost as an evil and never saw a necessary evil. They looked at retailing from a new perspective, moving an entire step up the food chain of retailing. Negotiating the contract was tough. Hans's salary was to be nothing but stock for the first year, they both agreed, but the amount of stock took several days to negotiate. This might have been more interesting if either had realized that the ten percent Hans got would become worth hundreds of millions in the next decade.

According to Price, the store concept worked because of limited selection, not in spite of it, and because of the large sizes. Accounting is easier, inventory is easier, and best of all, fewer customers buy more of the product. Price says, "Losing customers pays. . . . Suppose 10,000 customers walk through in a day. Assume that 10 need some light oil for around the house. If you carry a 12-ounce can, an eight-ounce can, and a three-ounce can, you'll sell oil to 10 customers.

"One buys the 12-ounce can, three buy the eight-ounce can, and six buy the three-ounce can. Add it up. You've sold 10 customers 54 ounces of oil by stocking three sizes.

"But at Price Club, we might only carry the 12-ounce can. Half of the 10 buyers won't buy. 12 ounces is too much. So we only sell five customers, but at 12 ounces each we've just sold 60 ounces. That's more oil. And the better part is, now we get a deeper discount from the vendor. They have to ship only one size to Price Club, and they ship more of it. Drives down their costs. So we pass along the break to our customer. And now we sell even more oil due to that lower price. That's how losing customers pays, and everybody wins."

Price Club (now Costco) earned deep price cuts from suppliers for making their life easier with less packaging. If suppliers refuse, that category is not carried. This keeps a sense of discovery in shopping. It may not always be in stock, but when it is, it's a buy. Adds a little adventure to the visit.

It worked so well that Price Club had no inventory expense. Items sell in two weeks or they are not reordered. Vendor payment is usually due in 30 days. Most products sell in half that time. Memberships are sold as a Price Club or Costco comes to town, paying for the building in advance.

When the customers started to come to Price Club, a second outlet opened. It was packed with people immediately and nobody knows why. Ditto for a third. *Forbes* magazine picked Price Club as the most profitable growth company of the 1980s. Sales in 1994 passed $10 billion. That's not bad growth for the first 18 years. In 2001 Costco is on track to book sales beyond $50 billion. It's beginning to look like this startup from my neighborhood just might make it big one day. Especially since they are still looking to cut costs.

Even after the company made multimillionaires out of anybody who invested $2,500 in the early years, the annual report was still done on a copying machine. The president's office kept his college bookshelf, two planks across a matched pair of bricks. Okay, the planks were painted in a nice gloss.

One day Sam Walton came to San Diego and asked Sol for a tour. Sol showed him, and a few years later, Sam's Clubs started appearing across the country. Success bred competitors. Costco soon appeared. They, too, grew huge in a few years, and merged. Everybody won.

What Sol and Hans knew on their way to the megazillionaires club is that there is no such thing as a fixed cost. No savings is trivial. Each sets an example, and rarely is there a motivating feature stronger than finding the best price. Hardly ever are nonregulated businesses blessed with a market so strong or isolation so great that price is unrelated to cost. Cost reduction, therefore, is the greatest market-developing activity that exists.

Sooner or later every washed-up, burnt-out marketing executive like myself starts to realize that accountants, those nerdy bean counters, are better at questioning and reducing costs than we flashy marketing guys. Therefore, accountants are better marketers than we marketers. Gulp.

Here's how you can boost profits immediately:

1. Cut management salaries by 5%. Drop CEO and vice president salaries 10%. Add monthly profit bonuses based on profits. When monthly profits beat last year's by 10%, give a 10% bonus. When 5%, give 5%, and when 20%, give 20%. Watch requests for expenditures drop. This gets everybody rowing in the same direction.

2. Put together a new committee each month to come up with different cost reductions. Use a cross section of employees. Pay for their time, give them 30 days to deliver the five most important cost reductions possible, and publish the recommendations. Post a list of all suggestions actually used along with committee members' names. Split 20% of the first year's savings among the committee members.

3. Set an example yourself. Use excursion airfares, schedule Saturday travel meetings to drop hotel and airfares, and check alternative long-distance services. Cut back the trash and janitorial service, buy used furniture and office equipment, move your office to a cheaper location, but put in more plants and brighter paint. Organize purchasing so everything costing more than $1,000 is a bid. Finally, stop replacing departed employees for 180 days and see what happens. Your remaining employees might prefer keeping the work themselves and getting bigger bonuses.

CHAPTER 9

JUMP-START NEW PRODUCTS

When Kodak announced its 110 Instamatic camera at a photo show in Chicago, we at Honeywell felt pressure to develop our own. You didn't have to be a Fulbright Scholar to figure out the 110 would sell; it fit a shirt pocket and took excellent pictures.

We were scared. We would meet at work, after work, in a bar, or at the bowling alley. We became obsessed, but as this do-or-die effort progressed, we began to talk about more than just the camera. "What if," somebody in our nervous little group asked, "we could make it focus automatically?"

Well, sure, duh. Nirvana. But we kept coming back to this autofocus idea. We finally stumbled onto a way to do it, just by rehashing it over and over. Autofocus started as a secondary obsession that outgrew the original dream. The 110 had already been built. And although our main goal was to make a better 110 camera, we found our real energy slipping to this ambitious tangent.

I was the Director of Product Management. Dean Peterson was the head of one engineering section for Honeywell's photo products division. I remember a moment when Dean stood among us near his drafting table after a particularly frustrating design review when he suddenly flung a drafting pen up. It stuck about a half inch in the ceiling's acoustical tile. "We've got to do something different," he barked. "There's nothing breakthrough here, there's nothing here that is going to move the world even one degree."

Peterson was a big talent at a small division of Honeywell. It was as if Michael Jordan had been invited to the hood to shoot some hoops, yet

Peterson flourished at Honeywell because of his freedom. Peterson, who had already designed the first Instamatic camera at Kodak before coming to Honeywell, was haunted by nightmares of slipping into anonymity. Pentax was threatening to drop us and Vivitar was chewing into our electronic flash franchise, so we were all twitchy and not feeling like winners. The idea was to design a camera that had features Kodak didn't, price it higher, and survive above the yellow-box boys. Everyone kept thinking about the possibility of automatic focus. Peterson had three other engineers working on it. Their names were Stauffer, Wilwerding, and Ogawa. They and I met every day for 18 months, but they were isolated from the rest of the company. Finally, at the end we had a good camera, but it was 8% over the budget. Couldn't get the costs where they had to be. If we had only known about Prozac. Beer sufficed and we killed the camera.

But sometime during those 18 months, we figured out the essence of focus. None of us remembers an exact moment, so it wasn't like a lightbulb over someone's head or even a grand vision. It was just a lot of brainwork and discussions.

Focus, we reasoned, is nothing more than the moment of maximum contrast. It was easy to measure contrast by sprinkling light meters all over the image on the ground glass and measuring the contrast between them. If the lens started at maximum close-up (totally out of focus, so it began with a gray image, no contrast) and then started moving until the moment of maximum contrast arrived, perfect focus would be achieved. (Since there's a question about which part of the photo should be in focus, we spent bleary-eyed hours at photo labs, watching prints roll off the end of processors to discern where most photo subjects are positioned.)

While scrapping the camera, we knew autofocus still could shake up the industry more than yet one more Instamatic camera, so we battled to invest another $85,000 to prove it. We had already invested $15,000, so that brought the total investment up to $100,000. (You won't find anyone today who'll admit fighting this expenditure, or dragging their heels, but I remember them all and stick pins in their business cards every few years.)

It took another eight months to build a working prototype, and then it was assigned to a separate marketing group that went about making presentations to other companies. Every camera manufacturer was interested, but some didn't believe a disheveled little band of Rocky Mountain engineers could possibly conceive something as earth-shattering as automatic focus. Many refused to consider paying royalties.

Some eighteen years later, after testimony from Peterson, Ogawa, Stauffer, Wilwerding, and myself, one of those companies, Minolta, handed Honeywell a $127 million check for royalties. Others like Kodak, Canon, Sony and more settled with Honeywell. All in all, it totaled just under a half-billion dollars of payments. In just 1993. Not bad, a half-billion-dollar profit on a $100,000 investment. (I'm no dummy. I got $31 gas mileage for my days of testimony.)

This created the biggest patent royalty award in American history up until that time.

It's funny thinking back to that moment. We were in a funk, watching Vivitar outhustle us, Pentax wanting to go direct plus other problems . . . like a slide projector that wouldn't sell, partially because it wouldn't work and partly because that market was dying as prints got better. Maybe it was lucky that those slide projector sales missed forecasts by so far, since our engineers managed to put twice as many parts in it as the Carousel used, making it impossible to build economically. Sigh.

When we set out to build a 110 camera, we had a new rule that helped direct product development: Before spending a dime, write the announcement headline in 20 words or less. Half the pending projects were immediately aborted. It's startling how much stupid development can be exposed by that test. If you can't write a compelling headline, the product is no good. Period. In any industry. We let that lead us, and a half-billion dollars in profit resulted.

Dean Peterson came farther west when we started a toy business and designed the world's best-selling tape recorder and record player, which we marketed through Fisher-Price Toys, who acquired that startup after a few years. Another friend from that engineering department, Chuck Taylor, whose department managed much of the electronic design, also migrated to join the evil competitor, Vivitar. He left them later and today heads design work for Sharper Image.

Guess what Sharper Image does today before spending a red cent on any new product? Correctomundo, friends. They write the selling headline in twenty words or less. If you can't do that, with a meaningful benefit, powerfully expressed, there's no product. Period.

Here's how to make development pay off big-time:

1. Put tight direction into research and development. Write the announcement headline with specific, unique benefits for every product before it gets money. Review precise dates, expenditures, and progress for each project every week. Then get out of the engineers' way. Focus on the project in every business report you issue. Profits are history. The new product is your future.
2. Stay loose and reexamine unexpected breakthroughs. Development can and must be scheduled. It not only leads to progress on the

stated project, but that intensity fosters unthought-of spinoffs that never come from aimless tinkering. Honeywell's pocket camera was killed, but autofocus spun out of that energy.

3. Isolate the design crew. Let them have no other mission or distraction. Make their careers hinge on success, and terminate projects and departments if they miss major benchmarks. One-way tickets only, and you'll get the best from them.

CHAPTER 10

MANAGE MORE THAN LEAD

Three men and three car companies. Two lost money. One didn't.

It whacked me upside my head in January of 1982. Detroiters were the "Bad News Bears" of the '80s and '90s. Losers. Cars that would be boring if they didn't fail so often. Roger Smith, Chairman of General Motors, was to speak at the Advertising Club. I was invited. I stood outside talking to the club president when a massive black tractor trailer rolled under the awning of the Mission Bay Hilton. I'd heard and seen the General Motors slogan thousands of times, but this time it registered. Five-foot letters on the side of the huge trailer said, "General Motors Mark of Excellence."

Inside, another crew unloaded a second truckload of audiovisual equipment, set up, and tested it. They marched out for this next load.

Bob Salt, president of the ad club, turned to me with a wry smile. "We knew he was already scheduled to talk in L.A. We knew January in San Diego beats January in Detroit. So we gave it a shot and look, two trucks."

Two trucks for one speech by one man.

The Mark of Excellence.

It was a breath-quickening presentation. Rhythmic drumbeats and trumpet blasts through the stereo as the screen exploded with zoom shots so quick you could barely tell how dull the cars were. Smith talked about the new Saturn project, advertising for the coming year, and how wonderful General Motors was now that he, Smith, was in charge.

Smith, once an introverted financial guy, loved the podium. Besides two truckloads of audiovisual equipment, Smith came with an entourage of PR flaks who made lots of money communicating inspiring anecdotes about their boss, Smith. This beat Broadway. It was staged to awe, but even in "Surfs up!" San Diego it was awful.

You see, some folks in other parts of our globe who didn't speak the same language were shipping autos with far fewer defects and better pricing, although none had as many coffee cup holders as our domestic offerings. So the pitch had lots of red, white, and blue, and "what's good for GM is good for America" overtones. Detroit is the heart of America, they pointed out.

And you know, I was mesmerized for awhile. The guy got my heart pumping when he talked about the Saturn project and its vast potential. He spoke for 30 minutes while this huge, trucked-from-Michigan, wall-to-wall, ceiling-to-floor video screen flashed professional graphics and photographs illustrating every point. Lights were arranged so that Smith's diminutive profile became an incandescent giant hovering onscreen in the muted convention room. Often, the screen flashed a huge Saturn with strobes. This was three-dimensional, audiovisual, turbo-glide charisma.

I sat, liking it, buying it for the most part, until another image flashed across my mind, kind of a loose connection. I thought of Lee Iacocca, president of Chrysler. Way more famous than Smith. A leader. What he is famous for are two books, the Mustang his starring bill in Chrysler television commercials, and his role in raising money to refurbish the Statue of Liberty.

That year, both General Motors and Chrysler lost money. Lots of money. General Motors laid off 12,000 workers and cut the benefits of most remaining workers. Except top executives, of course. The privileged class, each with two commas on their W-2s, all received bonuses for a job well done. It seemed their bonuses were for helping sell Smith's strategy. What else could they be for? Results?

There was one guy who stayed in Detroit that year. Donald Peterson never wrote a book or starred in a commercial. He tried his best not to give speeches and those he did were mostly in Detroit. His talks cured insomnia. Peterson was unassuming and had no desire for the spotlight. He only wanted better cars first, and he assumed profits would follow. Never heard of Peterson? He was CEO of Ford.

His philosophy was simple. He told his designers to forget about profits and instead design something they would like to see in their own driveways.

Ford had a slogan, too: "Quality Is Job One." Quality became the mission of the company, and Ford's quality, by most standards, soon surpassed General Motors and Chrysler. Incidentally, so did profits. No contest.

Peterson retired and was replaced by another hands-on guy you've never heard of, Red Poling; in 1992 Poling's new Taurus became the number-one seller in America. Poling was succeeded by a third guy you don't know, Alex Trotman, who kept the Taurus on top and led Ford to more record profits.

While Ford thrived, introducing the Taurus and Sable, good cars with record profits, General Motors and Chrysler faltered, losing huge amounts and a dozen plants. (Sadly, in 2001, Ford seems to have forgotten quality and the mantle slipped.)

What hit home as Roger Smith put on his traveling jamboree was that this was the most fraudulent of all skills, leadership without management. He was the snake-oil huckster spinning yarns about the joyous culture of General Motors and its success. But, of course, it was a promise from another empty suit, isolated in the executive lunchroom, who never stepped onto the assembly lines unless klieg lights and cameras were in place. The scariest thing is he probably believed what he said. Probably learned about cars by asking his chauffeur.

Leadership is necessary but leadership can be a seductive ego-massage. I've tasted it on a tiny scale myself. When I have been CEO of various companies, vendors, customers, and old associates who should know better became ridiculously deferential. My jokes were just as bad, but the laughter grew. It's easy to lose perspective (until you leave).

Management is work. Management is listening and digging for problems.

I once asked a sampling of CEOs of both large and small companies which task they preferred: giving a speech to new employees or participating in a customer negotiation. The CEOs of large companies went for the speech. The small-company CEOs wanted to mix it up with the client. The way I see it, large companies are laying people off, small companies are getting some work done, growing and hiring. The job creation in America through the '80s and '90s came from small business. Large companies could only boost profits by throwing employees overboard. The big companies only grow by acquiring others and then "right-sizing," which has something to do with your paycheck stopping.

Leaders deliver impressions and play to the desires of the masses. Managers inspire less and accomplish more. Japan's had its ups and downs, but their economic growth since World War II has outpaced ours on average. Think about how many great Japanese business leaders you can name. What are they like personally? There aren't Asians out there working the masses. They are too busy managing, working.

Here's how you get your corporate physique back in shape, to match the cosmetics:

1. Fight adulation. Encourage opinions. Any employee who always agrees with you is redundant. Replace him or her with someone who will contribute.

2. Eliminate public speeches except when it helps business. When it advances your business, then knock their socks off. If this takes more than 10% of your time, sorry, you're ego is deluding you. Speak often, internally, to smaller groups where you can ask questions and listen. Listeners win; talkers lose.

3. If the choice is between settling an employee dispute or meeting with the chamber of commerce, get with the employees. If a disgruntled customer wants to see you, reschedule that employee luncheon. Given the choice between symbolic acts and work, do the work. That's symbolic in itself.

CHAPTER 11

CRAWL INTO YOUR CUSTOMER'S SKIN

In 1982, when software sales across the country were skyrocketing, State Of The Art was a startup. State Of The Art made accounting software. Their first-year sales were $1 million, and their second year hit $3 million. Third-year revenues reached $10 million, and profits nudged an unheard-of 30 percent.

Franklin Press printed the instruction manuals and documentation that go with the software, and was constantly rushed by State Of The Art to put everything else aside and attend to their emergency orders.

Late one Friday, Polly, the no-nonsense buyer from State Of The Art, barked at Karen, the Franklin Press sales rep.

"Karen, we need them Monday," said Polly in a tone of voice that defied her 4'11" frame. Polly glared. "Monday. Period."

Karen pleaded, "But if you could just give us a one-week lead time, we could save you 50 percent."

But Karen didn't get it. It was the opulent early '80s and software was chic, as was life. State Of The Art had contemporary glass offices with a swirling modern art sculpture exploding in a crystal fountain across their lobby. The founders were energetic and determined. They worked 14-hour days, six days a week. On the seventh, they played extravagantly.

The CEO was particularly smitten. Newly rich, he wanted to recapture his youth. He hired a private investigator to track down that nostalgia; the investigator found the exact '59 maroon Ford Fairlane the CEO cruised in during high school. The CEO bought the old car, refurbished it, and had it stored under transparent wraps in the company warehouse as a shrine to his youth.

"Hey, you don't understand," Polly, the buyer, told Karen. Despite Polly's diminutive size, her comments echoed into the next zip code. She had frazzled hair, no makeup. She looked tough and acted tough, mainly because she was, a graduate of the streets of New York. "That ink and paper costs us only $8 a set. We sell it, with the disk, for $500 and we're back-ordered. Eight dollars is nothing. I can't afford to be a day late just to save $4. We need it now!"

It was delivered the following Monday. Franklin's bindery worked Saturday, Saturday night, and Sunday. The customer paid twice too much and was happy. But Karen went back the following week and made another pitch. She didn't have to make another suggestion, and in fact many companies would have stopped her. They would take the extra money and run. They would be wrong.

Karen told Polly, "You are making a lot of money, but we're shipping you $12,000 worth of printed material in an average month. Look at this. If you could just, for five minutes every Monday, forecast your needs with me for a couple of weeks running, I could cut $6,000 in rush fees out of your monthly bill."

"But . . ."

"Look, I know you are back-ordered and making huge profits. But for just five minutes a week you could save $6,000 a month. That's not trivial."

The buyer, even in her gruffness, got it. A lesser salesperson wouldn't have bothered. But Karen looked out for the buyer's deeper interest, even when the buyer didn't have the perspective.

State Of The Art tightened their ordering. Sales continued up and profits did even better. In 1990 they went public. Polly had survived a cutback forced on the company by the temporary slump of 1984. She might have been let go had there been sloppier buying practices. Instead, she went on to earn stock that became worth $250,000 in her first few years.

At the time of this incident, State Of The Art was wildly successful, and so was Polly. But neither the company nor the buyer was so bowled over by success that they wouldn't listen to a sales rep talking sense.

State Of The Art remained successful, surviving a few dips, because they were willing to listen. It became the only PC-based accounting software company to be publicly held and a decade later was acquired by a British consortium, making shareholders wealthy once again. The company took a couple million to start, made a lot of happy users, and generated over $100 million in returns for shareholders in two decades.

Karen, the sales rep, also enhanced her career. Within three years she became dissatisfied being a sales rep (for my company, gulp) and formed her own brokerage business, representing many printers and calling on the same customers.

Much of Karen's success came from old-fashioned hustle. She always made more calls than her competitive sales reps, thus learning more about her customers and their needs. She understood the economics of printing and her customers' business, nearly always better than the customers. She learned never to keep her mouth shut when the customer is wrong, and she knew that the customer can be wrong.

Customers often act for the moment without thinking of their longer-term wants. Sometimes they don't understand what they are doing to themselves. You must know them better than they know themselves so you can deliver to their truer desires without offending.

Here's how to save your sales group from choking on success:

1. Take a look at your special orders. Nothing elevates a supplier more than exceptional emergency service. You must do this to save customers. But they should pay extra because nothing kills a supplier quicker than delivering a superior service without charging for it. Many won't see it as special until it is priced appropriately.

2. Stop all discounts given when shoddy product or poor service happens. Replace or redo it, and do it right. Customers who are delighted with discounts and lousy service are lethal. Get used to that habit and you're within inches of becoming a schlock merchant.

3. Cut your commission schedule in half. Replace that half with bonuses based on customer interviews, repeat purchases, and displaced competitors. This is a bitch to administer, but the resulting arguments are more relevant than any you've had yet.

CHAPTER 12

CHEAP IS SUCH
A PRETTY WORD

C'mon. Don't you avoid the word? Aren't you always substituting phrases like "value" and "economical," fearful of sounding, well, cheap?

Stop it. Cheap is good. It's a compliment. I'm thrilled to be a minor, minor shareholder in a company run by my classmate, Frank March.

When Frank bid on the contract to build replacement urethane bumpers to protect the piers of the San Pedro, California, shipyard, he was already $77,000 ahead of his competitors.

March's plant manager in Virginia had just paid $77,000 for a urethane sprayer at a bankruptcy auction. Along with the functional motor and gadgetry, there were some rusty pipes and cracked hoses. It was part of the deal. March spent another $3,000 to scrape and paint the rust and replace the hoses. Then it performed like new, for a total of $8,000.

All the competitors, however, had shiny new sprayers, for $85,000. They didn't get any rust or cracked hoses, but Frank March got a $77,000 head start. The San Pedro project was awarded in its entirety to March's company, SeaWard International. All the other companies found less work and higher payments for those expensive, shiny sprayers. This led to more work, millions and growing, over the next few years.

March is one of those directional types who believed, before he scored a perfect 800 on his math SATs, that science and business and life are logical. He went to MIT, became class president, ran the Harvard co-op store while in school, and finished with a bachelor's degree in chemical engineering and a masters in oceanographic sciences. The chemical engineer in him made a chemical product. The oceanographer in him made a marine product. Scary. Life goes straightforward for March.

For instance, equipment savings such as the sprayer add up to roughly 2% a year. "It's a goal, and we meet it," said March, "every year, in new ways."

Bumpers for ships look easy but are tough to design and even tougher to improve. A controlled combination of flotation and resilience without flex-fatigue is needed to protect both the ship and the pier. The bumper must give just enough to protect it, without giving so much it crumbles prematurely. Certain proprietary combinations of varying urethane layers make SeaWard's bumpers more effective than any others, and seasoned mariners know it.

March always buys low. SeaWard bought an abandoned paper mill for its factory in rural Clearbrook, Virginia. The price was right and labor is good. More important, the isolation protects the secrecy of most projects.

The money saved by buying used and abandoned facilities went toward factory automation. In an industry built on cheap labor (many companies use untrained immigrant labor), hand-processing, and inconsistent results, SeaWard is computer-driven and automated. Its bumpers' performance is way more predictable.

March is involved everywhere. "We spent the better part of a year programming the trimmer that cuts sheets precisely for each size bumper," he said. "That is one year's work but it is worth it. We now use 50% more of what we used to throw away as scrap. That's savings of 3%. A 3% price advantage gains us 10% more sales. It just goes on and on, how cutting costs leads to earning. The 10% volume increase lets us negotiate urethane prices down further." It is wonderful to watch costs go down while volume and profits go up. It is self-perpetuating.

The few customers who have seen SeaWard inside advised competitors to simply drop out of the business. Most competitors took heed. A few, like Yokohama, plugged on but lag miserably. Yokohama, Dupont, and others have new sprayers. Some have new buildings. SeaWard, though, has new customers. March is smart enough to know that money is money, not some abstract accounting measure. The problem with accounting is that you can overspend and capitalize it, whether it is equipment or an acquisition, and the results don't entirely show for years. It gives businesses a fuse that is too long. When you hear, "That's okay, we'll just capitalize it," you know you're in a sick management environment that is hiding costs using perfectly proper accounting.

This attitude doesn't stifle development, it makes innovation possible.

SeaWard branched out in the '90s, and developed a proprietary system that turns empty Clorox bottles, baby diapers, water pistols, and Styrofoam cups into pilings for piers. These pilings don't rot like wood. Trees aren't cut to create them. Scrap plastic is transformed into a useful product and doesn't fill dumps. The piers last longer, flex, and bounce back from crashing ships. No creosote pollutes the water.

Several others tried this. All failed. SeaWard spent ten agonizing years developing and perfecting this revolutionary process, and could do so through such an extended period only because they cut costs regularly. That creates cash. Money fuels innovation. Now piers around the world are cleaner, stronger, and maintenance-free thanks to SeaWard's SeaPiles.

Here's how to trim some costs:

1. Never buy new equipment unless it's more productive per dollar spent than refurbished. Don't even buy refurbished if you can have outside sources do it for less.

2. Examine every service or part you manufacture. See if it can be bought cheaper than it costs you to make. If so, stop doing it yourself. Doing it yourself does not maintain control. If you can buy it cheaper than you can make it, you lost control of that process long ago. Your next step is losing customers if you continue to make it while timing and costs slip away.

3. Never acquire a company unless you can see a complete payback in five years based on their current earnings. More acquisitions fail than succeed. The inherent inefficiencies of mixing organizations into an unspecialized blob is one reason for failure. The primary reason acquisitions fail, though, is that the buyer simply paid too much.

CHAPTER 13

NUDGE VALUE UP

T his was white-knuckle time.

About a year earlier, Smiley Industries, which I now ran, won the contract to make part of the transmission housings for the Apache helicopter. The overall contractor for the Apache was McDonnell Douglas. They awarded us the subcontract.

Like all government deals, this was bureaucratic with two tablespoons of politics stirred in. First of all, the reason the contract went out to bid was because of politics. Once, there was one contractor making the parts of the housings. But in an effort to spread the wealth among more congressional districts, the housing parts were bid separately. It made sense politically. Gotta keep those projects alive.

Practically, however, it made life miserable. The previous contractor who had made all three parts had flexibility to mix and match, as long as the assembly worked. But now, each contractor had to make each part precisely according to specifications. This sounds fair, the old "standardization of parts" scam. But you should have seen the specifications.

It was humiliating. Perhaps a smarter outfit than we were could have figured this out by thinking harder while studying the blueprints. There were, however, a lot of other dumb bidders on this job.

The thing that threw us off was the use of an unusual alloy of titanium, nickel, and steel in a shape larger than normal. When we machined this larger part at an economic speed, it created vibrations that made it impossible to create dimensions within the required 10,000 of an inch. At economical machining speeds, the vibrations caused scuffed and chipped surfaces that came close to specifications. And the helicopters had a disturbing tendency to flip over, fall out of the sky, and send loose rotor blades careening through nearby homes, an awkward PR situation.

The more we tried, the more we struggled. We fell four months behind, and our cash was squeezed as a result. We couldn't beat the problem. We thought it must be doable. After all, somebody made these parts before.

Yes, but somebody was making all these parts and playing matchmaker, switching parts that were just off the mark until they fit. We had no such luxury.

At one point, a McDonnell Douglas officer visited. He brought with him a gaggle of managers and clipboards. He explained his dilemma and blamed it on us. "Mr. Sutton," he said, "40 percent of NATO's helicopters are grounded today due to your failure to deliver." He was right. Makes a guy proud.

But he, of course, hadn't explained that the previous supplier couldn't meet the specs either. He didn't say a word about their mix-and-match manufacturing. We had to figure out that part for ourselves and nearly went toes-up in the process.

We did finally get it, but it didn't solve the problem. We merely knew, after months and months of beating ourselves to death, that it was not solvable, period, so help us.

In all fairness, McDonnell Douglas probably didn't realize what was happening either. They were just frustrated and mad. Their attitude seemed, even to us, justifiable in the beginning.

After two more months of stumbling and cursing, we finally found an adequate solution. We used a sharper cutting tool at a higher speed. It took a while even to find the exact speed. We set the bite for a thinner cut. Then we had to clamp a set of weights onto certain sections of each piece while we machined. This dampened some of the bad harmonics that messed up the machining. It worked, but there was a problem. A rather significant problem. This new procedure took triple the time our bid indicated.

We went to McDonnell Douglas and explained the problem.

"So what do you want us to do?" asked the McDonnell Douglas officer.

"You have no choice," I said, "you have to double our price per part." His eyes bulged. I continued. "Your other alternative is to go somewhere else."

"You do realize you have a binding contract," he pointed out. I nodded. "Yes," I said, "and we've done everything humanly possible to honor it. Together, we've discovered a problem neither of us knew we had with this part. It's not your fault, it's not our fault. But it is a problem. A major problem. And we've figured out how to make you a much better part than you ever had before. Now it truly is interchangeable for the first time. That will slash your field repair costs. Unfortunately, we can't make it on the terms of that contract. We're sorry, but it is such a big contract that we would go bankrupt trying to honor it as is. If you choose to force us, you will be dealing with our creditors' committee when you want a spare part for NATO. And all those creditors are likely to be loyal tax-paying Americans, you know, but a couple of them may also be mad at the military for screwing them like this."

McDonnell Douglas relented. They even agreed to pay some advances to cover prior excessive costs due to the problem. Happy ending. The project lived, Smiley made better parts at fair profit, and NATO's forces remained at the ready.

If you understand operations and manufacturing, you're assuming that there was a real benefit to the outcome and that's the interchangeability of the parts. Sorry. That's only true when you have volume. We were putting out about thirty of these pieces a month, and dollar for dollar, it would have been more efficient to mix and match and build these assemblies by hand.

But the bigger point of the story was in the real battle. Inside Smiley it was a fight to get everyone to realize just how underpriced these parts were. There was a natural, yet irrational fear of losing the contract. There was not enough appreciation that we would lose our entire business if we honored the existing contract. McDonnell Douglas, with plenty of encouragement, did the right thing and Smiley Industries survived.

This was a price increase that was fair and correct, yet if put to either an employee or management vote the approach would probably have been more humble. The result of a humble approach might have been that McDonnell Douglas would never have fully realized the problem and the Apaches would never fly right. If Smiley had wobbled and failed, McDonnell Douglas would have had the same problem all over again with some other unlucky bidder. And Apache helicopters could have been a repair disaster, struggling to stay online, without interchangeable parts. Price increases are often necessary. They force scrutiny, which is healthy. It isn't always pleasant, but when there's a problem, nothing flushes out reality quicker.

Here's how to create fair prices:

1. Raise prices 10% on each product and service that isn't making money. See what happens. Some customers will be unfazed, and then the product is profitable. With other increases, you will lose some business but probably make money with the customers that are

left. And with some, it will kill sales entirely. All three results are wonderful. You've separated the winners from the losers.

2. Take the items that died with a 10% price increase and reintroduce them with a 25% cut. See if the increased volume makes it a winner. Watch this baby minute by minute and stab it in the crib if it doesn't work, which it often won't.

3. Sugarcoat the price increases. Somehow, a chocolate mint on a pillow makes an overpriced hotel room a little more acceptable. Your customers aren't dumb, but it's rude not to help them swallow increases.

CHAPTER 14

HUMAN RESOURCES IS NEITHER

As a maker of exhibits for trade shows and retail displays, Pacific Design Center had vast potential and opportunity. It was the biggest exhibit design center on the West Coast, but financial results were south of mediocre.

At Pacific Design Center, the personnel department was big and overbearing. When I was hired as CEO, there were nine personnel, each of whom had enough time to get in everybody's way.

For one thing, there was the manager's manual, an encyclopedic thing with jargon-filled text and a blue cover with laminated type that must have cost a couple bucks per. It probably took days for a committee to pick out the type style. The text was full of invasive, self-defeating techniques for "empowering" workers and management, little of which talked about objectives. There wasn't much in that stack of pages that had to do with anything produced by Pacific Design Center.

And there were evaluation forms, eight pages of unimportant nosy drivel that once again had almost nothing to do with results. There were 500 employees at the company, and one evaluation form had to be filled out annually by every supervisor for every employee. That's 4,000 pages produced.

Once a quarter, the personnel department held half-day training sessions with other managers, teaching them to manage better. That's two solid days of work a year for every manager, and nothing gained.

The nine personnel people had so little to do they actually went out finding studies showing that it was average to have nine personnel people for a company of 500 employees. Who said so? The American Personnel Association. That's who.

Title inflation from the impersonal personnel departments to the inhuman human resources was still years away.

One month after I arrived, despite all these manuals, training sessions, and forms, a forklift tipped over and destroyed a builder's exhibit for the Dallas Home & Garden Show. A couple of weeks later a worker lost control of his saber saw, and it severed a nerve in his wrist.

There were more problems. There were five trade unions, which tells a lot about how labor felt about management. Lots of employees seemed to come down with the Monday-morning flu and three-fourths of the worker's compensation claims were filed before 10 A.M. Monday, showing that even those who came in Monday morning weren't ready for work, and their claims were less than valid.

If you just walked around and kept your eyes open, especially in the bathrooms, you soon knew there were drugs pouring through Pacific Design Center. Sniffing. Capsules in the waste basket. Glassy eyes. Human Resources was busy creating forms and holding seminars, so they missed it, and the managers were too busy filling out forms to manage and observe the problem. But if you were half-awake you saw things, heard comments, and sometimes smelled it.

The final straw came after I had been there two months. We were holding a meeting of managers in my office, just going around so each could give an update on what was happening in his or her department. When it came to the human resource manager's turn, she gushed, "There's so much pain out there!"

Her body language hit about three major cheerleading poses. "We've started holding anonymous lunchtime meetings for people with personal problems. All kinds, any kinds. Our people are hurting. We get them to talk, to really let go. Just yesterday, we had two people crying."

She was into this. The more depression, the better. Without a shrink's degree, she was prying into people's psyche and getting her jollies. We listened to her, and we made some changes. One of the best changes we made was cutting human resources in half. Suddenly, managers had to manage again. If an employee wasn't performing, the manager had to discuss it before salary review time, instead of overlooking it and later blaming a puny raise on human resources' guidelines.

Suddenly, those left in human resources were busy without intruding on others. They might even ask references a few probing questions now, instead of calling and crashing through a checklist. The business flourished.

Managers and employees talked to one another honestly, and raises were no longer cloaked in secrecy.

We didn't fire the people in personnel. We found them jobs where they could be productive, in sales and manufacturing. You see, they weren't lazy, but they had a predisposition to forms, lectures, organizational charts, and structure, like nameplates and titles. Most changed when put into measurable jobs.

Six months later, everyone in management and supervision looked back and agreed that reducing human resources helped a bunch. Six months later, we did it again, reducing a five-person department to three. And things got better yet.

Productivity jumped. Costs for similar work from the previous year dropped by an average of 10%. In that first year, productivity savings were roughly $850,000.

There was a trade-off. Pacific Design Center lost a couple of wrongful termination suits that cost about $45,000. That's not a bad barter for $850,000 in savings, eh?

The truth is, the minute you create a department to tell the managers how to manage, you are automatically telling them to manage less. You are diffusing responsibility.

Don't do it. Set the people free. Let managers manage and make some mistakes; it's good for them and for your company. Don't create a new rule or policy every time somebody screws up. In fact, beware the employee who never makes a mistake. Learning means taking chances.

Here's how to boost productivity:

1. Cut human resources in half. Find those you remove other jobs within the company, if they're good, since growing that group was your error, not theirs.
2. One year later, do it again. Yes, it is possible and, yes, things will get better yet.
3. Create a philosophy of rewards for performance with your employees that all understand and write together. Don't let this degenerate into rules or formulas, but make it a clear manifesto that everybody gets a copy of when they join the company. Build the framework together from which individual judgments and actions can be made independently.

CHAPTER 15

HUSTLE THE HUSTLERS

San Bernardino—Late on a scorching morning in July of 1963, Jim Kennedy was hired by George Van Auken to work for the rest of the day. Van Auken owned Franklin Press. He needed 500 bundles of insurance brochures delivered to a client an hour away in Anaheim.

Kennedy was 20 years old. He pulled up in his red pickup. Clean, paint fading a bit, with tires that had seen younger days.

They talked briefly about the order and started loading. Van Auken carried a bundle, stacked it, Kennedy carried two, stacked them, and alternated the length and width so each layer overlapped and wouldn't shift.

Kennedy's eyes twinkled. He chattered while they laid the bundles in neat, alternating rows. He laughed easily.

"How long have you been working for this delivery service?" Van Auken asked.

"Two years, Mr. Van Auken, and they're a great outfit. Why?"

Van Auken dropped another bundle in the truck, squared it, and smiled at Kennedy.

"How would you like to learn the printing business?"

"Are you offering me a job?"

"Yes."

Van Auken recognized the attitude and the care Kennedy had, things that couldn't be taught.

So Jim Kennedy drove the load to Anaheim, gave two weeks notice to his delivery firm, and began driving for Franklin Press.

Van Auken never ran ads, checked references, used a recruiter, or gave personality tests. He just kept his eyes open.

Once he noticed a gas station attendant scrub a speck of pine sap from his outside mirror. Van Auken came back several more times, watched, noticed the kid always hustled, and he hired him. Taught him how to load paper in a press. Decades later the former gas pumper supervised a crew of three running a full-color press for Van Auken.

When a clerk for his CPA firm asked questions nobody had thought of during an audit, Van Auken noticed. He gave the woman a couple extra projects. She excelled and became Van Auken's accounting manager.

He had mental files on dozens of waitresses, Xerox repairmen, ink sales reps, painters, and others, all folks with a spark that brought them offers.

"I can teach them printing. I can't teach them what's inside," Van Auken said.

Van Auken built Franklin Press to just over 100 employees this way, one at a time over thirty years, and sold it 17 years after Kennedy first joined him. I was hired to manage the company, be CEO, not that this outfit needed managing.

Kennedy ran the shipping department with four truckers. His hustle remained. He picked up the tempo near the end of each month, wanting to get as much into revenues as possible, packing and trucking jobs from the night shift for evening deliveries on the last day. He'd call a customer and suggest a partial delivery with the rest coming when more convenient for the client and our routing.

Van Auken's spirit lived after he left. One morning I ran around a corner in the offices and bumped into a seven-foot gorilla. Not your normal occurrence. But this was Halloween and one of our drivers bought a costume and drove 200 miles inside this fur and rubber, making twelve deliveries. We heard from ten of them. It seems our driver spent a little extra time that day carting boxes from the customer's loading docks into the offices, generating shrieks and laughter and goodwill. He got back a little late that night.

Many years earlier, shortly after Van Auken moved into a building from his garage, he hired a dairyman who knew how to work the route. This fellow became one of the top producers in West Coast printing. He hired a kid out of high school who worked there summers and that youngster supervised 100 tradespeople a couple of decades later. Then he cashed out and opened a bar.

The dairyman retired to the lush fairways, pools, and dry air of Palm Springs. And the customers were always happy.

Employee turnover was nil under Van Auken and we managed to keep it below 10% per year. I left, we acquired a couple more printers, and finally got purchased ourselves.

Franklin Press grew and grew and just kept getting better. You see, everybody pays about the same for presses and ink and paper. It's the employees who make the difference, and Van Auken's spirit lingered for decades. Not forever.

Some seven-piece suits that were leveraged buyout experts bought Franklin Press. They immediately set out to boost margins and recapture their investment quick, but what they got quick is known in printing, and a few other industries, as bankruptcy. Padlocks on the doors. Big trucks and crews taking apart presses and rolling them away.

Day after day of steadily recruiting great people, reinforcing the ethic, and always working at it make a solid business. Leveraged buyouts, going public, mergers and splashy PR and advertising don't.

Franklin Press was good while it lasted. And those who made it solid did just fine.

Here's how you recruit best:

1. Remember it's a never-ending process. Keep watching your best vendors, customers, and employees around town. Woo them. Get to know them. When there's an opening, make an offer.
2. When you have a spot and there are no viable candidates, use a recruiter and give them a list of twenty industries that are similar to yours in pace and size. Exceptional talent excels anywhere. Spend lots of time with the recruiter defining the search, and review the calls made and the feedback every week. This is a big job. If you try to do it yourself, you'll be ignoring things at work and tiring yourself out until you grab someone out of frustration. This is the beginning of bad things. Don't hire a large firm. That impressive list of clients they show you merely proves how many places they cannot recruit from.
3. Cajole the recruiter into running some ads, and pay them to do so. They've got this thing against ads, and mostly they're right, the quality from classifieds is pretty bad. Read Chapter 1 to see how to handle this.

CHAPTER 16

INTERVIEW SMARTER

"**D**oes he have to know printing?" asked the recruiter.

"We prefer not," I answered, "we have too many people that already do." We were the largest commercial printer in the west, Graphic Arts Center of Portland, Oregon. Graphic Arts Center was part of US Press, which grew out of Franklin Press, cited in the previous chapter.

The recruiter was there because Graphic Arts Center, which had 500 employees, needed a new controller. He and I talked about what type we should hire. "Get someone who can manage eight people," I said, "who speaks well, is a CPA, and works hard. He or she must be able to communicate with nonaccountants. He or she should understand accounting is a service function to guide the business; it is not the business itself. But the person must also not let the areas and jobs that are hurting the numbers go unchallenged."

We agonized a bit over this. There were four of us who would decide, and we each spent time with the recruiter. I was CEO. The other three were Gayland in finance, Frank in production, and Don in sales.

"We need someone who has the courage to ask a few dumb questions about printing because the answers are sometimes dumber than the questions," I said. "It would be great if they came from a job-shop environment. That's what this is; we still spend more time on individual job-cost analysis than we do on the overall profit and loss. I'd like someone with manufacturing experience, in custom production environment. Also, get someone from a similar-sized business."

"Housing and steel fabrication might be good to pick through," suggested the recruiter.

"Bingo and bingo."

We talked about pay and profit bonuses and I summarized. "A boozer won't work. This is a pretty straight crowd. Can't be too slick or too dull, we're a down-the-middle group socially, same for aggression. There's a lot of interplay and this person must stand his or her ground without trying to dominate."

In four weeks, the recruiter had ten resumes in my hands. By phone, I cut it to six. We did background checks through Equifax Employment Services. One of the six wasn't paying his bills; another overstated her previous job. Neither seemed like sterling qualities for maintaining our integrity. The other four checked out, so we brought them in for interviews.

All four candidates came to Graphic Arts Center on the same day. Gayland, Frank, Don, and myself spent 90 minutes with each. Not a group interview. One at a time. We rotated them carefully so they didn't bump into each other in the hallway. We didn't talk to each other until all the interviews were over. Bang, bang, bang, bang.

There's this tendency to favor the last candidate interviewed when the process takes days or weeks. Forty percent of the time the last person interviewed is hired. This neutralized that. We each saw them in a different sequence.

Since we didn't compare impressions, none of us swayed the others before we saw them all. Don happened to be having a bad day. The computer burped, overbilling customers. His grouchiness showed, but guess what, it showed equally in the interviews with all four candidates.

For the rest of us, the day got better as it went on. The questions became more pointed with practice. So every candidate had a terrific last interview. The entire thing boiled down to compatible values, as it always does. We asked open-ended questions. "What's best about your job?" we asked. "Worst? When were you last angry? Why? What's your biggest fear about this job? What do you do in your spare time?" We hoped for glimpses of the inner person.

One guy's name was Bill Pattison. He had nervous energy, a quick laugh, and a sharp mind. More than once, I found myself enjoying his honesty. He was technically astute. Another seemed just as sharp and communicated more easily. A third caused discomfort. He had too many opinions that came from his prior job, they didn't all fit, and he talked more than asked. A fourth spit in the wastebasket. No kidding. Shouldn't matter. Does.

It was a good hire because it was a coherent process. By interviewing all at once, comparisons were fresh. We knew how each of the candidates thought, and none of them suffered by being the first candidate in or benefit by being the last.

So we asked the three nonspitters to give us a report. Tell us what's good, what's bad, and what they thought we should do to fix the problems. Four pages the next week and gave them each a check for $500 for doing so.

In his report, Pattison talked about friction in sales and the things that probably had to happen on both sides to stop it. Good, gutsy stuff, quite in contrast to the other candidates. One wanted to please everybody to get the job, and his syrupy report showed it, could've killed a diabetic. The third talked about the need to upgrade the computer system as his top priority. We didn't agree. That opinion may have been right, but it didn't matter since nobody else felt that way, and his report failed to convince. It did appear to be a legitimate weakness for his last employer, but that was them, not us. He also took ten pages to tell us. Time-killer.

We hired Pattison. He did superb work for a decade, made a nice nest egg on his stock, and management agreed the company progressed, partially due to his efforts.

You'll get a stronger team when you:

1. Do all final interviews in one day. It is tough to get everyone's schedules to match. But no other task is more important.
2. Don't talk too much; ask open-ended questions. Pay attention to the candidates' questions. Remember who asks the best.
3. Check each candidate's background through a service. For under a hundred dollars you can verify degrees claimed, credit, criminal records, job history, and references. Do it every time and you'll save yourself a disaster about once every dozen times. Twenty percent of resumes today, at every level, have false degrees or lengths of service. You'll catch some. You'll be surprised. That surprise is far better than the bigger surprises you suffer later if they slip onto your payroll. Also, pay each candidate to give you written suggestions for your business. It is a sample of their work, and you just might learn something. By compensating them you're not abusing the interview process.

CHAPTER 17

CINDERELLAS

Victor Palmieri won applause after turning around Penn Central. He deserved it and went on to start a turnaround fund.

Lousy idea. Inherently. Troubled companies need operational fixes, not money to subsidize bad habits. More cash means change is delayed.

Mr. Palmieri's fund first invested in Crazy Eddie's, a faltering electronics retailer, lost every penny of that investment within months, quietly refunded the leftover cash to his investors, and shut his office.

Q.T. Wiles was Hambrech & Quist's turnaround guru. Patched up one after another for H&Q, but decided to stay on with MiniScribe and do more than the turnaround. Using the same blunderbuss strategies that stopped losses to then accelerate growth, overeager and undermanaged employees started packing bricks in empty cartons, sending them to warehouses, and booking every shipment as a sale. Any inebriated, blind, and ethically challenged accountant shouldn't overlook this, but it went on for a couple of quarters.

Lee Iacocca did the fabled turnaround of Chrysler. Like Penn Central, there was just enough politics applied to question how much was fixed operationally and how much was the taxpayer's gift. (That's you, thanks so much.) Later, with fanfare, Mr. Iacocca took over Koo Koo Roo, a small and troubled chain of chicken restaurants, but didn't stay long. The company nearly went toes-up but was bought for a couple clucks.

Al Dunlap showed a dramatic financial improvement for Scott Paper, half caused by cost cuts and half by a lucky swing in commodity prices, made too many speeches, wrote the book, bragged about how tough he was, and destroyed Sunbeam in his next assignment. (Oops. Wrote the book? Hmm.)

Sanford Sigiloff nicknamed himself "Ming the Merciless." There's that tough-guy thing again, and so proud of it. He took Wickes over after its record-setting bankruptcy, shuffled off assets, threw some bodies overboard, moved the offices closer to his home, and pronounced a victory. Wickes was primarily a lumber and home supplies company. Two of the incompetent executives he eliminated started a new business. They named it Home Depot.

Jerry Goldress was such a skilled turnaround guy, heading Grisanti, Galef and Goldress, that he was not recognized as "the guy who saved . . . ," like so many other experts. He's done too many to be connected with any single victory. Jerry's one of the best, but has done so many he now understands publicity is a distraction. News about you brings resumes but not new business. So he's harder to track; I've seen several victories but suspect even he's stayed too long somewhere, sometime.

These guys are energetic, bright and intense, magnitudes more than me, for one, and are twice as tough and three times more rational than your run-of-the-mill CEO. As a practitioner myself, I believe these six to have been the preeminent turnaround experts from 1980 to 2000.

But each stayed too long somewhere, and none ever has built a lasting business or accelerated a saved one on into supremacy.

Why?

These personalities thrive on change. Change is great when things are bad but lethal when times are better. This gang will fix it whether it's broke or not.

Keep them moving along. Reward them. Praise them. But move them along.

CHAPTER 18

SECOND OPINIONS

John Carrington, Bruce Coleman, Craig Crisman, Dave Prolman, and Bill Gibbs are the only turnaround managers I know. This is after twenty years of doing mostly turnarounds, but some startups as well.

This lack of peers proves turnaround people don't hang out together much. The level of self-confidence required means that it's pretty hard to squeeze any two of our egos into the same auditorium. We are not social types.

John and I worked together at Honeywell three decades ago. He put me on a board of a company that he drove to the next level after Bruce Coleman, the original six-month fixer, stabilized it. That's how I know and respect John. Bruce's approach, never staying beyond a half year, struck me as brilliant. In my past, all fixes happened in the first six months and it was a different ballgame after that, one played better with a different coach. I didn't quite grasp this until I saw Bruce had contractualized it. So I shamelessly stole his approach. Thank you, Bruce. Bruce takes only one assignment per year, using the rest of the time to salvage his golf game.

Craig turned around a wheel business as CEO while I was CEO of a printing roll-up; both companies had common ownership, so we met decades ago at the owner's annual meeting, only to discover we had unknowingly been college classmates.

Bill Gibbs worked for GE in jobs that switched him from company to company twice a year. This lead to his perception that they're all the same. Bill's acceptance of an assignment is often built around the proximity to the fly-fishing season.

Turnaround firms exist. It's not just us individual cowboys. They come and go, but the rationale for belonging to a group only makes sense when half of the partners love to sell while the other half hate to sell, so you get a business where the deal-getters make much of the money and the fixers are happy with smaller slices because they don't have to knock on doors, so they just grimly grind out their work.

There's nothing wrong with that. I prefer writing this book. It's the most efficient way for me to attract some, repel others, and mutually select.

With the firms, just don't assume you'll see much of that commanding personality, that fellow you felt so good about, once the contract is signed. And don't expect the practitioner to be loaded with charisma. Yet, like CPA firms and law offices, it works. Division of labor pays off here as anywhere, but there are no economies of scale, so the practitioner gets the benefits more than the clients.

Firms are fine, but one person does the turnaround. I've traveled much of the world and walked many parks. Most have statues. I haven't yet spotted a statue of a committee or a partnership. Great change is an individual act. In the history of mankind, only one partnership ever lasted, that of David Packard and Bill Hewlett.

There is a Turnaround Management Association, headquartered at Suite 1880, 541 N. Fairbanks Ct., Chicago, IL 60611, phone 312-822-9700, www .turnaround.org. The TMA has an annual convention and a monthly magazine in which you'll spot several ads for turnaround firms, each beating their breasts over how many certified turnaround managers they have, whatever that means. Apparently there's a process, but it's hard to imagine opinionated, calloused loners like myself spending much time with an association.

See for yourself. Call for their publication, "The Journal of Corporate Renewal." Visit their site. Check out a couple firms. If you're thinking of bankruptcy with minimized pain, some of these outfits are superb since they specialize in that.

Most TMA convention speakers seem to be service providers . . . lawyers, asset-based lenders, and CPAs with bankruptcy experience . . . and far fewer turnaround managers.

My web site, by the way, is www.sixmonthfix.com. Sorry, being a turnaround guy doesn't mean you don't know how to promote. My weakness is having never worked through a bankruptcy, and my quirk is always working for shareholders. That limits where I should go.

If your vendors have studied your financials, swallow some pride. Talk with a few of them about turnaround managers they've seen in similar situations. Just remember the narrow vision each creditor must have, as described in Chapter 2, and filter their advice accordingly.

Call up a few. Ask them to show you every place they've been for a couple decades along with lists of the shareholders (if you're a shareholder; ask for the lenders if you're a lender). If they won't, the interview's over.

Here are the perspectives on turnarounds from John Carrington, Bruce Coleman, Craig Crisman, and Bill Gibbs. Union Bank just introduced me to Bill, although most of his work comes from a pension fund, not banks.

There's a West Coast bias here. I live in San Diego. John Carrington's estate is on the coast in Orange County. Craig Crisman resides in San Francisco, Bruce Coleman in New Mexico, and Bill Gibbs in Steamboat Springs, Colorado. Here's what they say:

Sutton: "John, you're known for your 20-20-20 formula. You want $20K per month, 20% of the equity, and the company should be within 20 minutes of your Newport Coast home. And you'll only do software companies. Let me test that: If you had two choices, a diesel manufacturer in Detroit with a billion dollars in revenues, but in need of a turnaround, or a $10 million dollar software company in Laguna Beach, minutes from home, which would you take?"

Carrington: "I stay with software. It evolves faster, can meet new customer needs, and has a propensity for acquisitions since time to market is paramount."

Sutton: "What was your easiest turnaround?"

Carrington: "The last one! Because I knew more then than I knew with any before. My Rolodex grows with numbers to call for tips. By trial and error I learn more about missing things in contracts. Experience has value."

Sutton: "What was the toughest?"

Carrington: "Earlier, I couldn't see the positioning as easily. Switching Cogenesis from financial software to insurance is obvious to me today. We have, however, sold every one I took over."

Sutton: "What patterns do you see?"

Carrington: "Too much VC money given an inexperienced founder. VCs accepting unrealistic next-quarter projections for too long."

Sutton: "Bruce, your formula made me realize all my best work has always been done in the first six months. You won't stay longer. Why is that?"

Coleman: "I stabilize. My deal is make changes and find a competent CEO. This happens to take around six months. I make the first wave of changes . . . expenses, management, performance problems, etc. There is always more to do. How stable the company is within six months is a function of how screwed up it was in the first place."

Sutton: "What was your easiest?"

Coleman: "Probably WebSense. They had some cash. The product was in fairly good shape and competitive. It was a growth market. There was a decent core of management. Some changes needed to be made but there was a good team of believers.

Sutton: "And the toughest?"

Coleman: "Probably Information Sciences, an HR software firm. I was the 12th CEO. The company products were poorly written and were three generations behind. They did not run on IMS, Sequel, or client server. We had no cash, and the employees were tired.

Sutton: "Any trends that create troubled businesses?"

Coleman: "The obvious problem with all of these companies was the CEO. The boss casts the longest shadow and no problems can be solved until this is addressed. Companies reflect their leaders, good and bad. If you like what you see in your company as a CEO, it may not be your fault. If you don't, it is certainly your fault.

"Most turnarounds require that the new guy reestablish trust, show by skills that he belongs there, make things better, and deal with the tough people issues."

Sutton: "Why do you prefer software?"

Coleman: "There is too much to learn about this industry to start from scratch. There are turnaround people who do companies from rivets to research because many of the fundamentals are the same. It is more difficult in high technology because of the speed in the market and need for fast decisions. Having a background, people to ask, and industry relationships makes the job easier."

Sutton: "Craig, you've engineered dramatic turnarounds that I watched, Dynamark and Applied Magnetics. Both slipped back into trouble a couple years later. Is there a lesson?"

Crisman: "Dynamark turned around so nicely that the owners got all their investment back in my second year. They were so grateful that we releveraged it and the owners gave me half of the equity. The company made steel wheels for the aftermarket. Public taste shifted to cast aluminum very quickly, which required massive capital for the casting machines and automated lathes. Our debt-to-equity was already 60:1. We tried to keep up, but ultimately couldn't cash-flow the business.

"Applied Magnetics made heads for disk drives. When I joined in 1994 there was only 45 days' cash in the till. The previous five years reported losses of $150 million. It was capital-intensive; in three years depreciation went from 30% of operating expense to 40%.

"There were a handful of customers in the whole world. Applied had three with the largest controlling 70% of our revenue. New products came out every six months. When I joined in 1994 disk drives had capacities of 200 MB per disk. By 1999 that hit 10 GB, an increase of 50× in five years with dropping prices.

"But our stock went from $2.50 in 1994 to $60 per share in 1997. This came from a $96 million profit that year on a 44% sales increase to $496 million.

"I tried to shore up the balance sheet by selling some convertible debt and attempted several acquisitions using stock; this didn't work. Our largest customer insisted that we stick with an existing technology where we had a commanding lead. That was wrong for both of us. In twelve months, together, we went from leaders to disaster.

"During this same time, demand grew 15% to 20% per year. But the capacity grew so much faster than users needed that the number of disks dropped per drive from 5.5 to 1.5. So true demand dropped like a rock and we were without the most advanced technology.

"In the 42 years of the disk drive business, the sum total of the net worths of all participants is negative. We applied for Chapter 11 in January of 2000. The company will emerge in 2001 as a manufacturer of microswitches with a valuation of $55 million. Often the best you can do is chapter the company and sell off the assets or maybe dress the company up for sale. It's difficult when you start out with a turd and no cash."

Sutton: "What was the easiest turnaround?"

Crisman: "There is no such thing. Small companies with declining sales and asset-based loans usually don't have the mass to get around the corner. Larger companies that are going concerns are susceptible to a quick fix by cost reduction, which requires an experienced turnaround manager. In almost all cases, the long-term fix requires some sort of change in business strategy. At Applied Magnetics there was a quick fix that yielded spectacular results, but I could never implement the strategic fix I knew was needed.

Sutton: "What puts companies into trouble?"

Crisman: "There are six broad situations:

1. Rapid-growth companies, where sales outrun cash flow.
2. Leveraged buyouts. Cash is key. Whoever is at the helm must constantly create fallback positions.
3. Companies in decline. The typical turnaround.
4. Businesses transitioning from entrepreneurial to professional management.
5. Startups.
6. Organizations built by acquisitions."

Sutton: "What are the traits of troubled businesses?"

Crisman: "Some that come to mind without thinking too hard are incompetent CEOs, grossly excessive operating costs and no budgetary control, bad morale from lousy leadership, ineffective business strategy, poor quality and bad customer relations, excessive inventory with high receivables and uncontrolled payables, political infighting on the board, and executives with different agendas."

Sutton: "Bill, you're making me look bad. You say six months is too long."

Gibbs: "I've done four turnarounds. One in four months, one in four months and two weeks, one in five months, and one in six months. The timing is determined by finding a new CEO. That search starts upon my arrival. My goal is to hand off to a new CEO in four months.

"I will only accept with a good CFO or have the investors provide a proven CFO. The person becomes my partner, someone I can trust. That provides more immediate cost controls. It allows me to focus on evaluating management, projects, new products, strategy, customers, etc. It also lets me have flexible time to fish, ski, and dance. I usually work three to five days a week and in later stages let the CFO mind the store.

"I let the board handle the recruiting. I input skills and experience I think the company needs and interview the final candidates. The board uses a recruiter and screens.

"Overhead walks through the door on two feet. Everybody must understand that if we don't fix it, our replacements will."

Sutton: "What was your toughest turnaround?"

Gibbs: "A tax recovery consulting and software company. The reason was, as always, poor management. No brain power.

"Commissions gave up to 50% of sales. Total commission expense ran to 25% of revenues. A sustainable business would allow 10%. No money, no bank line. This did not make the plan I put in place. Previous year lost $8 million on $13 million in revenue. Plan was to make $500K on $21 million in revenue but we lost $1 million on $22 million. Difference was all in commissions. I thought the new CEO could implement the new plan, but should have stayed involved until all agents signed. The new CEO was not as aggressive as me. He did hit 2001 numbers.

"Here's my dream. I die. My direct reports are the pall bearers. The casket opens and I sit up as they carry me to the grave. 'How many pall bearers do I have?' I ask. 'Six,' the minister replies. 'Lay off three,' I reply."

Sutton: "What was the easiest?"

Gibbs: "A software company. They hired an excellent CFO who reported three weeks before me, so I hit the ground running. Most employees were bright. And the previous CEO was so dumb I couldn't help but look like a hero.

"Philosophy is nice, song and dance a travesty, but action is our destiny. On the bathroom wall of one of my turnarounds:

'To be is to do, Aristotle.

To do is to be, Socrates.

Do be do be do, Sinatra.

Do, do, do, Gibbs.'

"I'm proud of that."

Dave Prolman runs a turnaround firm, Prolman & Associates, with offices in Los Angeles, Orange County, and San Diego. His forte is financial restructurings while he inserts experienced operating executives from various industries, who are his associates.

Sutton: "Where does your business come from?"

Prolman: "Most of our business is referred to us by lenders followed by insolvency attorneys."

Sutton: "What's been the toughest?"

Prolman: "Owners realizing that they've lost their business, effectively, with nothing to show for it, to a buyer or to liquidation. Both are rare, but do happen. Also tough has been fraud. Easiest have been those clients with large, cash-rich parent corporations."

Sutton: "Common causes?"

Prolman: "Almost every business we assist is in trouble due to incompetent management. Some were good at a smaller size or in previous generations, but all have grown into entities that put management in over their heads, with inadequate support in people and systems."

This group of five are likable folk. They don't eat ground glass for breakfast or enjoy firing employees.

Each of them get to the heart of the matter in seconds, and don't take up time with idle chatter. If attention deficit disorder had been invented during their youths, they'd probably have all been doped up on Ritalin.

Bruce Coleman does one six-month contract per year. He spends the other half of each year lowering his golf score.

John Carrington goes nonstop from one turnaround directly into the next; despite his 20-20-20 filter, he's been busy every day I've known him for the last thirty years. John and I discussed the tax problems of turnarounds once; there's no way to plan because the bonuses come in big chunks at unexpected moments. I had been thinking of a Lake Tahoe, Nevada, residency to avoid overpaying the California state bureaucrats. I still check that out from time to time. John won't consider it. His solution is simple. Just make more money.

Craig Crisman was doing his taxes when I last called. I expressed amazement. He expressed amazement at my amazement. "Your tax bill is your single biggest cost item as an individual. How can you not do it yourself?" One of Craig's earliest turnarounds was a winery; as a former farmer he got to liking the craft and owns his own winery today.

As a firm, Prolman & Associates are typically running several turnarounds at once, most assignments running several months, creditor-assigned and fee-based.

Don't try to hire Bill Gibbs in July. He starts serious fly-fishing then for several months and disconnects his phone until November. If the snowpack is good then, it may be tough to remove him from Steamboat Springs.

These are fun folks, turnaround people. Bright, tough, and human.

I note that Crisman and Gibbs are engineers. So's Goldress. Sigiloff majored in physics. The quants are more prevalent among turnaround people, no surprise; they're the ones who worry about cause and effect more and obtuse social things less. And, as reported in Chapter 1, those pedigrees are more common with successful CEOs of any time and place.

Carrington and I, with softer degrees, also seem better at the later game, selling the businesses and marketing. Maybe that's where art replaces science.

CHAPTER 19

CONTRACTS ARE SALES LITERATURE

Every significant transaction ends up with a contract, right?

So why let a lawyer draft it? They're clueless. They want to keep you out of any possible trouble. Death is one way to stay out of any possible trouble.

Never taking any avoidable risk is another way to avoid one kind of trouble. This assures a bigger kind of trouble, in that you go out of business, while your competition takes a risk or two and leaves you sucking your thumb.

Half the time you put a deal together, the person you negotiate with won't be the signer. It'll be her boss. Or his boss's boss. Or legal or maybe a committee.

In other words, the folks with the final say-so don't really understand the background, and your contact might be so exhausted after you've beat him/her up so badly, that they don't explain it so well. And the whole thing falls through.

Business goes on in any turnaround, and the restructuring of existing deals is frequent. So you need to hone your writing skills and understand why control of this process is important.

Control the structure of the contract. Let them do the typing and editing if they want. Put the terms that are most favorable to the other party in the first few paragraphs and in the ending clauses. Start 'em and finish 'em with positives. You want their heads bobbing up and down at the start, and you want them smiling when it's time to reach for the ballpoint.

Explain this to your attorney at the start. You need the lawyer later, as an unoffended and understanding worker on the final draft.

Now maybe you plan on being there at the close. Let's hope. But as often as not, it gets delayed. Right? Always. So the Director assigned to approve this deal is out of town and it gets faxed to his hotel, maybe in Taiwan, where he's jet-lagged. You cannot count on being there and you cannot count on your counterpart having the selling skills when needed.

Use plain English. No seven-syllable words. Say "agreement" instead of "contract," it's friendlier. Say "help" instead of "facilitate," "Widget Industries" instead of "party of the first part," and "sale" instead of "transfer of ownership." Those are understandable words.

Then the bleary-eyed Director in Taiwan will actually understand what the document says at 3 A.M. And if you ever get in a fight, so will an arbitrator or jury.

By the way, also mention the other company first. And favorably. We're just talking polite here, and selling courtesy.

"Amalgamated Metals, the leading zinc producer headquartered in Buffalo Breath, Montana, with unique processes, and Widget Industries, a puny little casting outfit in Lexington, Kentucky, who's just thrilled to know Amalgamated, both agree that . . ."

There's never a reason to say "whereas." No sentence in any contract needs to contain over thirty words. You would throw away any newspaper article written like that, and writing a readable contract makes things easier and more pleasant for everyone, a mood you want when closing deals. The preceding was a thirty-word sentence. And it was too long.

You can go too far. Just as there's this irrational, factual thing in all of us that feels anxiety over a banker in saddle shoes, getting too simple in language makes folks nervous. Go in the direction of simplicity, just not all the way.

Here's one example:

1. "Gary Sutton hereby grants to (one of my real publishers) during the full term of copyright and all extensions thereof the full and exclusive rights comprised in the copyright in (real book) including any 'Supplementary Materials' (as defined in Paragraph 2(a) below) and any revised editions, including but not limited to the right, by itself or with others, throughout the world, to print, publish, republish, distribute, and transmit (real book) and to prepare, publish, distribute, and transmit derivative works based thereon, in English and other languages, in all media of expression now known or later developed, and to license or permit others to do so."

This is the actual language from the first contract draft from a publisher. They were good people, so I signed the contract pretty much as submitted, but would argue the above sentence could simply say:

1. "Gary Sutton gives (real publisher) exclusive publishing rights to (real book) worldwide and for all media during the copyright term."

Their lawyers' extra words weaken the publisher's rights. They also create language that's hard to follow. And if you and I can't follow it, a jury comprised of unemployed and retired people will be easily rattled and vote for the little guy. That's me. Here's why:

The first line says "hereby," a silly word that adds nothing but fog. Delete it. Next it says "grants," which is okay, if a bit lofty, so say "gives." Then the draft says "during the full term of copyright and all extensions thereof," which probably makes lawyers happy when they study the paragraph, but, since a later clause negates it if the book goes out of print, it's wasted and contradictory. If the book doesn't sell, as most don't, who cares? If it does sell, the publisher will want a sequel shifting the power to the author, so what's the point? Renewing the copyright is under the author's control anyway. Copyrights are good for seventeen years. A few bestsellers last a year. Maybe. Too many words that will never mean anything.

Next it says "including any supplementary materials as defined in Paragraph 2(a) and in any revised editions," which is a nice thought, but, unless the publisher and author are happy with each other, other stuff will be written from scratch to avoid falling under this restriction.

Hold on. We're still analyzing the same sentence. Now it says "including but not limited to the right, by itself or with others, throughout the world." Well, "including but not limited to" limits. Any legal dispute will ask why, if the contract intended to cover other rights, it mentioned some but not others.

"Throughout the world" is redundant. "Full and exclusive" earlier in the same sentence covers the world.

Then the contract says the rights are "to print, publish, republish, distribute, and transmit (real book) and," which is fine, except "publish" means "publish, republish, distribute," while transmit might but, if relevant, needs better definition. Does that mean email or radio or the Internet? If important, say so, don't leave it vague for the lawyers to haggle over later.

It goes on and on, this single first sentence. Next it talks of other languages which "worldwide" would seem to imply. The "all media" to ever be known is so broad it's weak and should say Internet, DVD, and CD-ROM, and leave others that may appear up to negotiations and the good mutual experiences thus far between the parties.

Don't garbage up the contract with words that don't work.

Put in some disarming concessions before they're asked for. Suggest that the law of their state govern. It makes little difference, and speeds up the process since you're not quibbling over trivia. (Yes, your attorney will say they'll have the home bias, but that may be for them or against them and, more likely, is unlikely to have any effect.)

If, after offering up some of these unrequested favors, the other side asks for more, say no. Period. You're now getting a preview of their behavior as a partner, and you better correct it before the wedding. Ask if they want to start over. Mean it.

Put in the terms you want most with a deft sentence or two that help sell them.

"Since Amalgamated Metals enjoys more financial strength than Widget Industries, and borrows for less, both parties agree that payment terms will be net 90 days, and these prices from Widget reflect that assistance." Something like that. Don't overdo it, just put a little explanatory spin on the critical phrases. You won't be in Taiwan to remind that guy why.

If you're one who starts out demanding a long list of outrageous concessions, and then slowly yields on half to arrive at final terms, get a life. This kind of game-playing suggests you don't have enough to do, and the childish glee you get from pretending to be a tough guy is just that, childish. Worse yet, it makes you inefficient. The best contracts are quick ones. And more deals are hopefully better than fewer, so get on with it.

Put in a binding arbitration clause. Let the other side pick the city and you pick the arbitrator, or vice versa. Limit the time for arbitration to a few days.

Lawyers hate this. It's way too fair and efficient. Juries today are the unemployed, bored corporate workers, and doddering retired folks. These panels are made up of voters, many of whom cannot push the chad through a punch card. So if you prefer juries, then something's wrong with you.

The jury system, by the way, became obsolete along with the dumbing of America. Most professional wrestling fans are eligible to vote. Voters become jurors. O.J. was found innocent. In the McMartin case, the day care center owners spent decades in prison after preschoolers testified that they were forced to have sex with dead zebras. The evidence of dead zebras in the windowed school was never found, but the McMartins were not released.

Some argue that juries are better for the large, deep-pocketed partners. I say not. You can always launch the David vs. Goliath sympathy appeals. If it really matters, the Fortune 500 guy will use Madison, Harrison & Foster. That All-Ivy firm will play tough, but will bill your opponent so aggressively that they'll actually notice. Madison, Harrison & Foster is often distracted by other cases and SEC filings. You can hire young Jerry Schwartz, just out of a New York City law school, where he bused tables to pay his way, needs the work, wants to make his mark, and has the disposition of an alligator with an abscessed tooth. Pay his modest hourly fee plus a percentage of the award. I'm betting on Jerry.

Better than any of these shenanigans, however, is binding arbitration. Quick. Rational. Trials are only fun for the first few rounds, and nobody ever enjoys the judicial process; most leave it feeling a little emptier, whether winning or losing.

CHAPTER 20

DOWNGRADE EDUCATION

W hat cheer. Linda Billings, recruited years earlier from Wells Fargo Bank, handled Montron's checking account along with 1,000 other clients there. Linda came into accounting at Montron as our most upbeat and always hustling clerk, and later became controller, overseeing growth rates of more than 100% per year. Then Fisher-Price Toys bought Montron, and she became materials manager.

Her new job was to run warehousing, distribution, purchasing, and production. That's all, just everything inside.

Her biggest challenge was to install the MRP (Material Requirement Planning) system in the factory. To do this, she needed the cooperation of all 600 workers. Cooperation and dedication. In English and Spanish. She needed timely, accurate reports on all sorts of manufacturing data, entered in a computer system that automatically ordered parts based on projected lead times. It was a tricky system to coordinate, but when it worked it made factories hum and inventory fly.

This is no small task. She coordinated scrap rates, engineering changes, and the best-priced ordering quantities. She charged straight into it. I remember stepping into the warehouse one time and seeing her on the loading dock, with a Pacific sunset backdrop, asking a worker why it took two weeks, instead of two minutes, to clean up a pile of pallets. The worker tried to explain why they (the pallets) and he were both sitting idle. "I was gonna get to those tomorrow," Audie protested.

"Little late," said Linda. She swung a pallet over her head and slammed it into a dumpster. All I could see was her silhouette. That's all I could see of the other worker. It felt like backrow seating in a small theater with dramatic lighting and action.

The worker stood frozen. Linda stomped over to the pile and hoisted another pallet. "Do you think I enjoy doing your work for you?" she asked.

Her arsenal included more than one method. She could be hard, tossing wooden pallets; she could also mesmerize you with a soft question or polite logic. Her smile could melt icebergs, even an occasional accountant or engineer. Linda constantly quizzed you and rarely gave orders, but when she did it was commanding.

She was a leader and a manager, always striving for agreement, commitment, and vision. It was a kick to watch her stop a production manager in his tracks and change his priorities after a couple of words. Inevitably, the production manager would nod and smile and then head off in a new direction. I never knew what she said. But it worked.

When she first put the MRP system in place, she brought a withdrawn and intellectual engineer onto her side. When she first went to him, he seemed grafted to his drawing board. At lunch, he strolled out to his car for a nap. Not one of the boys.

Linda needed his support for the system to work. He tracked the engineering change notices. These documents determined type and quantity of parts ordered, and if out of date, your inventory could never be right. She showed him how this could work. Sold him. He started walking the halls, collaring people all day long to make sure they were all getting their part done. Everyone tried to stay a step ahead to avoid disappointing this reborn zealot who suddenly didn't need naps. His follow-up probably saved thirty days in the setup.

Thirty days in a twin plant operation that sends several truckloads of plastic parts, solder, electronic components, and cardboard across the border every day . . . and pulls back seven semitrailers full of finished toys daily . . . six days a week . . . makes a huge financial difference. Better toys. More of them. Less idle time. Happier kids at Christmas. Ecstatic shareholders.

Linda Billings enhanced manufacturing efficiency in a plant that went from 30 employees to 600 in two years. Scrap dropped to below 1%. Inventory turned over 30 times per year. Productivity steadily improved at a time when chaos might have triumphed. She coordinated everyone and nurtured a team, bought pizza and soda every day after the first shift for a month. This kept the team talking, figuring what the supervisors needed to do during the next shift for a smoother flow.

Linda does not have a college degree. In most companies, this would have sidetracked her. Or made her ascent slower. It's oxymoronic, no, just moronic, that in the name of fairness today a perfectly legal way to discriminate is to require a certain level of education.

Bill Gates didn't get his college degree. The boy's doing okay. My pal Ed Tuck, founder of Teledesic and a dozen other companies, didn't have time to finish high school. Fred McClain, the cofounder of SkyDesk, loves doing differential equations and dazzled professors with his postdoctoral math theories, but didn't finish a thesis so he never got the Ph.D. Oh, he also forgot his bachelor's degree along the way.

Let me confess to attending a Harvard program for a few years with a hundred other CEO/entrepreneurs who were prominent but not exactly all rubbed with ivy. Forgive me, the damage wasn't permanent. But we had a couple classmates who struggled with the case studies. One didn't finish. We later learned they both suffered from dyslexia. One was Paul Orfalea, better known as Kinko, who drove his copy business to the billion-dollar value range within ten years of our classes. The other was Craig McCaw. We did a cell phone case study one night, this was 1983, and Craig didn't come back for the second or third year. He apparently spotted something the rest of us missed, started McCaw Cellular which within ten years sold for $14 billion to AT&T. And he did even better with Nextel.

Limiting candidates by their degrees isn't very bright. The only certainty between two candidates is that the more educated one will be less excited by your offer.

The rules are, there are no rules. Keep an open mind and see what you can find. Education as a success factor is highly overrated. Intelligence and drive are much more important; compatible values are critical.

Education is fun. I drank my way through a B.S. degree in the '60s, lived at Denver University for a few weeks of business in the '70s, did the Harvard Business seminar for three years in the '80s, took more work at Berkeley and Oxford in the '90s, and view it all as interesting but marginally relevant. Fun, yes. A recess. Occasionally useful. You make great friends. Both our daughters are recovering M.B.A.s.

But all your employees need is motivation in every position, experience in many, and smarts in some.

Your group will be sharper than your textbook competitors if you:

1. Drop the educational requirements by one notch for every job. Spend more time interviewing a larger group of candidates. Pick talent and proven results over degrees.

2. Cut your seminar and training budget in half. Seminars give managers an excuse to delegate training that they should do themselves. Worse, it is delegated to an expensive outsider. Pick one, the expensive outsider or the manager. You don't need both.

3. Always pay for employees to take job-related classes on their own time. Cover all tuition for an A grade, half for a B, and nothing for anything else.

CHAPTER 21

REVERSE DISCRIMINATE

September, 1978, Tijuana, Mexico—Truck fumes choked the air. Inland winds swept that grit and oil into sandy dust devils that pelted my windshield.

It must have been on steroids, that tumbleweed, bouncing across the brown dirt field, flying over the ditch, jumping the road, and crunching under my left front wheel. And in its last mighty act, flattening my tire. The thermometer swelled mercury red. My feelings were up there. I was headed for the factory. This had been a bad month.

Weeks earlier, AFI de Mexico hired 200 new workers. I was the Managing Director and General Manager of Fisher-Price Toys for the West Coast. Finding workers was no problem. Applicants lined up 30 rows deep at the front door, starting at five every morning. This went on for days.

Despite the overflow of applicants, it was tough. This was a different culture. We spoke the language, sure, that was the rule for every gringo crossing to our factory. This seemed only polite. And, in my other, brief, international experiences, it always seemed the highest-ranking bilingual was the one who really ran things. Other officers merely observed and hoped they understood half of what was happening.

There were moments. We had our nurse teach new employees, mostly young women, how to use toilet paper in the bathrooms. They had not encountered it before. As a result of poor hygiene, some of them carried tuberculosis or even illnesses less imaginable, like mange.

As we worked our way through the medical problems, we found out the doctor giving the physicals to applicants was molesting the prettier women.

We dealt with this by complaining to the government. Nothing happened to the doctor, we were just reassigned and I think it stopped.

Somebody stuffed a packet of cocaine in the undercarriage of a truck and the border guards on the south side, strangely enough, caught it. They threatened us. This was so outrageous a charge that my arm-waving and anger got us out of trouble, but that could've gone either way, looking back.

Weeks earlier we slipped up and dumped a pickup load of scrap cardboard at the dump. This was wrong, absolutely; part of the maquiladora deal was that all waste returned to the United States. However, the Federales suggested that delivering $20,000 in a bag to a courier at the Guadalajara airport could settle it. We indignantly refused, requesting a hearing. The state announced they were shutting us down. When I called the governor to let him know, as a courtesy, that we planned to hand his home address to all 600 fired employees as they walked out the door, so that those who chose to plead our case personally with him might do so, the government decided one pickup truckload wasn't such an international offense after all. When in Rome, you know.

By the way, when we instructed the workers to use toilet paper, we soon after had to advise them to flush it. Used paper was piling up ankle-deep. In a lesson they may have understood but we didn't, as soon as they started doing this, the plumbing plugged up and sewage spilled over the floors. Maybe they knew better than we. International business gets glamorous at times.

AFI de Mexico was six years old, a growing part of our twin plant operation mentioned in Chapter 20. Three of our toys became best-sellers for Fisher-Price. Those items were a movie viewer, tape recorder, and record player, and they sold over two million units a year for over a decade. Three of the top ten sellers for Fisher-Price were those of AFI de Mexico. Altogether, Fisher-Price then sold 140 items, so this was a big deal to them, part of the reason why they acquired us, a lowly vendor.

We ran fast, running two 56-hour production shifts a week. The employees loved the overtime. But two days before, several dozen workers suffered food poisoning from the cart vendors outside our plant.

While changing the tire I imagined other changes.

We had a production problem. The setup at AFI de Mexico was that the production line for most items was entirely female, yet the Latin machismo culture put men on as supervisors. The women worked hard. The guys were above it.

Male supervisors were normally standing around gabbing, talking up their weekends at jai alai or whatever. Paying attention was a bit below their status.

Yeah, right. I put up with it at first because I assumed it was the culture and nothing could be done without disrupting their social fabric. We experienced this when we paid bonuses to the workers following the Tijuana floods. Two weeks' pay if the water came up to your knees inside your home and four weeks' if it reached waist level. This wasn't legal. Disruptive capitalism. The government fined us. The penalty wasn't unexpected but another result startled us: Nearly half our employees disappeared when they got the bonuses, not to be seen for weeks. When you live hand to mouth and suddenly get a windfall, why work?

But there was somebody who thought this good-old-boy monopoly on management should be turned upside down. Her name was Cecelia and she caught my attention as soon as I arrived late. I spent only a few seconds staring in amazement at that exceptional tumbleweed thorn, but changing the tire and discovering the spare was low threw me off stride.

"Senor Sutton," she shrieked, "la linea esta debajo. Sin partes. Siempre!" The production line was without parts. Again!

Pablo and Jorge stood by themselves. They didn't see me march in, and they were pointing and laughing, telling stories with chest-thrusting theatrics. I huffed over to the folder with the records. Pablo and Jorge had failed to record production rates for the past two hours. Cecelia told me we had only three boxes of springs left and we had run out of labels a half hour earlier.

That was it. I had thought about getting rid of this layer of male arrogance many times before; now there was nothing to lose. I fired Pablo and Jorge and promoted Cecelia. But I didn't stop there. I fired 14 of 17 male supervisors. Each was the same, a combination plate of macho and lazy.

So, with reasonable severance, a legal amount, we terminated the male supervisors and promoted females.

Life turned into a cakewalk. Production per labor hour went up by about 20 percent within 30 days. Problems seemed to get caught about a decade earlier and were usually easier, certainly with less pain.

More often than not, females outproduce males, Asians beat Caucasians, and youth beat their elders. Take advantage of it.

Minor minorities are terrific. My wife had a bedspread business that, due to a neighborhood quirk, used only Dutch Indonesian seamstresses. They policed each other and berated laggards over dinner. When work slowed, one would quit, and when it got busy, they'd bring in cousins or in-laws to help. My San Bernardino plant had quite a few Jehovah's Witnesses on the payroll, and they made sure each member got to work ahead of time and produced more than the others and never gave me a *Watchtower* to read in two years. You lose this effect with larger segments.

Here's how to fill your office with a more productive group:

1. Inject new energy into your business by making it resemble your marketplace or neighborhood. These productive ethnic groups often work harder. We're so stirred up today I'm not sure what ethnic means, but let groups clump a bit by country, religion, or language. Do things differently and watch your company thrive. Hire a female truck driver, a male secretary, or a 70-year-old sales rep.
2. If the new hires don't cut it, replace them as you would anybody.
3. When there's a productive ethnic or cultural group nearby, hire them in batches. They'll police each other. Move one of them into management and let that culture perform for you.

CHAPTER 22

WALK THE FLOOR

David Packard and Bill Hewlett understood a lot more than mere technology when they started their company in Palo Alto, California. They understood people.

It was because of this that they grew their company from a small garage in Packard's backyard into the leader in test instruments, engineering, calculators, medical products, and computers.

Can you name another partnership that lasted as long as this college-to-death partnership? Me neither.

Their success became legendary by the early 1980s, and therefore it attracted attention from all comers. Management consultants, business book writers, and columnists studied Hewlett-Packard and all came to essentially the same conclusion.

It was simple, even had its own acronym—MBWA. Management By Walking Around stressed listening skills and participation in the day-to-day operation of the entire company. There was no magic but that.

Bill Hewlett kept walking all areas, such as shipping, to see how the river of orders in and orders out was flowing. He learned a lot on the loading docks. Hewlett moved on from shipping when he was satisfied.

Next, he strolled through production to find out the quirks of hard-to-solder joints from the workers on the floor Monday and the variability of resistors on Tuesday. Often, he would spend days with production. He always tried to think of how any specific design change would affect all those in production.

But Hewlett was a scientist by trade, and it was there that his philosophy really came through. One Saturday, he stopped to examine some sub-assemblies and found he needed a microscope. The problem was that all microscopes were caged up for the weekend. Hewlett was frustrated. This was his company. Those were his microscopes and they were everybody's. They belonged to anybody in the company qualified to use them. But the microscopes were locked away, and this made no sense at all, so Hewlett did the only thing he could think of. He took a crowbar and pried open the lock that closed the chain-link gate over the equipment area. He took his microscope, but before he left that room he wrote a note for the first person in on Monday morning. It said, "Please don't ever lock this equipment room again," and it was signed Bill Hewlett.

Dave Packard had the same commitment to improving the operations. He was always looking to improve, trying to learn more about the inner workings. Sometimes he checked receivables to see if any customers were slowing up. Other times he went with a new salesman on a cold call to get to know him and to keep a feel for the field.

Profits at Hewlett-Packard hit $1.6 billion in 1994 as Dave and Bill faded into the background. Not bad for two college kids with an idea for an oscilloscope. They walked the floor and built a culture that did the same.

There are signs today that the giant isn't keeping up and is trying to reinvent itself in a technology world that's accelerating. The moment may have passed. But for fifty years, it just got better and better and better as Bill and Dave just walked around.

If you like the idea of fifty years of increasing profits until you're earning over a billion per year, here are the tactics to steal:

1. Walk the floor day and night and ask questions. Don't always go at the same time, or even same shift. The night folks have different concerns and problems and different suggestions. Share the dirty work. Go along on a sales call to Buffalo in January, or to Louisiana in July, just to show you're there for business.

2. Get rid of the sign-in book at your front desk. It has no use, except to help visiting salespeople discover their competition. Open the place up, get rid of the paranoia.

3. Visit remote locations instead of communicating by memo. If it's not important enough to visit, it's not important enough to keep. Use as little electronic and paper communication as possible. Talk more, dictate less.

Recognize that these tactics, pure Dave and Bill, may be attitude symptoms more than the cure. This kind of activity probably comes automatically from simply caring more than your competitors. If you have that, these tactics will happen automatically, and when the world changes you'll find your tactics changing. Just in case you don't care enough to be this special, copy these tactics. By doing so, maybe you'll learn to care. Meanwhile, try not to demotivate the troops by walking around. Get interested or die.

CHAPTER 23

RAISE PAY, CUT BENEFITS

In the late 1980s, Dave Cohen opened his second Greentree Foods, a health-food store in New Hampshire. In many ways, it mirrored his first store.

They both carried sprouts and roots and herbs plus the dried-fruit-and-nut mixes. Blackwort juice. Ginseng powder. Both stores had 2,000-square-foot layouts in well-traveled strip malls near younger neighborhoods and both were staffed by wholesome granola kids.

But at the first store, Cohen noticed that his clerks stayed only an average of six months. Sure, he was dealing with young employees, and, yes, his clerks stayed twice as long as the average for a fast-food place. But that was small consolation.

Every year, he had to spend chunks of money and time training people and worrying whether they were offending customers because they didn't quite know where the organic ketchup was or what to do with the biodegradable paper straws. And every time there was a new hire, he had to spend the first few days worrying whether the trainee would work out or show up for a second week.

So when he opened his new store, he tried something. He raised pay and eliminated all benefits.

New clerks at the original store made $8 per hour. If they worked 48 hours a week, they made $18,768 a year, including overtime. Plus they got medical coverage, 10 holidays, and a week of paid vacation during the first year.

At the second store, clerks received nothing but cash. No benefits, no vacation, no sick days. Only more money. They were paid $10.40 an hour.

If a new clerk at the second store took as many days off . . . ten holidays plus a week of vacation . . . as a new clerk at the original store, the clerk at the second store made $24,211.

The clerks at the new Greentree Foods enjoyed more freedom. When employees worked more, they made more. They took time off when they wanted, and they made $5,443 extra per year. No, they don't have medical insurance, but that $5,443 could pay for some great health care, cover the taxes, and leave some extra to stuff in the knapsack. Employees win, employers win.

At the new store, clerks stayed twice as long. Things were sharper on the floor as customers found things quicker and got better advice.

There was no increase in cost. Even though salaries were 30% higher, that was offset by savings from insurance and vacation and sick pay. And there were none of those hidden costs for administering the programs. The employees were happy to receive the money up front and there was no clamor for benefits or change. Win-win.

There was a coed at the new store who dropped back to 25 hours and relied on a group policy purchased through school for medical coverage. She took a three-month vacation to go home every summer, and her job was waiting each year when she went back. She made $9,000 during the school year and another $3,500 at another job every summer. This helped put her through school and let her visit home every summer.

Others went to longer hours. One took a two-week vacation every three months. Without benefits and the rules they require, the job started to fit the individual, instead of vice versa. That's nirvana.

Now, let me confess failure to implement this when I tried, even in a startup. Cohen's plan was rational. Kids get it. Middle-aged fogies with families don't.

In my last five companies, the actual health benefits paid out vs. the premiums paid in have not yet reached a 40% payback. Put in a buck. Get twenty cents, maybe thirty back. And we've had heart surgeries, cancers, and multiple sclerosis, the normal range of afflictions and disasters. The healthcare problem is simple: excess paperwork and not enough individual responsibility.

So when starting SkyDesk, I tried to hire engineers with $800 per month added to their monthly pay but asking that they get their own insurance, urging them to get high deductibles. That way they're protected against the significant problems, but don't bleed to death on the minor afflictions and probably pay more attention to those more frequent problems and cures, since they then pay for them. On average, they should gain several hundred dollars per month, after tax. The company would save a couple hundred.

Their savings would more than pay for the minor medical services and their catastrophic policy protects them against the major possibilities.

These were engineers, not sociology and literature majors. They could do the math.

No interest. Repelling thought. And no coherent reason why, just an emotional need to feel that their family was covered by the company. Yikes. When you hit that irrational feeling in your group, don't fight it. You're not dealing with logic, so you may as well pay them lower and spend far less for the premiums. They lose but feel better, and you can get back to business.

But if you have a younger crowd who prefer choices and have lower rates anyway, or perhaps you have employees who tend toward individualism, due to your trade, let everybody win.

1. Form an employee committee to help you plan a dramatic pay increase coupled with a drop in benefits. Announce, one year in advance, an across-the-board pay increase of 20%. Also announce a canceling of health benefits, seniority rights, sick days, and paid vacations. (Use the savings to prepay health policies for those few who may be uninsurable.)

2. An alternative is to offer a bonus of $1,500 per year to employees who will drop their health insurance and show proof they are covered by a working spouse. This cuts the health expense by $3,000 per participant per year. The company saves $1,500 while the employee pockets $1,500. Every year. Minimum.

3. Give the same benefits immediately to new hires as to 20-year veterans. All pay and vacation and pension fringes should depend on performance, not on how long they've been breathing company air. If you overpay long-term employees, you short-change new blood. And that's no way to build a strong company.

CHAPTER 24

INCENTIVIZE EVERYONE

In 1986 sales flattened at Checks To-Go, and the attitude of the telemarketers grew flatter. They did the job. They left. They responded like they were treated.

Telemarketers were paid straight salaries, and poor performers were sacked. There was no recognition given to top performers out of fear they would want more money or become difficult to manage. The only incentives were negative, scowling and scolding and verbal abuse. The supervisor normally entered their room from a back door so the telemarketers couldn't see him coming. He loved to slip in and watch.

(Turnarounds are often so poorly run that a C student like myself can look like a valedictorian from the get-go.)

After awhile, he'd stroll over to a cubicle, look at the operator's call sheet, and stare accusingly at it without eye contact. When he finished his inquisition into the log books, he would toss them on the desk with a condescending shrug and move on to the next employee, always asking, "How many calls have you made? Why not? What's wrong with you?" If only our medical plan covered personality transplants.

There was no reason for these people to strive, so we tried giving them a reason. The first thing we did was show the door to their sick supervisor, handed him a road map, and wished him well. Sort of. We promoted his abused assistant who knew a thing or three about people and sales. Instead of threatening to fire employees every other day, the new supervisor showed her interest in their opinions. "What are your customers saying?" she asked. "What can we do to make that better?" She knew that those in the trenches understood the business better than anyone, including the flashy new turnaround guy, me. So she just listened until her ears hurt.

But there was more. We cut their pay. It was a significant cut, from $10 per hour to $8, but we also gave them back 1% of their revenues. The new system meant that even if sales were merely flat, at an average of $2,000 a day, it was a modest raise.

But suddenly sales were no longer flat. I'm talking the next day. And employees started pocketing an immodest 25% extra.

Maybe more important, the new sales manager created weekly contests. When envelopes became overstocked, the person with the most envelope sales that week was given a weekend in Catalina. When things slowed down, whoever created the highest average order size received theater tickets. Everyone was always thinking about success rather than wondering if the grinch was spying from the back of the room.

Sales growth and customer satisfaction reflected the new attitude that came from the incentives. Once, we gave the group a complaint-reduction goal and, when they met it, I cooked everyone a lobster dinner at my home. The meal was, well, we didn't repeat that one, but the evening was a giant kick in the pants. (Too much garlic in the butter, lobsters were okay, never try to whip up a new sauce you've never made before.) Life became fun for the telemarketers until two years later when Rocky Mountain Banknote acquired Checks To-Go. One of the first things the new owners did was eliminate the incentives, and that's one reason the entire business vaporized within 18 months of their acquisition.

The thing about incentives is they have to be handled delicately. Several years after installing them at Checks To-Go, I ran Knight Protective Industries.

Sales at Knight were flat and declining and I thought I knew the cure. Done that, been there, no problemo. This outfit had 80 telemarketers on the payroll, each making 250 calls per shift. I cut the base salaries by $2 per hour and increased incentives enough to guarantee they would at least break even on the change for identical performance.

Déjà vu? Nope. It cratered.

The problem was that Knight telemarketers already had some daily bonuses. More incentives made the top performers wealthier for the same effort, they couldn't hustle any faster, but it hurt the average performers, the ones we were trying to motivate.

(Stars always star, the losers always lose. Get that mass in the middle to move, and you've done something.)

By then it was too late. We tried to go backward to prior programs where the incentives were more moderate, but all that did was disgruntle the top performers. They jumped ship. (This accomplishment may never make the highlight section of my resume.)

The truth about incentives is that the first dollar you pay is the most effective. A little incentive always works. A lot of incentive works sometimes with some personalities, but backlashes with others. Incentives also work best when they remain subservient to teamwork. Positive feedback helps, but helps most when combined with incentives. All praise and no pay makes a mockery of your words. All cash and no praise gets empty fast. Too much incentive fosters greed.

Here's how to energize your whole place next month. Start now.

1. Publicly recognize one employee for outstanding work every month. Reserve a parking place near the door for that person, almost as close as the customers' spots. Put the person's picture in the company newsletter with a story about his or her particular customer service act, cost savings, or production.

2. Make at least 5% of every employee's pay a monthly bonus for his or her department's specific goals (that is, the number of error-free transactions in accounting without overtime, units shipped minus 10 for every return in production, days outstanding in collection, beating budget and schedule in research, and so forth). Tie these bonuses to groups of 20 or fewer individuals to develop peer pressure and teamwork. Don't create lone wolves with individual bonuses unless a task is clearly a solo effort. Then do it big.

3. Post department goals in each area on bar charts or graphs that can be read from 30 feet away. Make these the center of attraction in all tours and walks through the offices. Always stop, look, comment, and discuss.

CHAPTER 25

TIGHTEN THE SHIP

In the spring of 1988, Rocky Mountain Banknote acquired Checks To-Go. I was CEO of Checks To-Go. Both companies produced bank checks. Rocky Mountain Banknote printed for banks in huge quantities. Their buyers were sophisticated, placing huge daily orders. They were the third largest, behind Deluxe and Harlan.

Checks To-Go created checks for small PC users. We bought checks in bulk and then personalized them for the customers. But our customers often didn't know their account number, how many to order, what type of forms they needed, and how to load them in their printer. They ordered only once or twice a year. They needed handholding.

When the transaction was complete, I ran the new division Rocky Mountain Banknote. In 1987, Checks To-Go made the highest profits of any company in the check industry. Our net profit percentage doubled Deluxe's, in spite of heavy interest payments, while Deluxe enjoyed interest gains. Checks To-Go had lost money for its prior ten years. Rocky Mountain Banknote bought us to enter the faster-growing but smaller PC forms business.

In the first meeting in their boardroom in Denver, when I officially became part of what they called the A team, we talked about, no, not checks. Not customers. We talked about hotels. They didn't like the one I was staying in. They squirmed upon learning I was a proud Priority Club member at Holiday Inn.

The executive vice president smiled and explained, "We prefer that someone of your level stay at the Marriott or Hilton. We need to keep up an image."

This guy was splendid in his French cuffs, monograms, and braided red suspenders. Never bet on a guy wearing designer suspenders to understand cost controls. Or to want to.

I knew that a night at the Denver Marriott or Hilton ran about $80 back then. (Some of this is historical, alright?) Holiday Inn was running about $50. Their choices cost about 60% more.

All had clean beds and a bathroom. Breakfast too. I thought of this as the executive vice president continued. "You are now part of a new team. We need consistency in the organization, so you should stay with the Marriott in Denver and its equivalent elsewhere." He expected I'd be eager to join this upscale group.

Image ruled. They changed their name from Rocky Mountain Banknote to ROMO because they were expanding beyond the West. The Chairman showed me the logo and asked my opinion of the switch, and I said, "It has all the charm of International House Of Pancakes calling itself IHOP."

This was one of those memorable moments in a career. The heads circling the boardroom table reminded me of one of those little plastic dogs you sometimes see in the rear window of a car, with the head bobbing up and down. All around the table, heads bobbled up and down, never horizontally, vertical, bob, vertical, bob. The room didn't exactly go silent. The VP Ops coughed. Two chairs on both sides of me squeaked a bit as their occupants tried to slide them away from me without being obvious by lifting them. The Chairman puffed on his pipe.

"Well, Gary, what kind of company car would you like? At your level, we authorize an Oldsmobile Cutlass or a Mercury Sable."

I replied that I didn't want a car, but would settle for mileage.

They fired me six weeks later for disagreeing with their business strategy. They viewed Checks To-Go as a production business, needing economies of scale. This reflected their primary business.

I viewed it as a service business.

So I left the company for a medical reason: They were sick of me.

In 18 months, Checks To-Go was gone. Kaput. The business disappeared. This, in spite of the fact that Rocky Mountain Banknote could have sent some of their overflow work that fit to Checks To-Go, let us handle and bill it, make even more profits, and pay no tax. Checks To-Go's prior losses, ten year's worth, meant the carryforward would shelter any income for years. But they blew it all up. Nice image, eh?

Look, there are few companies in America that make as much as 10%

profit on sales. Most make about 3% to 4%. With that tiny margin, everything counts, especially a chance at 60% in savings.

And remember, the Marriott is not just the Marriott. The Marriott is like one small hole in your bucket, but its mere existence leads to other spurts. Need new equipment? Go for it now. Then another leak, nicer offices to keep up the image. Pretty soon your pail is empty, and that fire is just starting.

Uncontrolled costs destroy any business, and limos and Marriotts and luxury are uncontrolled costs. If your competitor has a limo and you don't, you are already winning. He has a leaky bucket.

There were five self-made multibillionaires (say that five times fast, just for fun) in the United States during that story. Sam Walton founded Wal-Mart. In 1991, he drove an eight-year-old red Ford pickup. He always fetched his own coffee. One time, when a friend of mine was in the Wal-Mart lobby, he watched as Walton accidentally spilled his coffee out of the machine, grabbed some paper towels, and mopped it up himself.

Ross Perot paid himself $70,000 a year as president of EDS. When Perot sold EDS to General Motors, the president of General Motors, Perot's new boss, made a $2.4 million salary plus a bonus. Finally, he paid Perot $2.5 billion to go away because GM executives were embarrassed by the folksy Perot, who didn't want a big salary or office or specially tuned cars. Worse yet, Perot invited employees home to dinner and talked with them constantly. The president of General Motors announced layoffs of 72,000 that year.

David Packard never had an enclosed office before he left Hewlett-Packard for government service. It figures.

Bill Gates of Microsoft often rode coach on planes, until they finally got so big they ran their own fleet of aircraft. Warren Buffett manages Berkshire Hathaway's billions and billions with a staff of 24. When they lunch together, it's McDonalds.

Okay, yes, right, the Silicon Valley gang recently, and the Wall Street crowd forever, have lived lavishly in everything they do. So if you're one of those, go ahead. You've got sinful margins and may as well waste some. It's just that most businesses can't support that. Did you ever really admire a sheik?

Here's how to boost your bottom line right now.

1. Downgrade hotels one level. If your customers stay at the Holiday Inn and your competitors are at the Marriott, whom do you want to know? But if your customers stay at the Ritz Carlton, sip a house wine at their bar, meet and greet them there before quietly slipping back down the block to your room at the Sheraton. It's okay, if you know

your stuff better than the other guy, you'll survive the night there. The bus gets downtown from the airport just as fast as most cabs. Get rid of the company plane. Commercial flights get you there quicker, they are seven times safer by the way, and they don't isolate you from other people, some of whom may be your customers.

2. Stop building and equipping new offices. If somebody absolutely has to have an assistant, let him or her share a desk and space. (Watch this cut requests for new hires.)

3. Do little things: Shut off the lights; cut express mail costs by using economy when possible. Withstand the jibes and ridicule for counting paper clips and keep it up until the attitude spreads. Don't spend a lot of time on these items. Do them quickly and quietly, then refocus on the bigger picture.

CHAPTER 26

PUBLISH A FIRING POLICY

For six months in 1974, business at the Broadway Bowl in Littleton, Colorado, doubled. The alleys weren't packed, but between 4:30 and 5:30 P.M. engineers with pocket protectors, marketing guys in tasseled loafers, and production supervisors in short sleeves and clip-on ties draped over the bar. The number of daily kegs at the bar jumped from four to eight.

The Broadway Bowl was at 5499 South Broadway. Next door, at 5501 South Broadway, sat Honeywell, and anxiety reigned. Thirty seconds from our front door poured just enough hops to help us deal.

For over 10 years, Honeywell sold Pentax cameras in the United States. We operated out of an old supermarket that had been converted into offices and warehouse space.

For awhile, that was the way of the Japanese camera market. But Minolta dropped their U.S. distributor two years earlier, and Canon canceled their distribution contract with Bell and Howell seven months after Minolta. By foregoing profits and pumping money into advertising and price cuts, they hoped dominate sales in America.

Good plan. This faced Honeywell in 1974, a year before our Pentax distribution contract expired.

The strategy was a tax strategy as well as one of growth. The change meant that Canon and Minolta would realize profits only in Japan, eliminating taxes here.

Made sense. I'm always for reducing taxes. Until it jeopardizes my paycheck, when it becomes subversive, Communist, Fascist, and toxins in our apple pie.

Sales at Canon and Minolta jumped. Sales at the Broadway Bowl jumped.

If Honeywell followed their marketing tactics, dropping more into advertising while slashing prices, we'd lose our kimonos.

Something had to give. Pentax wanted more sales in the United States, while Honeywell artfully dug in its heels. Honeywell wanted profits, so it continued with modest advertising and what seemed to be fair prices. Pentax balked.

In this particular division of Honeywell, almost all the profits came from Pentax. Pentax wanted more sales than Honeywell could afford so Pentax threatened to break away.

Were they bluffing? If not, our business was kaput. Every employee knew this, and quite a few eased the tension with pitchers of Coors at the Broadway Bowl. Maybe they were bluffing for better terms on the next contract. It wouldn't have been the first time in history. The other question was, if Pentax was really going to drop Honeywell, would they hire most of the current employees or would they start a new company with entirely new employees?

Coors poured fast and slid down easy.

And then one day K. Chiwata showed up. He was Pentax's export director, a Japanese who spoke five languages. He popped in wearing a loud plaid sport coat and a mastery of English slang that made him seem more like one of us than us. He absorbed alcohol in mythical quantities and remained coherent, happy, and confident.

Staffers went to dinner with Chiwata and he brought the predictable but bad news from Japan. Pentax wanted to control their own distribution, and the cancellation was no bluff. Chiwata announced that Pentax would drop Honeywell in one year when the contract expired. They would start their own distribution, using many Honeywell employees. They would also keep their corporate offices in Denver, a huge relief. Most jobs were safe.

"We have been friends for many years, and I hope this planned change does not upset you too much," Chiwata said that day. "We will take over and manage the distribution as Pentax Corporation next year.

"I will here move from Hong Kong and we will build a distribution center 10 minutes away in the Denver Tech Center. And I promise we will have fun. All of you will be kept on the payroll. The way we will do it is to guarantee every job and pay rate for the first six months. After that, some positions will disappear, and I have no idea how many or which ones. If you stay through the first six months and your job is eliminated, we will give you six more months' pay as severance. If your job is kept, you will make at least as much and probably more, but you may have more duties. If you quit before the first six months, you get nothing."

The deal was clear. On the table and more than fair. Suddenly, employees all stopped worrying about the economy and instead began, again, concentrating on our jobs. Nobody worried about what the government or competition or other outsiders might do to hurt the business.

Smiles returned. Productivity soared, and errors dropped. Few workers wanted their positions eliminated but at least there was nothing to worry about for six months, and those dismissed would be cushioned with cash.

The only problem was at the Broadway Bowl, where beer sales plunged.

Most companies have hiring policies. Few have firing policies. Hiring is a pleasant process and is written about and overwritten about in detail. Firing is more important. It establishes a company's soul.

Every company does it. Oh, yes, there are those happy aberrations like Japan was for a couple decades. And IBM. Later PeopleSoft. Nothing's forever but death, and companies that pretend otherwise or, worse yet, believe differently, are setting everybody up for deeper tragedy when the ultimate reality arrives. Markets change. Life is transient. It's easy to have a hiring policy, since hiring is a positive move, yet firing is more controversial and therefore should be better understood. It's time to eliminate paranoia.

Here's how to get the workers working again:

1. In practice, give specific written warnings for habitual problems before terminating. Employees should be given a chance to respond and correct the problem or challenge the complaint. Policy violations or dishonest behavior should not need such a warning. If a firing is a surprise, management failed.

2. Accrue severance for all employees as a liability in the range of one week for every year's service. This means that when a layoff is necessary, some earnings have been set aside to ease the blow for employees. Then there's no temptation to be cheap and dishonorable when a recession or sales slump tempts you to scrimp on severance. Accounting practice guides a company to do the opposite under the theory that all businesses are ongoing. The assumption is wrong, so the practice is wrong.

3. Make it clear in the employee manual that employees are free to quit anytime with a two-week notice. Also make it clear that any employee can be fired for any reason at any time. This is at odds with real practice, as previously stated; you really do need to have a reason, but this is an example of how excessive laws require some hypocrisy. There is no alternative. This is not a nice thing to say, but it must be stated publicly to legally protect your company.

CHAPTER 27

BEAT THE UNION

Roy ran Arts & Crafts Press. Ironically he was a 30-year union member who had joined management eight years earlier, but that didn't make him one of the guys. His dad started the business. Roy studied the numbers. He opened the mail himself and picked it up at the post office. We're talking shy.

One year Roy negotiated the next labor contract. Me, I was the headquarters guy who stopped by one day a month. I tried to stay on the sidelines and watch, and did pretty good at it. Man, was it tough that day.

"I don't even know you," said the union worker when he sat. Not a good beginning. He was talking to Roy.

It was true. They had rarely spoken. This was a small company of about 100 employees. It was astounding, and it was apparent to the employee that if Roy hadn't talked with him, the employee representative, he had probably never spoken to a few of the other workers.

Yet there they were, trying to reach, in theory, an amicable agreement on numerous matters of supreme importance to both sides. They shook hands, but it was obviously, and tragically, an impersonal negotiation.

It's not as if there weren't chances before the negotiation for things to be discussed. It's just that Roy never took advantage of the opportunities. Instead, he went reclusive. And please understand that Roy was one of the nicest people I've ever known. Not a bad bone in his body. Problem is, that doesn't matter much when you don't know your employees.

Now he paid the price: irrational demands that destroyed the business.

This negotiation turned sour at the negotiating table, but the real battle was lost months earlier at the company picnic. It was lost every day in the lunchroom, in the halls, wherever Roy walked and averted his eyes from direct contact with those he led. He may have been bashful but the employees didn't take it that way. They saw aloof. And you know, it just wasn't so, but it doesn't matter. Perception is reality.

The problem with unions isn't with the unions or the employees, it's with management. Always has been. The problem is self-created by lazy, disinterested, and sometimes unfair management. Mismanagement creates unions.

But it doesn't stop there. There is a reason to beat the unions and that is that once the mistrust takes hold, it snowballs. Unions are adversarial by nature. Without conflict, union officials are out of work.

We saw it at Arts & Crafts Press, two years after the aforementioned negotiation. I was CEO of the parent holding company by then, and I was invited to sit in and observe what my managers told me would be an interesting spectacle.

There were seven of us around a yellow Formica table. It was an instant-coffee moment. Two were from management, two were outside union representatives. The other two were the shop steward and the guest of honor, a platemaker who had been fired and was filing a grievance.

It went on for three grueling hours. I tried my best not to get involved. It wasn't really my fight but, gee, I was there. One of the union representatives repeatedly claimed Arts & Crafts Press unfairly dismissed the worker. Roy, being a true gentleman, didn't respond.

"Wait a minute," I blurted out, "this guy was caught stealing. He was caught red-handed, reported, in fact, by other union workers. Not only was he stealing our materials but he also set up a competing business outside."

I'm rarely called a gentleman.

I slurped some rancid coffee. "And he's been using nonunion labor to undercut our prices and cost your union jobs. You call that an unjust firing? I've got an idea. How about if we go to the newspapers with this travesty. I can see the headline now: 'Union Leaders Defend Stealing and Support Scab Shop.' "

"No newspapers," said the union representative. He scratched his chin. "Look, we don't care about all that. You abused this worker's rights. It is our sacred bond to protect him."

Sacred bond? Hmm. Well, the meetings went on for two weeks. Finally, the union agreed that the firing was justified but maintained that the termination was wrongly handled. We settled. I guess the union realized that . . . naah, forget that . . . unions are like boards of directors, they're political . . . they have to spend time making it look hard and don't really care about the result.

A larger problem was that all this wasted time was spent debating a matter that wasn't debatable. The guy was stealing. Case closed.

Here's what else happened during those two weeks. The strongest local competitor, a nonunion shop, snatched away two major jobs because we were too busy dealing with this problem to dedicate time to a customer. And all the workers at the competitor didn't pay union dues, so they made more money than those at Arts & Crafts Press.

There is only one way to beat the union. Earn employee trust. That's the game. It's about being real. If you deserve their trust, you can win in the market, together. If you lose, you set up adversarial situations that only drain energy.

Here's how to get labor working with you:

1. Set up a 401(k) retirement plan that beats any union fund. It's easy. Any 401(k) is better than every union plan, numbers being equal, because workers keep it whether they stay at the same shop or not. When a 401(k) is set up in a union shop, it should be offered to all, union and nonunion. Many union workers will see the benefit and leave the union. They must continue to pay dues, though, and they essentially receive nothing in return for that expense. Eventually, when half the workers have dropped the union, you can stop recognizing it without a need for a vote. Slicker than a peeled tomato. And fair. Strikes become illegal, and cooperation becomes a reality. Finally.

2. Never hire outside experts to lead your labor negotiations. This should not be a battle. Work is collaboration. Certainly, there needs to be some outside consultation at times, but negotiations are ultimately based on trust, not authoritative bullying or legal trickery.

3. Participate with employees in more than just work. Go bowling, to ball games, picnics, charity work. Play cards together. Don't fake it; that will backfire. It has to be genuine. Mix it up with different departments and different levels. The only way to succeed is to enjoy one another.

CHAPTER 28

FIGHT POLITICS

It started as Bill Lear's dream. In the early 1960s, the Swiss government quit competing with Americans and Soviets in the weapons game. They cut funds for a proposed Swiss fighter-bomber. Lear took advantage of this retreat and bought the designs and tools for the jet from the Swiss government. It was a fire sale and he got it cheap.

His idea was simple and so was his premise. He would build the world's first affordable private jet, betting that there were lots of successful people and shameless governments who would want one or think they needed one.

Lear brought all his tools back to Wichita, Kansas, and he established Learjet. If you stood it on its tail, it could reach 30,000 feet in five minutes.

Lear had a great idea, but he ran out of money. So he went to Charlie Gates, the owner of Gates Rubber of Denver, who bought a franchise to sell Gates Learjets in the United States from Stapleton Airport in Denver. Everything else about Learjet, including production, remained as it was in Wichita.

It was a marriage of convenience, but it collapsed $20 million later because of a clash of egos and refusals to share information. I know. I was part of it.

Politics is a popular sport, with disinformation, whispers, and nasty names. When you're in it, it seems necessary and sometimes even fun. With the benefit of hindsight, after a collapse, it looks childish and counterproductive.

(I'm talking normal business here, not boards of directors which are inherently political.)

In 1968, I was hired as manager of public relations by Gates Learjet in Denver. It was a kick. The tough part was mental. I had to sell the idea that Learjets were practical business tools for a fast crowd of business and government types. First I had to sell myself. It took a while, but I understood. I ski; others fly Learjets. A small difference of cash.

We sold the jets by stretching some assumptions about money and time savings and then putting the stretches into a three-ring binder and calling it a travel analysis. The assumptions couldn't bear close scrutiny, but they seemed to neutralize bankers and potential shareholder critics. Then I got publicity. I flew with the *Business Week* bureau chief for the Rockies to Wichita for lunch and back in one day. I did a similar trip with a *Fortune* freelancer.

It was fun and I spewed tidbits for the press, such as how Bill Lear redesigned the leading edge of the wing and then ignored engineering quotes of $200,000 to build it. Instead, he hired a local body-and-fender guy and paid him more than the guy had ever seen in a year, but Lear still saved well more than $150,000. He also got it done in two days instead of 18 months. The problem with my factoids were that they weren't only mine. I had competition.

The problem with my competition was that it was from the same company. I worked for Gates Learjet in Denver. My competition was three other PR flaks for Learjet in Wichita. It wasn't pretty.

No one was in charge, so we all put out stories to the press. To the same reporters. And because there was competition among all of us and not nearly enough real news to go around, we got creative. Sometimes devious.

We were in the same company but we rarely talked. Everything was secret. It was obvious when I sent out a press release claiming we sold 22 planes the previous year. A reporter from *Fortune* called. He said he had a press release from Wichita claiming only 18 planes had been sold. "What's the deal?" he asked.

It was a good question. Who knew? Everything was based on orders, but some were firm and some soft, and there were projections for both companies.

We all battled terribly to see who could get the most ink. More press releases meant more chances for contradictions. Once, heart-transplant surgeon Michael Debakey of Houston wanted to buy a jet. His business manager talked with us in Denver, and he talked to the folks in Wichita. We told him there was no way to put a bathroom in such a small jet. The people in Wichita knew better and told him they could. Of course, when they worked out the new option a year earlier, they never told us. In fact, when we asked, they told us bathrooms were impossible.

After the bathroom incident, the Wichita people ran to owner Charlie Gates and called me and my Denver colleagues incompetent and claimed they could do a better job by themselves.

We in Denver weren't exactly Boy Scouts. We interfered with production, all done in Wichita, by calling the General Electric factory that made the engines for the jets. After Wichita had ordered engines based on their forecasts, we guaranteed we could sell an additional dozen engines, and GE made those extra engines.

But sales slumped, as the folks in Wichita suspected could happen. When Wichita tried to slow down deliveries of more engines, they learned that the Denver dreamers, as they derisively called us, had guaranteed the orders, and they had to take them. One dozen extra engines, at $200,000 apiece, sat around for almost a year before they were needed. Oops.

Everybody complained about everybody. It was constant, mean-spirited, and counterproductive. Gates Learjet was gone in a few years, a $20 million lesson in the expense of politics and vague responsibilities. Learjet was sold and then finally took off when the new owners did away with politics and instead devoted that competitive energy to develop new models geared to the changing market. What a concept!

Every business faces politics to some degree, and nothing weakens an organization faster than politics overshadowing results. The successful ones know how to deal straight without the games and one-upmanship. When perception becomes paramount and results irrelevant, it's time to step back and reset priorities.

Here's how to establish the drill:

1. Pinpoint responsibility for every job. Make goals clearly stated and as measurable as possible, then support every individual in his or her effort to meet these objectives. Encourage teamwork and discourage political games of "Gotcha!"
2. Never set up shadow governments or intercompany spying. Every worker should be responsible for his or her own work. This reduces the expense and harassment of too many supervisors. Eliminate every position that has the words assistant, coordinator, or liaison in it. Give them real jobs or get them gone.
3. When employees complain about other employees, make them do it in the other person's presence. Make sure everybody is hearing the same problem. Don't play Henry Kissinger, jumping from one side to the other. Avoid shuttle diplomacy; force face-to-face talk. Remember that shuttle diplomacy of the '60s and how it brought us peace in the Mid-East? Right. Face-to-face.

CHAPTER 29

DANCE WITH THAT DEBT DEVIL, ARM'S LENGTH

Intermark was a holding company in La Jolla, California, traded on the American Stock Exchange. They always borrowed and bought. They had a magic touch. They borrowed to the limit, and they bought more and more.

I was CEO of Franklin Press, a well-run $7 million printing company in dusty San Bernardino (described in Chapter 15). I knew about Intermark because, well, they bought Franklin Press and hired me to run it.

Intermark promised we would combine Franklin with Arts & Crafts Press if I managed to learn printing without stumbling too badly. The goal was to eventually find another printer to buy after that and ultimately take the group public in five years. It was my baby, and amazingly, it almost worked. Almost.

It looked as if it was going to work when Intermark was booming in 1983. Intermark owned about a dozen companies and was rolling when it decided to take a couple of giant steps. It seemed great, only Intermark decided to step in another direction.

I wanted only $3 million cash and another $8 million in notes to acquire Graphic Arts Center. But Intermark first went for different and far bigger acquisitions. They bought a $50 million wheel company. And then there was a huge sporting goods distributor. The next acquisition was Pier 1. Suddenly, there was about $300 million in new debt just to pay for these companies.

When I first approached the management of Intermark about Graphic Arts Center, the executive vice president screamed that it was "crazy." Eventually, I talked them into negotiating and we bought Graphic Arts Center reluctantly, and at a trifle higher price than we could have had we acted with more enthusiasm.

The first year, Graphic Arts Center's profits jumped from $1.5 million to $2.2 million. Profits plummeted the next year so we slashed expenses, and the following year profits passed $3 million. The acquisition was half paid for out of its own cash flow in three years, then sold for $25 million. Intermark did just fine.

On the other buys, though, Intermark wasn't so lucky. The glamorous acquisitions that they jumped on never came close to paying their way.

In 1992, Intermark entered bankruptcy. On the one hand, anyone who invested $20,000 in 1973 was worth a cool million by 1983. Of course, if you put in a million in 1969 it was worth that same $20,000 by 1973 and a big goose egg, a cipher with the edge erased, by '92.

The problem was simple. When you play double-or-nothing forever, the result is always the same. In the steady-growth '80s it worked for a moment. Kind of like the dot-com boom of the '90s.

Winds blow in the right way and we're all geniuses. For awhile. But as soon as the market hiccupped, Intermark was in trouble. They pushed debt too far. I helped.

If Intermark had simply stopped buying and borrowing in 1983, it probably would have been a nice little money-maker today. Maybe doing a half billion and netting 5%, with debt all paid down. And shareholders would be smiling.

Debt is your ultimate fair-weather friend.

Here's how to keep debt from destroying you:

1. Put together a 10-year flood plan for every business, much as a city planner does. Guess the worst possible year for your business and then set the debt levels needed to survive that year. Attach the number to every plan you ever do, and never exceed the debt levels it allows. You'll miss a couple of opportunities, but you'll survive the unexpected—which you should always expect.

2. Examine your competitors' debt levels when you set yours. If they are slugs, put yours higher and outrun them. If they are leaner and meaner than you, invest internally, cut your debt, and don't butt heads with them as much in the marketplace. If the market allows peaceful coexistence, ignore their debt levels and set yours to maximize growth without getting swamped in that ten-year flood that comes every five years on average.

3. Anytime that rates are low and you are tempted to borrow, don't. Take a long walk, shower, and go to a movie. Never borrow money because it is cheap. Borrow only when forced to by overwhelming opportunity.

CHAPTER 30

DUCK COMPUTER TRAPS

Metaltreet is a subsidiary of the Precision Machine Company of Seattle. Precision Machine is the largest manufacturer of metal parts in the western United States.

It was January and the slow rain was colder than usual in Seattle. I had become CEO of Precision Machine the day before. As the new CEO, I replaced a 33-year veteran who had slacked off the last two years. It wasn't his company anymore. It was being run by his CFO. It was being run by numbers.

In the previous two years, Precision Machine had grown fast. The company had splurged on equipment. Sales jumped, but debt grew faster.

I was hired because the veteran CEO was fired. His demise came when the economy burped and profits disappeared. When I was hired, I had 33 years' less experience in metal manufacturing than my predecessor.

As I started on the job, I saw that people at the company worked hard, but the hard work was misdirected. The hardest worker of all was the CFO. He was a maniac on the mainframe. He was the CFO and his purpose was to create reports. All else would fall in line if there were just plenty of reports.

The day after I took control, I went to visit our subsidiary, Metaltreet. Metaltreet specialized in treating parts after they were made.

The treatment could be heating the parts to relieve internal stresses, deburring sharp edges, or shotpeening the surfaces to eliminate surface irregularities. Pacific Metals did all these for its parent company and other competitors.

I met the general manager, Bill Holiday, in his office. He was wide open and friendly, happy to have some attention. We shook hands and sat. I noticed a stack of computer printouts on his desk. I asked about them. It was innocent. Just curious.

"Bill, how do you use those reports?" I asked.

He looked at me. He grinned, and then held it back.

"I get my paper clips from them," he said.

"I don't get it."

"Watch."

He picked up the report of green-and-white-striped computer paper. It was at least a quarter-inch thick. Bill pulled the thick metal clip off the report. He reached into an upper desk drawer and pulled out an oversized coffee cup. He dropped the paper clip into the black cup and put the cup back in the drawer. And then he pushed the report off the side edge of his desk. It plopped into the circular file.

"I never complain, and they never complain," he said. "I've got a lot of other things to do, and it saves me searching for paper clips." He smiled.

I understood where he was coming from, but it was a deception. All of it was, especially the reports. The IT group felt good for being so productive in generating reports. Division managers loved them for the paper clips and nothing else, and top management never heard anything about it so they just assumed everything was under control because there was so much information in the reports.

Most of it was useless and irrelevant.

Here's how we solved the problem. We demoted the IT guy one level. Now, the managers of sales, production, and accounting could shove him around a little. IT became a service again. It responded instead of dictating.

IT always has its own agenda. Since they have knowledge others don't, it's like any techie area—the power of knowledge corrupts the best of them.

IBM's cleverest move to help this was their PR campaign of the '70s and '80s to create CIOs, Chief Information Officers who never reported to anybody but the CEO or, better yet, the board. Wouldn't that be a market-sensitive outfit?

This stuff beats logic too often. Right now giant companies like Hershey's and others are stumbling over their adoption of SAP, the IT of all IT systems, with presumed efficiencies nobody's seen yet, but all techies have imagined while few look at history. History says markets change. Companies merge. Divisions appear and disappear. Putting a cumbersome IT system in the middle is a dodo bird answer.

Another IT trend du jour is the ASP. Application Service Providers are the wave of the future, everybody can tell you. Don't buy it. This is a concept that was called a service bureau twenty years ago, and it died then when disk drives got so big there was no reason to send the company jewels outside. It's been resurrected today under the guise of all of us being so connected and wired that your software is better residing somewhere else.

Two problems. First is the premise is wrong. Yes, connectivity is getting cheaper and faster and better. But not nearly as fast as storage is getting cheaper and faster and better. And the smaller drives get cheaper at a rate the huge boxes can't match. In February of 2000, as this is written, I can buy a 30GB drive for $99. There's a reverse economy of scale going on here.

Second problem is that the software you use wasn't written to be used online and remotely, so there's awkwardness, inefficiency, and errors using a service this way. Look out.

Computers are great where they fit. Airline reservations. Financials. Spreadsheets. Banking. Word processing. (I think that means typing, but any business that says "user-friendly" instead of "easy" probably doesn't hang out with its customers much. You've all seen the jokes about users' stupidity with PCs, like the customer who thought the CD drive was a coffee cup holder. PC companies circulate these jokes and laugh about the unsophisticated buyers. A car company would respond by installing coffee cup holders on the box, and would never dream of ridiculing its customers. PC users remain awed; there are signs that's slipping away, and an entire industry is going to have to get serious about making things easier.)

But twenty years ago, when Lotus 1-2-3 shipped its twenty-millionth spreadsheet, that was a promise that productivity was dropping. Any civilization that has twenty million people doing spreadsheet is doomed. Somebody's got to build the cars and bake the bread and generate the electricity. Everybody can't measure it or forecast it.

Email, on the other hand, has more than counterbalanced this by making decisions quicker and meetings fewer.

Some of this automation reduces thinking. Back in the dark ages of the 1970s at Honeywell, where I was director of product management, we were arguing about cost vs. return on a potential new slide projector. We fought. This would sell better than that, we argued. No, that had a better sales potential, they countered. Passions rose and people stood up for what they believed. Over two prototypes, we stood nose-to-nose and talked about their respective financial merits.

One group supported building the projector that cost $99 retail and was expected to sell 50,000 units per year. The other group supported the $149 projector that was expected to sell 25,000 units per year.

Why the debate? Because it had to be decided before the bean counters could get to it. There wasn't time to do a bunch of detailed what-ifs. Once we decided the most likely unit sales for each price and what the most probable cost to produce would be, the accountants took those numbers for two prolonged weeks of manual spreadsheet agony. Imagine, if you can, doing a manual spreadsheet. We're talking weeks and take your phone off the hook.

Not today. Have you seen a bad pro forma recently? Every manager has a PC. Most have spreadsheets that spit out instant answers. If the return looks bad, just change the assumptions: Raise sales or lower costs with keyboard magic until the return is acceptable.

The agony is gone. The mental anguish has vanished. That's the problem. The thought process hits a stop sign. Nobody thinks about the assumptions anymore. They are created to fit the desired results, and bad products are born.

Here's how to free your outfit from computer tyranny:

1. Simplify. Kill any computer reports that aren't read. Find out which by killing each one in sequence and don't regenerate any until requested. At least once a year hold a report-killing meeting and don't let anybody leave until three or four are buried. Ask everyone which reports are used and then ask what actions were taken as a result. Anything that's not read, dies. Anything that is read but doesn't lead to action also dies. Put counters on your intranet that audit the frequency of visits to each report and suffocate those that have no audience except the proud authors.

2. Stop buying more stuff. Use what systems you've got for a year. Let workers buy PCs but stop adding software and hardware that supposedly will enhance your business. Wait. It'll cost less next year and maybe you'll be lucky and a competitor will have debugged it. When there's a commanding argument for full-scale strategic moves, like Wal-Mart and Toys R Us beating everybody, due to their superior knowledge of sell-through, do it. If you can speed design processes dramatically, and it's been proven elsewhere, do it. Don't do the marginal things. Every computer makeover causes more grief and downtime than predicted, simply because the folks who dream these things up operate at a theoretical level. They find disruptions fascinating, intellectual challenges, and moments to be heroes. Disruptions cost. Techies see these surprises as enhancing their heroic status. You can never beat this. Just understand it.

3. Cancel any meeting that reviews pro formas or projections. Don't allow group discussions of those numbers. Change the subject to discussions of the assumptions (market, costs, price) that go into the calculations. After a consensus is reached on the assumptions, anybody with a PC can do the pro forma in minutes.

CHAPTER 31

KILL MEETINGS

When I arrived at Checks To-Go, they held no staff meetings. Such heaven.

Except it didn't work. Too bad. How blissful that would seem to be. Problem here was that nobody committed. They guessed.

Production didn't know what sales was hoping to do next month. They guessed.

Accounting didn't know what productions costs were likely to be, and accounting never told sales that the low prices offered were costing profits. Nobody talked and everybody, when necessary, took their best shot.

So, gulp, I called a meeting, and the conversation went something like this: "We're losing money."

"What do you mean we're losing money? Sales are up 30%."

"And why do you think the owners hired me? You gave away 40% more in promotional expense to get that extra 30%. And not only that. None of it was scheduled so we had to special order Peachtree forms and pay a premium."

What a surprise. We kept at it. The first meeting had rough edges when we sat and tried to explain our different perspectives. They sure were different, sometimes strained. But we kept at it, one hour at a time.

That's right, we had a one-hour meeting; when it ended, it was over and the large lady sang, as that great philosopher, Yogi Berra, sort of said once. And then we held another, and another, once a week for sixty minutes, no more. Finally, after two months of melting acrimony, the managers began to understand teamwork—what they need to do, and what they deserve to expect. The purpose was to fix problems and not blame people, and when everyone bought into that, things opened up.

Finally conversations went like:

"Can we do another promotion for June on the Open Systems forms?"

"We're a little short but if you can push it to the second half of the month, we can get ready for it without needing a special order."

"That's great. If we do a mailing today, at bulk rate, we should get some extra business at just the right time without much extra expense."

"We'll be ready."

We made money in the first quarter. This followed, seriously, 53 straight quarters of losses. In 1984, Checks To-Go was picked by *Inc.* magazine as one of the nation's 500 fastest-growing businesses. For our first full year, 1987, the company had the highest operating profits in the industry. That was with huge interest expense, not the gains competitors enjoyed.

In March of 1988 Rocky Mountain Banknote acquired Checks To-Go and reasoned that if one meeting worked so well then a bunch of meetings would work even better. They increased the meeting schedule to 16 hours a week on every conceivable subject. The scene was wonderful, employees staring at employees while forecasting and reforecasting. They planned and replanned. They talked and talked and talked about work.

I lasted all of six weeks under the new regime. They talked enough about work to insure nobody worked. Jaw exercise leading into posturing and that old death spiral when articulation wins and results become bothersome. For two days out of every week, the managers were all meeting and boosting their social skills while production waffled and customers were ignored.

All that planning didn't help because they lost their customer base, and 18 months after being the profit leader of the industry, Checks To-Go vanished. Kaput.

Keep coordinated without overcontrol. Try to:

1. Spend between three and six hours a week in meetings. Three or more people talking is a meeting.
2. When there are six or more people scheduled to attend a meeting, publish an agenda and exact times in advance. Stick to it. Have separate conversations take place outside the meeting. If two or three people can solve a problem, don't bother everyone else at the meeting. Randomly pick a person at the end to write up action steps assigned to each person.
3. If anybody attends to listen, ask them to leave and summarize for them later. Meetings sop up time. There's no reason to let that metastasize.

CHAPTER 32

KICK DOWN THE WALLS

I was dragged in to salvage Monument Industries, Broadfield, Nebraska.

My motel had four rooms. Striding out the front door one morning, I heard rapping on the glass window of the office. The owner pointed at my room. Sure enough, I forgot to turn out the light again, so I trudged back, clicked it off, and headed for the plant.

Monument made architectural marble ornaments and did well until the stonecutter founder died two years earlier.

He was replaced by his son. I was called in by the bankers two years later.

The founder's son must have picked up some hermit in his DNA somehow. He probably didn't really want to run the business. But he felt a sense of duty and mom thought it proper. So he took over and began to put his imprint on the company. He had a new office built in the back of the building. It had a private entrance. Profits slipped away, steady as cancer, and Monument Industries began laying off some of its 300 employees. These workers were farmers from the nearest few counties, some farm offspring, and Monument was the only factory for fifty miles in any direction.

When I arrived, I found a place filled with unguided missiles. Production built what seemed most efficient, delaying less standard orders. Junior want the place to be more professional so sales and accounting appointed liaisons and coordinators to make things smoother. Well, maybe that was the idea, it usually is, but the only certainty is payroll expense grows.

That first day, two trucks unloaded finished slabs onto our dock. This wasn't right. We were supposed to send out finished slabs. Not take them. It turned out, of course, that they had been returned by troubled customers.

"What went wrong?" I asked the shipping foreman.

"Uh, ah, you'll have to get that from my supervisor," he said. The guy fidgeted from foot to foot as he looked away.

It had to come from his supervisor. This was like government. He knew. He was afraid to tell me. Not his responsibility.

Inside, our building was little more than a hallway of closed doors. My desk was buried under a pile of memos. Most several pages. Why get to the point?

When people talked, they did so in furtive conversations, ducking their heads behind doors so as not to be seen. They all practically genuflected before me—not in honor, but in fear.

Before leaving that day, I went to the head of maintenance. "Take off every inside door tonight except for the restrooms and IT. Stack them in the parking lot where everybody will see them for a couple of days, and then sell them."

"You must be kidding," said the head of maintenance.

"I'm serious as a heart attack."

Sure, it was theatrical. But this outfit was in dramatic trouble. Some show business was needed to open things up.

It helped. A month or so later a salesman from Standard Cutting, which made tools that carve granite, came into the building. For the previous two years, he had never gotten past the lobby. He had always come in, taken his orders in the lobby, and then shuffled back to the parking lot. But on this visit, things were different. He went from office to office, getting to know our people, listening to their situations and explaining his.

Before he left, he sprang into my office, which didn't have a door. "It's as if I'd never been here before," he said. "This is a new company." He smiled. "You know, I did a week's worth of business in one day. There's no waiting now. There's no hesitating. I love that you got rid of the doors." He loved it so much he cut our prices by 10 percent. He suggested the cut. Hmm. I wasn't quick enough to ask.

"I can deal with you quick and straight now," he said.

Okay, yeah, getting praise from a vendor is no great trick. Laugh? Your jokes are hilarious to that crowd. But the place slowly seemed to whisper less and yell a little more. Nobody said, "Can we discuss this in my office?" when questions were asked.

One afternoon the vice president of marketing pulled me aside. "Hey," he said, with a hopeful glint in his eye. I was hopeful, too. The look on his face told me he was onto something good for the company. He was sincere.

He said, "I hear you need a Cross pen refill. Here's one of mine." So sincere, it was unbelievable.

I couldn't hold back. "Listen. You're the vice president of marketing. It's your job to make sales grow," I said. He looked at me, surprised by my switch from the safe subject of my pen. So I went back to it. "I'm terrified that you think paying attention to my minor needs has any importance at all. I've failed tragically to communicate. Don't ever do anything like that again or we're both headed for failure. Your job is marketing. My only task is to help you succeed."

He stood there with his mouth open for about 30 seconds. When what I said sunk in, he smiled faintly. "Fine," he said.

It was blunt, but he understood. In fact, after the shock he was happy with the change, I think, ready to be an equal and fight for more sales.

Monument Industries showed what damage physical barriers create. This guy, Terry Randolph, designed and printed pages of advertising that went into reference books. He was expected to be creative, you know, maybe order an artichoke with his chicken-fried steak or go to Omaha for a play on weekends, far-out stuff.

As I surveyed personnel, I asked, "Who is Terry's boss?" I was told he works for production.

I went to production. They told me he worked for sales.

I was curious, so I went to accounting. I found Terry's file. I wanted to look up how much Terry made and who approved his pay. It turned out he hadn't enjoyed a raise in four years. His last raise was given by the previous sales manager.

I asked Terry, "Who is your boss?"

"I don't know," he said. "Nobody pays much attention as long as I get the catalogs out."

"Who fills you in on company objectives? Who helps you? Who gives you raises?"

"Nobody."

There were so many barriers that Terry became an island and nobody knew it. Nobody.

To keep in touch:

1. Anytime you see a closed door, knock and stick your head in. Ask if everything is okay. If company business is being conducted, nobody should be embarrassed. Just keep doing this until everybody gets it. Don't close the door when you leave.
2. Eliminate assigned parking except for one spot. That's for the employee of the month, near the front door. The only way to get a

good parking spot at a good company is to show up early. Close the executive lunchroom or open it to all.

3. Spend half of your time out of your office. Work in other people's areas. See what is going on and let everyone sense that you know and care. Don't screen calls; put direct lines into everyone's office. This saves time, cuts costs, simplifies phone bills, and keeps everybody in closer contact. Doors, guards, secretaries, and memos are little more than ways to avoid contact.

CHAPTER 33

WHAT'S YOUR BUSINESS?

In 1983 I took a course for small business owners at Harvard. One hundred students. Great group.

Paul Orfalea was growing a small copy business called Kinko's copy centers. He seemed to be a space cadet whose name came from his Afro, and attended almost half the classes. But if you talked to him, you learned he started as a student with a copier at UC Santa Barbara, and he could already forecast the revenue difference between copies required at liberal arts campuses vs. scientific schools. In the years to follow, he moved into cities and began to see that price didn't matter as much as high-traffic locations, clean and well-lit stores, and finally 24-hour service. His buyers valued the business at just under a billion several years later.

A second classmate, Craig McCaw, was a cable TV guy looking for creative financing ideas. He and I did a cellular phone case study one night. Craig hurried home, sold the cable business, and started buying up rights to cellular markets. Didn't come back for the second or third year, so he looked like a slacker. Ten years later Craig sold McCaw Cellular to AT&T for $14 billion. Apparently he spotted something I overlooked.

Later he started buying up taxi radio licenses, city by city, improved the technology, and turned that into Nextel. $45 billion today. Cost him about $1 billion.

Kinko understood that he was selling convenience, not copies. Craig believed there was a market for freedom. He saw no reason a phone number should be a place instead of a mobile person. Cellular was his first pathway and converting cab radios was his second. Kinko and McCaw were blessed by being the only dyslexics in our class, which gave them focus. They skipped the details, didn't read the pages upon pages of spreadsheets, so, unlike the rest of us, saw a bigger picture.

Understanding your true business is the toughest lesson of all. Example after example after example might make the point. Maybe. Stick with me.

Lucille Roberts, another classmate, was the queen of workout centers in New York City. She ran 18 physical fitness centers in the boroughs of New York. *Cosmopolitan* called her one of the nation's most glamorous business-women. What they didn't see was a girl who escaped from Siberia and came to the city unable to speak the language, was held back in grade school more than once until she became fluent and graduated at the top of her class. Today she spends weekdays in her five-story condo on the upper east side, some weekends at her Fire Island home, and others in her Southampton castle. I suspect she's added a mansion or two since.

The woman understood her business. And she got to know it better.

When we studied, she said hers was a real estate business, a gamble that paid. Back when New York City was broke, the city gave away delinquent and abandoned properties. Lucille's husband, Bob, was a real estate specu-lator. He picked up distressed buildings for free and Lucille turned them into workout centers.

Voila! A money-making business is born from no-cost real estate.

But those cheap leases didn't last forever, so Lucille learned the business.

It became clear that in our melting pot, customers are more comfortable exposing their bodies in a club where the others look like them. That goes for sex, ethnic, and physical condition. Here's a chance for big trouble. You cannot advertise or restrict memberships, but as each club finds its type of most comfortable clientele, more similarly shaped and similarly colored and similarly aged members come along and soon everybody's relaxed. Feels like home.

She took away the weights, just a few each month, until the muscle-bound and sweaty Neanderthal men cancelled and went to a gym of their own. Good deal. The ladies loosened up.

She learned which neighborhood ethnics were swimmers and which were dancers, and put the pool up front of some, but a dance floor and picture windows at others. Prejudiced? Sure. Smart? Of course. Happier clients? Yes.

(For those of you who insist diversity means pushing people in front of others they cannot relate to, let me make you feel better by mentioning that all eighteen centers had handicapped parking in front, as required by law, and not one space was used legally for her first ten years. So that economic inefficiency and waste of valuable space, which you love, should make you feel warm and fuzzy.)

So there's a great business, now making money, a taxpayer, and with normal rents.

But Lucille didn't stop. First she had a real estate business disguised as physical fitness centers. Now she had true physical fitness centers. And three homes, each worth more than the GNP of some small nations. Her managers promoted themes each month and were bonused upon attendance.

"Make these workouts part of their life," Lucille preached, always giving furs, plaques, and trips to managers who beat their attendance goals. Members paid $60 per month, usually by check.

But in a few years, Lucille tested a radical change, and switched the whole system over. She slashed prices to $15 per month, offering the same programs and hours. Payments came from automatic bank transfers or automatic credit card charges.

Enrollment skyrocketed. Memberships went up almost ten times, so revenues doubled. Usage dropped in half. Usage drives staffing, so total costs dropped.

When revenues double and costs drop, you've got a wonderful experience. My guess is that Lucille and Robert had no problem meeting new yacht payments.

But isn't this dangerous, with usage dropping? Nope. Not as long as you keep promoting to gain new members, and the cost of marketing to those new members plummets since your monthly price is lower.

And more important, you've got to understand now you're selling a dream, something most people intend to do but don't get around to. So you have an economic model where the users get a terrific deal, subsidized by the nonusers. So the users are happy campers. And the nonusers merely get irritated at themselves, but don't often cancel, because they know they should start and intend to next month. That's their dream. Workout equipment makers, diet book publishers, and movie producers live well by selling dreams, and their customers enjoy it.

I'm sure her business has shifted again. It went from real estate disguised as physical fitness to real physical fitness to the concept of physical fitness for many and real workouts for the few, and profits got better each step of the way.

I stole her approach one decade later when sales of a service I started, backing up PCs automatically over the Internet, didn't take off as quickly as we and our investors presumed.

All the market research in the world proved this would be a hot item, and all the market research was dead, stone-cold wrong.

But the beginnings of life came when we slashed price and bundled with others. The outcome cannot yet be known, but this understanding of the business being comparable to physical fitness memberships produced a quantum leap in acceptance.

Another lesson about high-tech emerged here. Among our partners were Intuit, Microsoft, and AOL. Real high-tech, right? Well Scott Cook, the founder and Chairman of Intuit, always walked around holding up a pencil.

"This is our competition," he repeated. Intuit published Quicken, Quick-Books, and TurboTax, all software for individuals and small businesses for managing their checkbooks, accounting, and taxes. He saw manual record-keeping as their only competitor.

Steve Ballmer, CEO of Microsoft, views everybody as his competitor.

Steve Case, founder and Chairman of AOL, says his company is in the entertainment business, and competes with the media.

It's interesting and never noted that these three high-tech leaders all started their careers with the same company. They all worked for Procter & Gamble, one of the world's largest advertisers.

So when you look at Microsoft's annual report, notice that their marketing budget is billions larger than their R&D budget, and you'll start to get closer to the truth about high-tech. It is high hype, a marketing game, and few engineering-led businesses survive.

That's why you've got to think a level deeper than your customers. Understand what it is that they're really buying and deliver it. My best customer in the printing business didn't quibble over price and wasn't really buying printing.

Understand this is art, not science, and there are no rules. It's instinctive, so let's look at a few more to see if we can develop that gut sense.

"What I get from you is a good night's sleep," Jim Krenek of Petersen Publishing said. He wasn't worried about the slickest colors or lowest price. He wanted the job done right, no errors, and on time. So that's all we worried about. Nobody delayed a job for the sake of a different sheet of paper, since that customer wasn't buying that. Petersen wanted it error-free and on time, period.

There's a $5 billion company headquartered in San Diego, SAIC, that claims to be a technology company. It isn't. SAIC is a company that has perfected the art of relieving the federal government of its budgets, the leader among the beltway bandits, and has more employees in Washington, D.C., than in San Diego. Several restaurants have stocked their wine cellars to match SAIC's requirements, and yes, the company does a lot of technology things. But they'll also snatch a contract for a million-dollar movie out of the Pentagon, teaching soldiers how to brush their teeth, and subcontract that to any of a thousand independent movie producers, none of whom understand which bottle of wine to order with dinner. And SAIC does quite well, thank you, netting $600 million on that $5 billion last year. Public service pays just fine.

At Honeywell, in the '70s, half the business was thermostats and half was computers. Computers in those days were IBM and the BUNCH. IBM held most of the market while Burroughs, Univac, NCR, Control Data, and Honeywell fought over the table scraps.

But in thermostats, Honeywell controlled over 90% of the market and was unassailable. Hundreds of engineers struggled year after year, knocking another penny out of the cost, and making the devices respond a few seconds sooner, meaning nobody else could compete.

As a bright-eyed employee who attended some management meetings, it soon looked to me like our division had a dysfunctional parent. The computer guys spent money like water and constantly wanted the Feds to break up the IBM monopoly, while the thermostat guys in short-sleeved shirts with vinyl pocket protectors didn't want anybody even whispering the word monopoly.

So what do all these stories mean?

You've got to understand the true business you're in, and once you grasp that, recovery becomes easier.

Honeywell floundered until they got out of computers and recaptured a chance to build a corporate culture. Craig McCaw made billions by selling cellular freedom, first to lenders, then users. Kinko sold well-lit convenience. Lucille sold the dream. High-techies AOL, Microsoft, and Intuit put more into marketing than technology, and they win. SAIC works their understanding of the government.

When you take over a loser, they've lost sight of their strengths, they don't really understand what business they're in. This is where a fresh set of eyes has an unfair advantage. Give yourself a few quiet moments each night, at the beginning, to think this over and find the true key behind the presumed key.

When I took over Graphic Arts Center in Portland, it was the largest commercial printer in the western United States and had a supreme reputation. It was a subsidiary of mine that inexplicably slipped into losses, which we reversed back to record profits within months.

There were four factors:

1. First was the distraction that grew into GAC by getting into too many businesses that were allied to printing. It had a publishing subsidiary, a typesetting subsidiary, and a bindery subsidiary.

   Vertical integration is great sometimes, but not if you have subsidiaries that need business from competitors as well as your own to profit. Nobody'll trust them with much business as long as you own them. So we spun off all three subsidiaries to manager/employees. Now GAC could focus solely on printing again.

2. A real advantage GAC had over the Los Angeles and Bay Area printers was labor. Everybody pays pretty much the same prices for presses and paper, but our hourly rates ran 30% less than the California printers, so if productivity could be equaled we had a 10% total cost advantage over them. Half of this was lost to transportation expense, leaving a 5% edge.

   One problem: Management had become a little isolated from the workers and a drug problem was spreading through the plant. So we began walking the floors through every shift, getting to know the crews better and put in an employee assistance program to clean up the drug users. This all worked, and it wasn't long before the labor union became an ally instead of an adversary.

3. The third change was recognizing that most of the profits came from alterations customers made after the jobs were bid, so we doubled prices for changes and doubled the sales commissions on alterations. Once the jobs awarded, customer worries over price diminished, and the ability to make quick changes to a job that's due in a day or two is a valued service, one that nobody objected paying more for. And so they did. It's like selling the shirt and tie after the customer agonized over the price of the suit. Or the side mirrors for the car. They don't care anymore. Our salespeople became adept at helping them, since more of their pay came from last-minute changes.

4. Finally, and fundamentally, the printing salespeople's salaries are extremely high. There were probably twenty salespeople who made more money at GAC than the president.

This is fair. In commercial printing, each job is unique, with decisions about layouts and formats, and options for binding and paper selections, that clients don't understand as well as the salesperson, who creates much of each job, hopefully in both the client and the printer's best interests. It's nearly an independent business for each person in sales, so they make money by the fistful.

(The top salesman for a Los Angeles printing competitor owned eighteen racehorses. He worked the entertainment industry and ad agency artists and was known as The Candy Man. One automotive creative type died in The Candy Man's Las Vegas condominium with a needle full of heroin in his arm. The Candy Man understood his niche of the business, sadly.)

Several large corporations have misunderstood this and lost many megamillions. RR Donnelley, Arcata Graphics, and World Color are each huge printers with more standardized product offerings than commercial printers. These big guys print magazines and don't deviate much in the types of jobs they produce, but as a service-sensitive business they still pay salespeople quite well. They just don't pay nearly as well as the commercial printers.

So when they acquired the largest commercial printers in Los Angeles, as all three of these giants did at one time or another, they immediately convert the commission plans for sales to a more professional approach with less incentive and more base pay, and time after time, once every decade, they go out of business within their first year.

Understanding that phenomenon made it clear that yes, GAC had customers, but the real customer was the salesperson. So we hired a few more and edged up their incentives.

Boosting the incentive a bit kept the veterans happy while some new sales folks competed with them for our available press time. Having more jobs competing for press time meant the average margin went up. And, within reason, once you understood the dynamic of the sales force being your customer, instead of fighting against them, you just hired a few more and paid them higher commissions. It's like hiring new customers, and it worked.

The industry experts, RR Donnelley, Arcata, and World Color all failed simply because they didn't get it. Printing is printing, ink on paper, they believed. That cost them hundreds of millions of dollars, each time in months. They didn't understand the true business behind the apparent business.

Most troubled companies don't. They've lost sight of what once made them good. Maybe the next group of management didn't understand what their predecessors were doing, and more likely, the previous managers didn't express clearly the secrets of the business. They were just too intuitive.

It was my fortune to hit three in a row like this, each described elsewhere in this book.

At Checks To-Go, it became clear, quickly, that the business of customer forms should be tossed overboard while the checks and invoices that fit Peachtree, Great Plains, and others, generated the most margin with fewer complaints. Moreover, speed was all.

We cut delivery times from two weeks to three days and raised prices. Customers loved it. Had the business not been acquired, we had a scheme ready for twelve-hour delivery . . . put a press near FedEx's hub . . . take orders up until midnight . . . run one shift from 8 P.M. to 4 A.M. to catch the outbound flights from Memphis.

With that setup, customers could fax in an order (today would be email) by the end of their business day, in any time zone, and get a batch of new checks and invoices before brunch the next day. That was the essence of Checks To-Go, supreme service, fast, and in any color you wanted.

Sadly, the new acquirer, Rocky Mountain Banknote, misread the deal. They decided any color as long as it's black would be the new policy, costs would be driven down, and they'd compete with Deluxe Check, the leader and their archenemy. Rocky Mountain Banknote paid a fat premium for Checks To-Go and vaporized the business. As a turnaround, Checks To-Go gave Rocky Mountain Banknote a huge operating loss to carry forward, and the business was netting over 20% when they bought it, so it would have made sense for them to divert other business to this, their new acquisition, and enjoy added and nontaxable profits for years. (Yes, with taxes you've got to be careful, even semidevious, but that's why the CFO gets paid so well and your CPA firm bills you triple what you pocket per hour.)

So Rocky Mountain Banknote lost millions and millions of dollars, in months, simply because they didn't understand a business they bought.

Smiley Industries was the next turnaround I fixed and sold. You can peek at bits of this in Chapter 13. We renegotiated contracts. Trimmed some costs. Flattened the organizational chart, which looked like a totem pole when I arrived. It was a schizoid business making $17 cargo door hinges for 747s all the way up to $60,000 missile guidance systems housings. This was classic. A hard-working entrepreneur scratches his way up, starting out with the easier stuff, and over many decades finds himself making a huge array of nonrelated things.

In Smiley's case a Detroit metal stamper had acquired the business, with an understandable desire to diversify beyond the brutal economics of hammering out steel parts for carmakers. The entrepreneur agreed to stay around, but predictably called in rich one day. They hired a bright new CEO from a perfectly wrong background, a retired military officer. His belief was that the business should make money as long as the chips were flying on the factory floor. That's one reasonable gauge, but only of activity, and activity is a distant cousin twice removed from profits.

Smiley lost 35% on sales in 1988. It lost 10% in 1987. The company had always made money before that, under the founder. I joined in the last quarter of 1988 and the business showed a profit in the first quarter of 1989 and was acquired that year.

Profits came from straightforward moves of flattening the organization, trimming costs, and using the trauma of a management changeover and clear danger signals to restructure the contracts. But the real win came by spinning off the blacksmith work, the heritage, to a liquidator, and the high-priced business to a publicly held aerospace manufacturer.

And that win began, I'm embarrassed to say, five months after my arrival when it finally became clear that the company had one unique strength: making intricate parts from exotic metals to tolerances of 0.0001″ in sizes from two feet to four feet. Pretty exciting, eh? Well it was. As soon as this became the guiding mantra, our bid activity dropped in half.

This was good. Our capture rate skyrocketed to nearly 78%, up from 18%. So the business became busier, but with more appropriate work. Returns dropped. Customers became less irritated with our bids on inappropriate work and the reputation crystallized, came into focus for all, and it was that simple. But when I say simple, note that it took me almost half a year to figure that one out. This part's hard.

If you remember the small business owners class at Harvard, we did one case study that proves you've got to understand the business.

Picture a class of 100 small business owners, all multimillionaires, and several like Kinko and McCaw headed for stratospheres above that. It's a room full of risk-taking, opinionated businesspeople.

Our professor, Marty Marshall, made this snarling group read the history of Gold Toe socks the night before his class.

You've probably worn a pair; these are the socks that yet today have a yellowish or Gold Toe created by the stitching at the end.

Well, the numbers didn't look so good for this company. The sales growth lagged the sock industry and the clothing industry overall. Most, but not all, of the high-end retailers carried Gold Toe socks. None of the mass-market chains stocked these socks. The sales force was a few guys in New York City who were about a decade older than most of the buyers, and they spent more money at La Cirque, then as now one of Manhattan's most outrageously overpriced restaurants, than the rest of the industry combined. They reserved two tables for lunch and dinner.

The costs of production for Gold Toe socks was modestly higher than others, not more than a few percentage points, mostly due to domestic production but a little caused by their distinctive stitches on the toe.

The hostility from the class reached incendiary levels. Professor Marshall let CEO after CEO rail against this company and its low aggression and high entertainment, good-old-boy wine-and-dine approach, while the market outgrew the business.

"Okay, you guys want to light a fire under this sales force," Marshall summarized, "and pay them for new clients and cut commissions on the old, right?"

Heads bobbed up and down, with several barking out yeses.

"So we expand Gold Toe socks from Brooks Brothers, Macy's, and Bergdorf Goodman into Target and JCPenney?" our professor asked.

The class nodded yes.

"Just like Izod did with their famous alligator shirts and disappeared in two years?" he asked.

"Huh?" we responded.

"Gold Toe socks didn't have the cost structure to compete on price," Marshall continued, "so the mass-merchant buyers would squeeze the life out of them. And if they survived that, Macy's would drop them about thirty minutes after seeing the Gold Toe brand being discounted at Target."

Now, when a professor tells 100 successful CEOs how to run a business, you'd better be careful. But it turned out Gold Toe, years earlier, had tried some forays like these seemingly logical ways to expand revenues. And nearly died.

If they wanted to compete more broadly, they needed lower costs. If they wanted a major share, they needed a unique style or benefit difference, a tough thing to find in socks. Better to reserve another table at La Cirque. Let the boutique chains make a better markup on a brand that's not discounted and feed the buyers crêpes suzette.

That's understanding what a business is about.

Your company might be the low-cost producer. Your product may be the quality leader. You are not both. Nobody ever is, for long.

You may be the fastest. You may be the tightest on credit, which is an advantage to buyers, because then their competition is reduced. You may be the loosest on credit, so anybody can buy, but you understand how to watch those shaky receivables better than any competitor, so you get business that they cannot risk. Binney & Smith squeezes paraffin into tubes. They dye it. They label them Crayola crayons and nobody can compete. They give 365-day terms . . . that's right, buy today and pay in one year . . . and have distribution that's so efficient nobody threatens them.

Maybe you control the channel. It could be that you're the most automated, which is just another way of saying the low-cost producer.

All any business needs to make money is one of the above. Any business that tries to be the leader in several is doomed. You cannot be the highest quality with lowest price and the best service. Even if you could, nobody would believe it.

When I took over Franklin Press, all the margin came from printing ballots and we purchased the company right after an election year. Took years to figure out why I struggled so much to grow some profits.

Knight Protective was supposedly a burglar alarm business, and it was, but the bigger reality was that they discovered radio ads worked. And they worked it until they had a great business. The freeway strangler was loose then, which didn't hurt sales. Then an election year came along, taking all the ad space away. Soon other businesses discovered radio advertising was underpriced and rates shot up. Then we morphed into a monitoring business.

Teledesic is a radical idea, but its biggest asset is the spectrum, or the frequencies granted the company for operating. The idea begat the spectrum. Now what to do with the spectrum? Stay tuned.

Enron was a pipeline company. Now it's huge in e-commerce. Makes sense. All those pipes have right-of-way already, so they can thread fiber through their tubes without expense and have the cheapest, fastest links between major cities imaginable.

When you step into a troubled business, find out which is the strongest and rebuild the company around that and nothing else.

If the company is truly the low-cost producer, which is rare with turnarounds because it's so hard to screw up that advantage, all you have to do is get rid of the distractions. Cut the advertising budget in half, ditto for the personnel department, retire anybody who's an "Assistant to . . ." and take a hard look at their boss, fire all marketing people who don't create sales, and make sure operations stays efficient. Try raising prices. The business will straighten out in months.

Just make sure you've got it right before doing this. Your production must be more efficient than any competitors. Your processes must be 10% better using methods that are not easily copied. Or your labor expense should be 20% less with comparable productivity. Slam-dunk for a turnaround.

If that's not in the cards, think about moving production. Send the claims processing to Ireland. Get the (East) Indians to write your code. Let the Chinese make your widgets.

If that doesn't fit, check your distribution. Ricoh cameras joined the top-six brands in the United States overnight when Ray O'Hannes restricted their distribution to the specialty stores, a channel with zero growth. Ricoh cameras didn't feel as good or last as long as Pentax or Nikon or Canon or Minolta. Ricoh didn't have any features those others didn't. Ricoh didn't have half the accessories, but it just didn't matter. With this distribution strategy Ricoh jumped from an unknown to the top ten. Grew fastest by specializing in a no-growth channel. That channel embraced Ricoh.

Sometimes your business flourishes by "going where they ain't." Sam Walton never put a Wal-Mart in a town with over 50,000 population for his first three decades, towns that Sears and Kmart scorned, and became the wealthiest man in the country before the first Wal-Mart went into a city.

Dig into the books to find a nugget somewhere. When you spot something that seems to have more margin than anything else, expand that product or service and drop the others. Yes, it's a smaller business then. It's also profitable, which means pretty soon it'll have some cash to grow. Don't rely only on the accounting records. Check customer service activity levels, see where most of the complaints come from and which service causes them; when you talk with your sales troops, notice which categories they talk about the most. Now you're getting a sense of how overhead should really be allocated. And maybe it is spread appropriately, but more often it's not, so the books distort profits and losses by product.

Understanding any business is tough. It's inexact. It's also do-or-die, so best of luck.

CHAPTER 34

TURNAROUNDS YES, STARTUPS NO, AND WHY

This is for you sick puppies who want to become turnaround managers. You're also smart, by the way, and will learn why in a few paragraphs. At the end, you'll get tips on starting.

In 1995 Crosspoint Ventures, a huge VC fund with great returns, asked me to look at a troubled investment.

This floundering company made audio and video mixers, used mostly in the entertainment business. Their offices were within a comfortable drive of my home, a rare pleasure, and the business enjoyed some revenues.

But the customers were filmmakers. The thought of spending lots of time in beautiful Burbank, the marketplace, going from one single-story production house in tan stucco, on streets so dreary that strip malls looked pretty, underwhelmed me, but where the opportunity is good the environment is rarely perfect.

So I checked the numbers. This startup's first product, the not-so-revolutionary one, was selling and growing. But the investors' hopes and dreams were built around the next-generation device. Faster, better, easier, but more expensive. Tough to build.

I counteroffered to the investors: "Instead of the 5% of equity up front and $200K salary, how about $100K and 10%? More important to both of us, you committed to putting in another $4 million if I join. My deal is that you keep your $4 million, but possibly sign a credit line for $1 million."

My thinking was that I could get the business to break-even cash flow, or better, on the first product and shelve the second one, watch and see, move slower, and risk a little less until we got smarter.

My phone sat there. Silent. No response. I called the lead investor. He couldn't get off the phone quick enough. That same month I started negotiations with a CD-ROM publisher in Arizona, one that with a packaging concept became the biggest disc distributor in the world for a brief, shining moment. They were making money but had a subsidiary that was bleeding to death.

Same deal. The owners couldn't stand the thought of not putting more money into their loser, so we never shook hands.

This was 1995. An epiphany. It was clear my skill, making money from a business that had no place to go for more investment, was being eclipsed. The world had too much cash.

So it seemed time to shift to a startup. Spend a few years building a business and absorb that money the world wants to give. We started SkyDesk in 1996 and raised about $59 million in the following five years with six financings, each one with higher-priced stock than the one before it. This was fun and it fit the times.

But it disturbed me to realize it in 1995, because turnarounds are so much more rewarding and pleasant than startups.

Huh? Yes. Listen.

When you join a startup, the investors are pumped up, the employees eager, and everybody's hoping to get rich on stock options. The CEO gets 7% of the equity in options, vesting over the first four years. The board meets monthly and since they're all investors, they've got ideas on how the business should be run.

When I joined a turnaround, I got 20% of the equity on day one of my employment. Sometimes that was a negative worth thing and the salaries were never anything to admit to your friends. The boards usually scattered like a covey of quail, thrilled that I was dumb enough to take the wheel. Board meetings were an interesting concept that we didn't experiment with.

Most startups fail. Most turnarounds I've done succeeded.

So why would you want a startup?

There is that rush of startup excitement and the chase of a dream. But reality is that most convert to nightmares. Yet, in a turnaround, grim hopes for survival are about as good as it gets. The employees do greet you and give you support you'd have to work for elsewhere, since you're their last hope, and any anger they feel is directed more at the prior administration. They know who got them where they are, and they know where they are.

I've done several of each. It's kind of like cross-training. Both turnarounds and startups move faster than traditional businesses. The anxiety levels are cranked up several notches. And I think doing startups does minimize the personality distortion that comes from a never-ending series of turnarounds, where you are grinding ahead doing the superrational things and the highly predictable moves over and over and over.

But the payoffs, on average, are better from turnarounds. And people think you're smarter when you do it. With startups, success was expected.

Okay, you want to do turnarounds, you think. Here's how:

First you've got to have general management experience. Period. If you don't have it, get it. Do this for your current corporation. Or if you're weak in one area, marketing or operations or finance or research, get a job that concentrates on that weak area first. Immerse in it so you understand each discipline.

Next, volunteer for every troubled division assignment that comes up. This isn't as lonely or challenging as a true, independent turnaround, but the world doesn't know that and you'll be able to sell your experience as a turnaround person once you make it work internally.

Now comes the brightest moment of your career. It's almost spiritual.

Get a legal pad, a half-full bottle of wine, either color will do, and close your door. Think about turnarounds. Doodle on the pad. Float. But push toward what you believe to be the most important things to do in any turnaround. Boil this down to three things. Write them down.

For several months, read nothing in the business press except tragedies and recoveries. See if you can sense what worked. Observe how your three keys seem to work in the world. Clip those that fit your approach.

Now you're ready. Write a one-page article expressing this belief. Use your own experience for one of the points. Refer to two cases you read about to buttress the other two.

Get this printed, anywhere. It doesn't matter who the publication is. All you want are the reprint rights. I was in an industrial park turning around a business when I did this. The park had a bulletin called "The Paper Clip." Circulation smaller than some dinner parties you've attended. Doesn't matter. In a way, it's better, because the editor is delighted to get some space filled, and will feel no right to change what you say.

Now turn this same article into a slide or flip chart or PowerPoint presentation, and start making presentations to financial groups.

Put a reprint of your article into every letter you send. Doesn't even cost an extra stamp. Put a link to it with every email. Do your presentation once a week, to investors and bankers and CPAs, wherever you can.

Now you're the expert, and in a field where there isn't much competition.

I've done enough that I don't work that hard at it anymore, but you will at first, spending more time finding troubled businesses with receptive owners than actually fixing them. This changes. Make sure your Rolodex knows of each victory and, to disarm them, tell your audience of prospects about one that failed once in awhile. The sophisticated ones—they also are the ones with more money and power—will appreciate this honesty and be more receptive.

And read the rest of this book.

Now you know why turnarounds are better than startups. Keep it quiet, okay?

CHAPTER 35

ONE BUBBLE OFF PLUMB

In *Confessions of an Advertising Man,* David Olgilvy tells how he excelled in his first job, a chef.

Olgilvy triumphed in advertising, founding Olgilvy & Mather, and did so well for clients that he spent his last years living in a French castle. (He owned it.)

But his first reputation, as a chef, came from a baked apple dessert that only he could create. His split the skin and spilled out over the plate in an explosion that was never duplicated. He revealed the simple secret in his book. He baked two apples and scooped the second one out, spreading the gooey insides over the first. Nobody could duplicate the effect.

There's a certain street-smart sense to that, a harmless, delightful, and fun aspect to business that produces satisfaction and raises profits.

Getting way out of your box works sometimes.

It dazzled me in the camera business to watch how our sales folks would work the retailers.

Charlie Grisafi waited until noon when his Manhattan dealers were swamped. At 12:15 he labored into the front door, tie over his shoulder, shoving a pushcart full of new Pentax cameras and flash equipment, balanced just over his head.

"Murray, where you want these?" he asked.

Murray, waiting on a line of customers three-deep at the counter, waved to a corner, Charlie ran the goods over, tilted the cart, tucked them safely out of foot traffic and shoplifters' way, wiped his brow, and walked over to

Murray. He slipped the receipt on top of the counter, under Murray's waving hands as he helped a customer.

Charlie waited. Murray glanced aside. Charlie pointed. Murray signed. Charlie left.

Now the only problem here for purists is that Murray never ordered the stuff. This was the presumptive sale elevated to the max. And that's how Charlie spent every noon in New York.

His Midwestern counterpart, Clark Owen, served Columbus, Cincinnati, Dayton, Indianapolis, and so on. Clark got to town about once a month. Each had about a half dozen dealers.

On his first day in town, Clark's routine was to walk past every dealer and knock on the front window until the dealer spotted him. Clark then waved, grinned, and walked away. Drove them nuts. He'd be back the next day or maybe two later.

Instead of waiting hat in hand, Clark had them wondering who he was spending more time with and why. Got their attention before trying to talk.

Ray Ohannes was another sales artist. He ultimately headed up Ricoh camera for several years, and while the industry was swinging to the mass merchandisers, Ray had the cool to go against that and sell only to specialty camera dealers, with counter-intuitive and astounding results described in the last chapter.

Ray was a big Cadillac lover. Once his dealer complained that it was getting tougher and tougher to know where to advertise. Ray asked where he spent most of his budget.

"Radio," the dealer said, "it's the only medium that works. But I don't know which stations to pick."

Ray took him by the arm, walked him into his service bays, opened the door of the first car, and hit each of the radio buttons. Then he did the same with the second, third, fourth, and fifth cars.

"There's your media plan," Ray said. Street smarts.

One of our downtown Chicago dealers, Altmans, was a particularly shrewd businessman. He also handled appliances. The city of Chicago was forever charging more and more for garbage hauling, and it became a serious business expense in the loop. Ralph Altman solved his problem. Each night he dumped their waste into an empty television crate and nailed it back up.

They left it near a light in the alley. Almost every morning they would discover their garbage had been stolen. A great cost-control program. Fun to visualize the crooks opening their prize.

I thought this was uniquely clever until learning that King Louis the XVI was frustrated that this new vegetable, the potato, wasn't being accepted by the French. This new plant from South America seemed hardy, produced lots of staple diet from a little land, but his subjects couldn't be interested. So the king had a large field planted, over a hundred acres of potatoes. He then fenced it off and posted guards marching around it. Not enough guards to constantly cover every section, but enough to be noticed. When the crop came in, most was stolen and eaten. And one day, the french fry.

Our camera dealers were typically aggressive retailers. At trade shows, we paid for an ice carving with caviar nestled in the fish sculpture, watched a tipsy dealer walk in, scoop his hand into the pricey stuff, and smear it across his mouth while his salesclerks howled. This was our customer.

So next year, we had equally lavish food and drink set up in a suite. There was one problem. The suite had two bathrooms. So we paid the hotel to drape over both doorways, hiding them. The bar was open with no limit. Their kidney limit, however, soon had them scrambling down the hallway to find a urinal, and few came back. We looked generous without busting the budget.

Another year was the opening of McCormick Place, the first show it held. Unions were always a problem in Chicago shows. Trying to budget for the show while carrying around a wad of cash to get an electrician to screw in a bulb was tough and aggravating.

We were shocked by the cost of this show. The booth space was $20 per square foot for one week. You could buy a house for that. (We're talking 1971, dear reader.)

So we designed a three-story booth, beating the rates, something that hadn't been seen in those days. It featured spiral staircases and two stories overhead and was the talk of the show. Best of all, the ground floor was steel. The second was wooden beam. The ironworkers and carpenters were still arguing over who had jurisdiction while the crane hoisted one story on top of the other, and it was bolted together before they could put on the squeeze.

Before bragging too much about a minor victory that seems laughably obvious today, let me admit that we were merely the second most creative approach to that show.

Our competitor, Vivitar, once again outdid us. They skipped it. That takes guts. Most people attend trade shows out of fear of not being seen. They buy booths, which restricts their mobility. Justifying the expense becomes a stretch.

Vivitar was the first with the courage to bolt from the crowd and simply not show. Instead, they created an audiovisual program, put it in several semitrailers and drove the country, one city at a time, hosting the dealers and showing off their latest products and deals. They may have spent less, they may have spent more, but it doesn't matter. They differentiated themselves and had exclusive time with the dealers, undistracted.

Two later trade show approaches worked best.

At Montron, a startup, we had a toy with an audiovisual market. So we went to the NAVA show. At this show, for our product, nearly everybody was a prospect. We couldn't afford anything beyond the minimum booth. So we hired Dot's Floral Shop, Las Vegas, to plant ivy walls around the edge of our booth and put picnic benches in the middle. We placed lemonade pitchers on each table.

It drew. Weary walkers thought they spotted an oasis. And they sat. We poured and demonstrated. The costs of that show were well below our smallest competitors.

Five years later, Checks To-Go attended its first Comdex. We made software forms. Checks that worked with Peachtree Accounting software, or Great Plains, among others. The trick was getting any attention from those accounting software firms. With most, we couldn't even get an appointment. And we couldn't afford a booth.

At that time, Price Waterhouse had an expert in-house who was viewed as the PC accounting guru. So we hired him for $500, asking him to speak for twenty minutes at a lunch. Title? "The Future of Accounting Software."

Every accounting software's executive staff attended, our room overflowed, and we made contacts that built a great business in the months to follow. Total cost for the lunch and speaker was well below booth expense.

In my earlier youth, working in a carnival booth, the public was invited to pick up a bamboo pole with a line on the opposite end. This line was attached to a hoop. For twenty-five cents, all the customer needed to do was loop the hoop around the neck of a Coke bottle that was lying flat and lift it upright. Looked simple.

To assure the crowd, I would demonstrate how easy it was. They'd pay their quarters and fail.

The deal here was that Coke's casting process for bottles always produced a few in every case that were off-centered. One side of the bottle would be thick and the other side thin. No problem, it drank just fine. And all you did was find a case of empties and sort through them, selecting the most out-of-balanced bottles for the day's work.

When setting up the bottle for myself, the thick side went down, making it easy to lift upright. When lining it up for our customer, the thick side went up, guaranteeing it would wobble away when lifted.

There were more sophisticated lessons from the carnival. Such as the time the papers in Springfield, Missouri, just weren't covering the circus events when we arrived in town. So our animal trainer took me with him one night while we released an elephant, guided him gently through several backyards and into a clothesline and a tool shed, causing some minor damage and making headlines the next day. Ah, the glamour of PR.

Eighteen years after buying a new home in La Jolla our water heater died and bled to death all over the garage floor. Who to call? Fortunately, there was a service sticker on the heater with a phone number. We called. New heater the same day.

That sticker, it turned out, came in the mail about ten years earlier. I congratulated the installer, saying it was a brilliant marketing mailing. He looked puzzled. Then I explained. He reexplained to me how it really worked.

It seems an enterprising fellow just mailed out these stickers to occupants with the number of his answering service. The letter suggested putting it on the water heater for convenience when emergency service is needed. When the calls came in, he referred them to the nearest plumber, who paid him $25 for each lead. Not a fast payback, but a steady one, and an inevitable call. And not a bad return on each postage stamp.

I'm not complaining, just admiring, and my water heater was replaced posthaste. It still gives warm showers every morning.

This printer in Pasadena ran a great shop. He made enough to build a cliff home on the island of Catalina. The guy also loved to fly his own plane. Fair enough. What gave me a huge buzz was how he threaded it together.

He started a burial-at-sea service. For a few hundred bucks you gave him your dearly departed's ashes which this printer then sprinkled over the Pacific waters.

Now can't you see the guy, gleefully jumping in his plane late Friday, heading for his island getaway? He tosses in a few small boxes of ash, slips the checks into his wallet, takes off, and tosses Aunt Helen out just after clearing the coast. Colonel Walters gets dumped out the window minutes later, and Sam Bixby goes into the drink just as the airstrip on the island comes into view. And our printer gets paid for traveling to his weekend home, expensing his business costs.

It goes on. When I noticed our neighborhood Mail Boxes Etc. offered a shredding service, I asked the owner if many customers used it.

"Just enough to eliminate my packing material expense," he chuckled. So he gets paid to create the material he used to pay for. Instead of buying packing material, he uses the shredded paper.

This kind of thinking cannot be taught, but you can encourage it among those rare few with that ability to think around corners and hear through walls. Before telling you how to do so, let's agree on what you won't do. First, don't push this out-of-the-box thinking overtly or with much effort.

Pretty soon those who cannot do so will try, and chaos wins. Teaching pigs to sing doesn't create inspirational music and makes the animals cranky. You want employees focused on finding the margin and discarding all else. Second, do not have brainstorming sessions. Those are painful. Generally worthless. Great ideas spring from the subconscious, loosened by a receptive environment and happen in the shower, at a stoplight, or dozing on a plane.

Here's how to loosen up your employees' brains:

1. Pay for lunch when one person from accounting and finance hosts a marketing type. Ditto if someone from operations takes a staffer from research and development. Encourage an engineer to lunch with an accountant by paying for their sandwiches. But never let employees expense meals when they're with their own departments.
2. Pay every employee's dues for joining one outside organization, no matter what it is. Never pay for two.
3. Give books like *The Art of Warfare* by Sun-Tzu and a Sherlock Holmes paperback to all managers. Circulate copies of Henry V's speech, as Shakespeare wrote it, before the Battle of Agincourt. Best yet, be a leader, and pick your own favored song, act, or speech to inspire the workers. Take them to the symphony or a boxing match. If you have retreats where there's tennis and golf, have all the golfers play tennis and the tennis players golf. Do all this for fun. The brains will free themselves.

CHAPTER 36

ELIMINATE SEX

L ove is blind. Office sex is blind, deaf, and dumb.

William Agee, chairman, proved that at Bendix when he lost all business perspective from an infatuation with his protégée, Mary Cunningham.

Cunningham was intelligent enough. So was Agee. The trouble was that the two of them fell madly in lust, and later, I suppose, in love, but in the meantime they lost track of what they were supposed to be doing for Bendix and, ultimately, lost it. Okay, maybe love preceded lust, I wasn't there, it doesn't matter, either affliction corrodes teamwork at the office.

One year when I was at Graphic Arts Center, we contracted to print the Bendix annual report: 32 pages, 40,000 per hour. It was a good order so we loaded up a railroad boxcar of paper and everything was in full motion when Bendix called. Cunningham had just seen the proofs of the report and she had a complaint.

I heard about it from our salesman. He took the call. When he hung up, he said, "We have to stop printing. Cunningham doesn't like Agee's picture. She likes him better when he doesn't wear his glasses." We stopped the press.

A private jet flew the photographer to where Agee would be that evening, with a matching suit for the officer's page. The same backdrop was used again but Agee was now holding his glasses smartly, folded, just at his lapels, instead of wearing them. The rearranging of press time cost Bendix $60,000. (Not our cost, proofs were signed and I thought he looked swell with his glasses on myself.)

Neither Cunningham nor Agee ever thought of the cost, even though both have business savvy, supposedly, and normally would know better. The money came from shareholders, who never knew of the minor miscellaneous expense.

Affairs are the ultimate betrayal of team spirit, and yet inevitably happen with energetic people. If you can keep your employees servicing the customer, not each other, everybody wins.

Here's how you do it:

1. Make sexual harassment painful for the higher-ranking participant. Race, politics, religion, and sex are not subjects at business. A superior never asks a subordinate of the opposite sex to dinner alone. (Change opposite sex to same sex if you're homosexual.) A superior certainly lunches with subordinates of the opposite sex, but never one more than others and does so more often in groups. Peers may ask coworkers for a date once. Never twice. Once turned down, don't even hint at it again. Save that persistence for reluctant customers.

2. When affairs develop within a department, transfer the higher-ranking lovebird and don't make it a promotion. It is more the responsibility of the superior to cool this heat.

3. Make sure your insurance doesn't get too liberal with its stress benefits or counseling. One of my companies was disrupted by the strange and simultaneous disappearances of a man and woman in our sales force. They denied anything was going on, even got huffy with me for asking about it. Both divorced their spouses and signed up for a year of stress counseling. Our premium jumped so high the next year that salary increases companywide had to drop by one percent. If the rest of the company learned about that, there would have been a mob solution. Gee, maybe I should have. . . . naah.

CHAPTER 37

ATTACK DRUGS
AND ALCOHOL

O kay, I'm sitting in the lobby of a San Francisco hotel while editing this, and feel I must admit to you that I'm sipping a glass of the house Merlot. Do as I do, gang, I write these books to give myself worthwhile goals and sometimes reach them.

There was this guy, Bill Madison, a talented fellow who did a little less work in later years and missed quite a few Mondays. But he was an experienced thinker and produced top-selling products so most people ignored his breath and Rand McNally eyes, and they dismissed his twitchy demeanor as just a creative person's quirk. There were many clues but everyone looked beyond. And so Madison's drinking grew, getting this silent support.

He ran one section of toy design at Fisher-Price Toys in East Aurora, New York. Two of his group's winners were the popcorn popper and the ring stack. Each still sells about a million pieces a year.

I was there from California. Fisher-Price just acquired our small toy company and we were learning to fit our product development into their plans. Madison and I had dined once before and negotiated several times previously when he was our customer. The night before at dinner, we swilled two bottles of Cabernet Sauvignon. Two of us, two containers of grape.

We had just finished three days of product review with the toy selection committee. The result of all that was that Fisher-Price Toys had pruned the next year's new offering down to 40 items from 110 proposals. This was about average. We had a couple of items to do; Madison's group had a dozen.

Decisions had been made, the tension lifted, and Bill said, "Hey, c'mon over for some drinks and we'll cook and hunker down and talk."

I went. In Orchard Park, just outside Buffalo, we followed a winding path through tall maple trees to a contemporary glass house with three fireplaces. Snow fell as we pulled in the driveway, which was accented by spotlights. The house was cheery, but no more so than we.

Bill's wife mixed a batch of rum toddies, and he started the grill on the enclosed patio. It was a beautiful winter night and Bill and his wife were in rare form.

We finished the toddies. I did my share, and a second pitcher appeared. Suddenly the fire was leaping about four feet out of the grill, licking at the rafters. Bill's wife noticed. Bill was standing nearby. His attention was elsewhere, but who knows where.

Mrs. Madison screamed and Bill ran to the garage for a bag of sidewalk sand. He tossed handfuls at the fire. It went out. His house was saved, though temporarily scarred. There was a big black smudge on the ceiling, about seven feet across. And the paint had bubbled up in a couple of places. "Oh well," laughed Madison.

We skipped dinner and instead had another round of toddies. Mrs. Madison brought out cheese and apples.

Bill didn't make it to work the next day. It was an important day, as we had scheduled and budgeted for the 40 items. His crew, as they had done many times before, covered for him. I was just embarrassed enough about the evening, and my part of it, to not mention it.

I participated, but with a few badly needed brain cells not receiving or sending signals.

I thought about Bill later when I heard he had made a spectacle of himself at a toy buyers' dinner in Manhattan. There was an open bar at Delmonico's, a lot of schmoozing, and some key buyers from the country's leading retail chains. Bill Madison had known many of these carnivores for 30 years.

At the dinner, as it was told to me in hushed tones, the drinks gushed and flowed, Bill became much louder than everybody else until a salesman quietly suggested Bill go to his room. The dining room was about three-quarters full but there was still time for Bill to slip away relatively unnoticed. Instead, he had another drink, then another, and then climbed up on a table on all fours and started barking like a dog. Then, between fits of laughter, he tried to bite one of the customers.

In Marketing 101 you learn that biting a customer's forearm, in public, is not listed as a proven sales enhancing approach.

Nothing had been done for Bill Madison until he tried to chew on a customer. Almost got him. By then it was too late. He was fired, although the company gave him a generous severance payment, and they paid for a rehabilitation program. He's probably either dry or dead today. My guess would be toes-up, his liver pickled long before I helped him along. But I've not heard, even though I hear from toy folks three decades later. It's one of those depressing, embarrassing things—with a loss of dignity not just for Madison, but for anybody who aided and abetted—that we don't bring up.

It's not about being a watchdog every moment of your workers' lives. What they do off the job is their business. This is about productivity and safety.

To keep your workers dry:

1. Put in an anonymous employee-assistance program. This is a switch from the last chapter, where you were advised against offering counseling for stress. Counseling for stress costs you money and the results are worse than questionable. Counseling for drug and alcohol abuse works, saves you money, and improves their lives.

2. Face reality. Your business has drug and alcohol problems. All do. The worst policy is a vague policy, the next worse is an unpublished one. It's management's job to spell out exactly what the company will do to help with substance abuse and what is expected of the employee in overcoming it.

3. Alcohol problems are easier to spot for those of us born in 1942 or before. It's our drug of choice, our pal. When it interferes with work, talk to the employee about it immediately. If you're of my vintage, you probably don't understand drugs and the telltale signs. Do yourself a favor and learn. Accidents, erratic behavior, puffy eyes, sniffles, and jitters could mean nothing. You can't wonder, especially around equipment. Check the restrooms and keep your eyes open in the parking lot. People and companies die from this stuff.

CHAPTER 38

STOP GAMBLING. OH, YES YOU ARE

W e had this cash manager who used our company's money like the white chips at a blackjack table. I'll call him Ben Feders and I won't bother to make up a name for the company. The organization is on the New York Stock Exchange, a Fortune 100 outfit, but we were a small division. Ben managed a lot of cash.

Each day, Ben guessed how much to drop into short-term deposits, how much into long-term, and when to borrow just a little. He was not your gold chain Vegas guy, but he played the market like a high-stakes game. He pushed cash into fixed rates when he thought rates might drop and borrowed some when it smelled to his trained nose like they might rise.

It turned into a regular talent show for management. Ben seemed to take off his glasses and wipe them with his handkerchief about fifty times an hour, carried spare batteries for his calculator, and had his name stuck on his wastebasket with a Dymo label.

But what did we know? Mortgage rates were interesting. Free checking with a toaster from the bank was a big deal to us. And being two time zones and from Wall Street, Ben's reports became a fascinating diversion for us corporate drones.

And you could see Ben getting more and more into it, embellishing his victories for us at staff meetings. Probably swinging a little harder for bigger returns during the rest of the week, going for a score to tell us about.

Ben became The Kid, and people in the hallways of the company looked up to him and his magic like a professional athlete or a genius scientist. This guy even, gasp, started wearing colored shirts, suspenders, and almost became charismatic.

He set up a display that he changed every day. He charted his projections, and he graphed the company's plans. Soon purchasing, production, and sales began consulting monthly with Ben. Then weekly, and finally daily.

There were daily meetings with Ben in front holding court and changing forecasts. It was entertaining, and sometimes his focus would go out to more abstract things, like Ben's read on America's economic challenges.

"Everybody's worried about the national debt," he observed one time, "but it doesn't matter. That's just money we owe ourselves. Our problem is the shift from being a creditor nation to a debtor nation. That displays a fundamental weakness that no amount of intervention from the Fed can ever fix." Huh?

Ben went from cash manager to company economist to global soothsayer in just two years.

It was marvelous. He should have sold tickets. Sometimes it seemed he did. When dealers came through, part of every tour was to visit Ben's war room—a jungle of computer screens, printouts, and jangling phones that could autodial bankers across the country. It was in this room that decisions were made to lend and borrow, short-term and long-term. The community college invited Ben to speak about cash management to finance majors. He lectured every semester. One year, he was president of the Financial Executives Club—a group of CFOs and analysts who gathered monthly to discuss interest rates, banking, and bonds. No whoopee cushions there. In that atmosphere, Ben was the star.

He was an expert, the wizard from his particular company, and no one ever questioned his intelligence or instinct for cash management. All you had to do was listen to him talk, spin his magic.

But one day the CEO of this company retired, and an outside guy was hired. First, the new CEO revitalized research, lowered inventories, and made a change in marketing. Then he took a look at cash management and our wizard of the markets.

The CEO asked the CPA firm to calculate the difference between the wizard's system and a more conservative plan of simply putting excess cash in CDs at prevailing rates and borrowing only at amounts needed for the time needed.

The difference? Try $14 million. There would have been an extra 14 million in the till if four years hadn't been wasted trying to outguess the market. It cost even more. Since the company was paid a week later than all the competitors—because of the time spent in Ben's office, speculating instead of collecting—there was a week's lost cash, and the interest expense on it, every week. This was an even greater loss than the speculation tragedies.

Ben Feders' gambling goes on in every business that operates without guidelines. There are controllers guessing the prime rate, plant managers guessing on fuel futures, production people betting on leases, and credit folks speculating on the economy. They're all distracted and therefore less efficient.

It's more fun than work, but it's not the right stuff. There are ways to swagger by loosening or tightening credit, borrowing long-term or short-term, depositing the same, signing long-term leases instead of buying, or vice versa, setting inventory levels, or negotiating energy contracts . . . pretending to know.

Business has enough risk without creating more. There's not one business in the world that has succeeded based on those bets, but plenty have been sucked under by gambling on the side.

Here's how to reduce risk:

1. Each year, get everybody together and agree on a plan for interest rates, inflation, and your commodity prices. Then everybody takes a blood oath to make every decision based on that consensus. If things change dramatically, call a second meeting to adjust the guidelines. Will those guides be exactly right? Never. But neither will others, and this gets the group acting consistently and eliminates distractions.

2. In areas where you must speculate, as with pension funds, put equal amounts into stocks, bonds, real estate, and CDs. Never buy or sell more than 10 percent of the portfolio in a year, and do that only to maintain the balance. Use outside managers to do this for you and pick them based on lowest management fee. They're no better at this than anyone else, so concentrate on simple administration, straight guidelines, and Spartan costs.

3. With credit, determine what level of losses you must experience to be competitive in the marketplace. If you can boast of a perfect credit record, you've missed some good business somewhere. Make sure write-offs and rolled-over debts get counted as bad; when you are pushing collections those are a couple of easy ways to lose chunks of money while appearing to bring receivables back in line.

CHAPTER 39

SEND GOD BACK TO CHURCH

The famous singing family called. That was the message on my desk at Montron, the toy company. That's right, Ma and Pa Smileyvoice wanted to talk serious business.

They wanted to talk about our toy movie viewers. Users could watch a three-minute cartridge just by turning a crank. Batteries not included because batteries weren't required. Originally, we planned to limit the marketing only to cartoon cartridges. But we made mistakes in startup and therefore were still paying for some tooling that had to be scrapped. Although sales were good, margins were not strong enough to cover past sins. So we chased other sales.

One popular series was a CPR set of cartridges that the Red Cross bought and sold with every training dummy and instruction kit. In addition, a couple of pharmaceutical companies bought the viewers to show doctors and patients how to insert a new glaucoma treatment capsule and the best way to apply severe burn bandages. Another was instruction in breast self-exams for the American Cancer Society, in which several hundred films got mixed by the factory in with Sesame Street cartoons, and I don't even want to think about that.

We were looking for business when the Smileyvoices called looking to make a cartridge and buy 5,000 viewers and cartridges. They wanted to make a cartridge of the milk-and-cookie group's recent European tour, and they wanted it to feature their youngest son and cherubic daughter.

The package called for us to edit the film down to a three-minute cartridge. Over the phone, I quoted $2,500 to edit, $2,000 for the printing plates, and $7 per viewer and cartridge, plus boxing.

"That's a little steep, but this is just a start," said Mrs. Smileyvoice, ever the negotiating businesswoman. "We have 200,000 very active fans. Can you do better with larger quantities after this test?"

Could I do better? We had missed two payrolls during the year. The travel agent required personal credit cards for tickets. Parts arrived COD only. Toy sales were dropping due to an inventory mistake at Fisher-Price.

"Sell these and you've paid for the editing and plates forever. Double the quantity and the price drops a dollar," I quoted. They bought 10,000 units.

I flew from our San Francisco office to their suite at Tropicana in Las Vegas. When I arrived, they were mostly lounging around, but Mrs. Smileyvoice was all business. She wanted to ensure that the youthful son and the wholesome daughter, who were more popular than the older kids, were featured in the cartridge. "Put their brothers in the background," she instructed. Cash was thicker than blood.

She had a contract. I read it and it was just as we had agreed over the phone. I signed it and started for the exit, since our business was complete.

Before I could leave, as my signature dried, Mrs. Smileyvoice asked me to pray. Actually, she said, "One moment, young man," in her best motherly tone. "Let us pray for success before you leave." She had a grave look.

It had been some time since I prayed, and somehow bowing my head while she delivered the words in her mirrored leather Las Vegas room wasn't how I remembered it. I had nothing against God, it's just that her Lord and mine weren't exactly tennis partners. But I bowed anyway and murmured and nodded in the interest of commerce.

God was on our side, she said. It was a good thing, too, because later Mrs. Smileyvoice told me she couldn't pay our bill. She assured me, "The Lord is testing us right now," and then added, "I just don't know where the money is going to come from."

Well, in the end His Fanclubness came through and people were moved to buy gobs of Youthful Boy and Wholesome Girl Smileyvoice toy film projectors. They sold the first 10,000 projectors, and reordered.

Despite their assurances that our prayers had come true, I insisted on the money up front for the reorder. I even had the gall to ask for payment on the amount due from the previous batch. A miracle happened and all the money arrived.

We cashed the check and delivered the second order six months later, the exact delay we suffered through waiting for their first payment. The Lord sometimes works in mysterious ways. In this case I skipped the New

Testament's turn-the-other-cheek advice and opted for the older book's eye for an eye and tooth for a tooth.

Religion is private. When your vendor proclaims religious fervor, double-check his or her most recent invoices.

Here's how to keep religion in the church and out of your office:

1. Make it clear that your company respects the individual above all. Any intrusion on personal beliefs are not tolerated. No prayers. No invitations to religious services. Of course, weddings, funerals, and bar mitzvahs are fine. But nothing more. Run a business, not a house of worship.

2. The pursuit of profit is often attacked by those seeking to impose their beliefs. Put up a defense against this by pointing out, in policy statements, that profits prove two things. Profits prove that the organization is paying taxes to help support the community and nation, not just sucking up free services. Next point out that profits come from providing services that are valued higher than the cost of the labor and goods consumed to create them. To not profit, therefore, means the organization consumes more value than it produces, which makes it parasitic.

3. Remember that religion comes in different guises with names like Amway, United Way, PTA, Girl Scout cookies, and political action committees. None of these have any right to intrude. Employees come to the job to work, and employers pay for these efforts. Anything else is an invasion.

CHAPTER 40

SLASH CONSULTING

A basketball coach invented the handheld movie viewer. He thought it would be a nifty training tool to help players visualize moves and shots.

He brought it to us at Honeywell, and we were intrigued, so we put our ad agency on it. They recommended a consulting firm, and soon we hired them to do the market research, primarily shopping center interviews.

Part of the deal, and the more expensive part, was creating a set of handmade prototypes that worked well enough to hold and use. The consultants came through with the prototypes and then they set out to consult.

Two tables were placed at opposite ends of the walkways into the Apache Plaza in Minneapolis. Interviewers sat with samples while one stood soliciting interviews. Each three-minute interview included questions about the product, choice of films, and what they would expect to pay. The usual rough information about income and occupation was inferred from zip codes.

A trailer was parked in the lot for more in-depth interviews with a dozen willing subjects who were promised theater tickets. So we had the quantitative batch of quick surveys plus the qualitative in-depth interviews probing their deeper psyches. Their modus operandi included broad, probing questions about attitude, plus collecting information about other products owned and not owned. Occupations and hobbies were noted. They also interviewed on weekends and evenings to ensure a broad cross section of people.

The report came in. The Blue Binder's contents advised, "This is a serious educational product. The biggest possible mistake you can make is to treat it as a toy." They also talked about the need for some point-of-purchase demonstrator, since it was an unfamiliar product.

Development of a full library of skill films was the key. The software had to sell the hardware. The message from the broad cross section of people was clear. This is a hot new product, but only if it is treated as a serious educational device.

Even though a lot of people at Honeywell were excited, it would have taken two tons of development money and the timing wasn't right, so we passed.

The inventor went back to northern California, where a leading venture capitalist who also happened to own a sporting goods store loved the idea. The venture capitalist told several people from Honeywell he would risk another $4 million to jump-start the project if they would personally join the effort. They joined. John Belden, the Honeywell sales manager, quit and moved to California to run the startup. Two of my best friends in the marketing department left to help him.

I envied them, but their departures opened up promotions for me, so I stayed in the corporate bowels and became a director, which seemed like such a big deal I'm embarrassed.

The first $4 million vaporized fast. Johnny Unitas was hired to do the football films. Jean Shrimpton did a series on makeup and modeling. Arnold Palmer handled the golf series. Historical names today, but these were hot personalities then. There were a dozen different subjects covered and filmed, each one with several cartridges. The dozen celebrity subjects cost quite a bit, and so did the marketing.

Tests were set up on the West Coast in sporting goods stores and department stores. All the bases were covered. Newspaper, television, coop budgets, retail spiffs, and radio ads were timed to coincide, and displays in the stores were each well stocked to service the broad cross section of buyers they expected.

Customers stayed away in droves. Maybe the only people interested were those weird few willing to answer probing personal questions for theater tickets. That's a miniscule cross section.

So the company altered its strategy and tried more advertising, different advertising, lower prices, coupons, sample giveaways to local schools, and direct-mail offers. Nothing worked, and another million in cash evaporated. Layoffs started. Merchandise was returned and stacked in the warehouse.

About January 1972, the company's UPS bill for return shipments exceeded that for outgoing shipments. That was special.

And then, by chance, Belden met people from Disney, who gave Belden some Mickey Mouse cartoons to try. Disney had no competing products in the category, liked his toy, and gave Belden the rights to their cartoon library in exchange for a 7% royalty.

By the time Belden hooked up with Disney, he had a handful of workers left, and there was just enough money to meet three more payrolls and buy some Mickey Mouse labels and packaging.

And just like that, the company rebounded. There was no advertising expense and no giveaways, but there was this other thing, a product people bought.

The investor put more money in, and better cartoons and packaging were developed. Within two years, an $8 million business was born, but it was delayed two years and sopped up an extra $3 million out of the chute. In addition, several careers were disrupted and John Belden's hair prematurely grayed. There was one cause for all these problems: a consulting report that confirmed exactly the wrong strategy.

The main difference between you and consultants is that you know more about your business, cost less to analyze it, and are responsible for the results. The captain goes down with the ship; the consultant rows back to dry land to seek more business from others.

Consulting is the great wimp-out of business. It puts decisions elsewhere, delays them, and costs more. Managers know how to find what is wrong, or they shouldn't be managers.

Here's how to ensure consultants feel a part of your business:

1. Put half of the consultants' pay on a performance basis. If the goals aren't met, no pay. Use consultants only when you have to know about new areas or unfamiliar technology or markets. Otherwise, you're chickening out.
2. If, as often is the case, you're hiring a consultant to tell you what you want to hear so you can defend a move to owners or employees or customers, don't pay on performance and don't pay until you have the final report. Let's not kid ourselves about what you are doing. Every consulting firm spends most of their time on projects like this. Just sell them personally on your viewpoint so they can spit it up with enthusiasm.
3. If you are looking for an honest appraisal, including an evaluation of your own management effectiveness, pay the consultants in advance. You can't expect honesty if their last check isn't due until after they submit.

(Now, let me state that almost all consulting fees are wasted, but a thin slice of it is extremely well spent. Extraordinary moments, like startups and turnarounds, require experience and insights that won't be around for the important day-to-day, one-click-at-a-time management later. We used two dozen consultants and three employees in the first two years of Teledesic. Only one stayed for the decade that followed, but all were underpaid in fees with stock that soon made all paper multimillionaires. That tends to flush out true opinions and incandescent energy.)

CHAPTER 41

USE LAWYERS LESS

Knight Protective Industries was the defendant for one primary reason: Knight Protective was guilty. The complaint was trademark infringement and from what I could tell after becoming CEO in 1990, Knight had infringed upon a burglar alarm company that also had Knight as its name. Knight Protective of North Hollywood, California, was a national burglar alarm company with accounts from New York City to Honolulu.

The previous year, Knight fought the case legally on its merits and lost. The legal bill in 1989 ran over $300,000 which made us think the cost of the battle was more than any possible cost of a loss. As a result of the case, there was an injunction against our use of the trademark in the plaintiff's territory.

Knight appealed, challenging the premise of the case because it was filed two years after the infringement. Prior to going to the appeals court, the other company filed another suit against us claiming violation of the injunction and therefore contempt of court. We went into a preliminary hearing in a state superior court.

The judge heard both sides give brief arguments, and then he shook his head. He stood up. "It seems rather silly to take this any further, don't you think?" he offered. "Here's what I'm going to do. I'm going to leave the room for about an hour. Let's see if you two can act like adults and reach some kind of settlement." And the judge strolled out.

The plaintiff focused two smoldering eyes on me. "I'll see you bankrupt if it takes every penny I have," he hissed. I guess the boy was miffed.

"I'll tell you what," I said, "we don't have any more money than what I already offered to settle. So how about this: We'll give you 20 percent of our company on top of the cash offer of $100,000 we already made." I smiled. "You can have a seat on the board."

"What's the stock worth?" he asked, sarcastically.

"About a negative $2 per share," I replied. "Once we suck you into owning some newly issued shares, that drops to only a negative $1.60 per share. Gives you a chance to share our negative equity. If you win in court, we can't pay, so you lose. If you lose in court, you lose. I can make that offer to you here and now, without even checking with my board, because if you accept, we've shifted some liability onto your books and the value of our holdings go up."

He marched out. I didn't care, even though he had won the first round. He who has less to lose in any battle wins. There were three weaknesses to his case.

One, he had neglected to complain or even bring up the infringement for two years.

Two, and he didn't know this yet, we had documented sales trends from his hardware suppliers that showed his sales increased when we started advertising in his territory. This concurred with his complaint, which stated customers called his sales office citing our advertising, thinking his company was ours. (This says a lot about our advertising, but that's another chapter.) That fact made his chances of winning stronger but reduced his potential for collecting any damages. It helped his case because a key to winning trademark infringement is proving confusion in the marketplace. But he was benefiting from the confusion. So no damages.

The third weakness, as I had told him before, was quite serious. Knight Protective was in the middle of a traumatic turnaround and had no cash to pay any significant damages. Never sue a turnip.

The plaintiff returned and five minutes later the judge floated back in and gave us a weary look. The plaintiff didn't say much but you could tell he was ballistic, on a hair trigger, when the judge asked what happened. His pudgy, balding lawyer simply told the judge that there was no hope to settle out. The lawyer jangled change in his pocket when he talked.

Knight beat this charge after a one-week trial. Then the appellate court unanimously overturned the first decision, which we had appealed. The appellate judges agreed that the original complaint was filed far too late. At this stage, with a unanimous appellate decision, it was 100-to-1 that another appeal would work or even be heard by the supreme court. But we were not dealing with a rational being here, so we offered $30,000 to settle forever. He accepted. Our legal bill was only $10,000 this time, compared with $300,000 the year before.

Our cardinal sin was that we let our lawyers get mad, and we cheered them on initially. Instead of letting logic intervene, the other side counterat-tacked. We were spurred on when our lawyers got mad because then we got mad, which made them madder. And all the time the opponent was doing the same. Everybody took personal affront and all meters were running.

At one point their attorney threatened to punch our attorney, who wel-comed it with a macho, "Go ahead, take your best shot!" I gotta believe there's a class in law school, taught by the dramatic arts department, teach-ing lawyers how to pose in front of their clients.

Everybody took their best shots, all right. With our shareholders' money. And we let them. That's key. Behind every spurious lawsuit sits an emo-tional client.

You've seen people and businesses who are quick to sue. Besides the obvious paranoia and persecution complexes these people suffer under, you don't want to hang out around them or talk with them much. That poi-son spreads.

Profits are inversely proportional to legal bills unless you're in a pretend business, meaning one that's regulated.

Here's how to settle, not fight:

1. Never buy legal work without an estimate in advance. This will cut your legal bills by about one-third for conventional work. Shop around. For unconventional jobs, and there aren't many of these, review the billing weekly and ask what's being done and why. There's not a law firm in the world that posts its partners' wins and losses. Ask and they won't know. But every partner in every firm knows how many hours each partner and associate billed last year. Nothing wrong with that. They're a business. Just keep that in mind.

2. Always test your firm's beliefs by offering some form of contingency before going after somebody. Also try incentives for a winning defense. It doesn't have to be a 100% contingency. Few will take that. But you can cover their out-of-pocket expenses without markup and let the firm keep 25% of the winnings. If the fire disappears from their eyes, you know the case isn't worth pursuing. (Don't show this offer around; you can always find some firm that is desperate for work and will take your deal just to cover expenses.)

3. When you have a legal bill that seems outrageous, don't pay. Pay what's right. Attorneys can't sue clients without seriously boosting their malpractice rates. Since attorneys invented the concept of mal-practice, there's a nice touch of justice to that.

CHAPTER 42

ROMANCE THE BANKERS

At US Press, we started getting the bankers ready to push money at us two years before we needed it.

At the time, we just saw it as a chance to cultivate relationships with several cash pools. Intermark, our parent company, held a "Banker's Day" at least once a year and US Press always made one of the presentations. We showed sales growth, cash flow, and profit, and then we would tour a plant and let representatives of three different banks see, touch, and smell the equipment. Bankers love to remind themselves that they are dealing with something more than numbers.

So we did it up. When our new Toshiba press was installed and purring in Portland, we let the bankers climb three stories of catwalks for a bird's-eye view. At the top, we set up a table of coffee and doughnuts, and we watched Bloomingdale's Christmas catalog whiz through the 270-foot-long press. There were cranes loading two-ton rolls of paper in one end and forklifts removing catalogs at the other. How can they not love your business after that? They never sipped coffee and munched doughnuts in such a vibrant setting before. Then we demonstrated more wizardry. We programmed the computer to print out catalogs addressed to them at their banks, and then we presented them to them before they left as new friends. That's right. No requests, just a future customer.

Another year, we brought the group into a prepress area where they watched a technician change the color of a Mercedes proof by tapping on a keyboard. Proofs were pulled both ways so one banker received a brochure with a teal Mercedes, the next a maroon. It was a kick for all. And, as always, key figures were presented and handed out so the bankers had a basic grasp of the business.

Continental Bank, Bank of America, Union, and First Interstate Bank came to the show. At each meeting, US Press sat next to a different banker to keep a scent of competition in the air.

When we were in downtown Los Angeles, we stopped for a visit and a quick update. Usually we would be calling on ARCO or Honda or Time Warner or Georgio. We could show the banks what we were printing for clients of ours who were sometimes also their clients. Soon these meetings became a forecast for when we intended to go public. As a subsidiary of Intermark, we always borrowed from Intermark. But when we would go public, we could need our own bank cash.

They listened. And they started wondering when, not if, they could shovel some money to us.

In 1982 the market dipped and caught US Press in a margin squeeze. We dropped our prices 4 and 5% just to keep the new presses busy. We slashed costs to the marrow just to make a profit . . . barely. At the end of that meager year, our paltry earnings made the company look less attractive.

But within six months things came back. We went out on our own and three banks were clamoring to loan us money. Here's why.

During the downturn, we scrambled for business and made some painful cuts to operating expenses. We spun off marginal subsidiaries. And, always embarrassing, we cut people. Shameful but necessary and better than bankruptcy.

Most important, we showed the banks our bad numbers instead of fading away.

We rebounded sharply a couple quarters later when sales came back and our costs were lower. And we mentioned that to the bankers.

Imagine. These bankers had already been through a tough moment with us, an enjoyable dip for them since there was no risk, and now they saw the recovery. We forecasted the following year, they nodded, knowing that all forecasts are wrong, but felt fine because they'd seen us stumble and get up.

When the economy turned, Linda Araiza of Union Bank said this: "Usually silence is our first sign of trouble. You guys are just the opposite. It's refreshing."

So was her attitude. When we finally asked for money, Linda smiled and came back two weeks later with $10 million at prime plus 1%. Two weeks for a new customer. New, but not unknown.

Bankers cannot make more than a few percentage points on the money loaned, but they can lose it all. That's why they're jumpy. They make more money by avoiding losses than by getting new clients. Help them relax by getting them familiar with your business.

Woo the bankers; it's their money you're using. To keep the bankers backing you:

1. Get to know your banker's boss. There's enough turnover at the account level that you'll find yourself starting all over every two years if you don't. Introduce several of your key officers regularly so the bankers can get information from several sources. Always be acquainted with several different banks to protect yourself when your banker changes jobs and forgets you, or when your bank gets squeezed by the feds. Talk to bankers that fund your competitors. They think they already understand your business.

2. Every quarter, give the bankers background information on your industry. Give it to them whether or not you need money. Give them quarterly financial statements and talk with them about the future. Soon, your bankers will anticipate your needs and ask you if you need a loan. It's much better than if they knew nothing about you and are surprised with your request for quick cash.

3. When things go bad, give the bankers more information than normal. This forces you to really tighten up your actions. The bankers will feel a stronger bond when you pull it through. (And if you don't pull through, it doesn't matter anyway.) When bankers see you beat a tough time, they view you as less of a risk.

CHAPTER 43

USE THE CPA AS MORE THAN AN ACCOUNTANT

"**Y**ou know, it would sort of put icing on the cake if somebody would buy this business now," mused Bob Jacobsen. It was a thankful time for Jacobsen and for the company he owned, Checks To-Go.

Jacobsen was already beyond comfortable, having created a tax software company that Burroughs Computer acquired in the 1970s. Jacobsen and his offspring created Checks To-Go as a hobby in 1976, and I was hired as CEO in 1986.

Checks To-Go went through two CEOs, and it required cash to keep afloat every month until the turnaround we did in 1986, when we redirected the business.

Finally, in 1987, Checks To-Go was gushing profits and Jacobsen remarked how wonderful it would be to find a buyer. It was nothing urgent. The future looked as bright as the PC market then, and should only get better. But the Jacobsens were typically relieved and somewhat disbelieving owners of a recovered business. They didn't want to test their luck.

So we started looking, quietly. Finding a buyer would be tricky. Several competitors would probably be interested, but if they knew we were for sale, a few would spread the word among our clients that we were troubled and for sale.

We went to an investment banker called Geneva. They specialized in small businesses, and were doing well, just enough to be ostentatious. They wheeled up to our dowdy stucco building an El Cajon industrial park in the first Mercedes and BMW our asphalt parking lot had met. When the doors swung open and the alligator briefcases swung out, all wore designer suspenders, a sure sign that they were overpriced. After we talked briefly, they pulled at those suspenders and told us they needed $20,000 to do the preliminary analysis of our business: an appraisal and optimistic projections.

We passed. We called Price Waterhouse, our accounting firm, and put together a plan. We drafted a letter that they would send from their Los Angeles headquarters instead of the local office. It was to go to every competitor and possible strategic partner imaginable. The letter described the size, profits, growth rate, and asking price for Checks To-Go, but it did not name the company. It gave a general description of the service, but there were no specifics. The letter hinted at probable economies of scale that this acquirer might expect.

Nothing happened.

Auditors are your best outside advisors.

We went back to Price Waterhouse and suggested they do a second letter to the same list. Since CPA firms, especially in the biggies, have credibility at stake in everything they do, we merely restated the sales pitch in the second letter and sent it to the same list. Price Waterhouse didn't ask, but we insisted on paying their costs plus a markup. Good thing.

The second letters went out and nothing happened. We paid the Los Angeles office about $2,000 to cover the partner's time to look over and approve the mailing as well as the cost of the postage, clerical time, and stationery.

We tried a third letter, repeating the proposition. Understandably, Price Waterhouse's enthusiasm was on the wane. This wasn't their business. But they were serving us as a client and, since we covered their expenses, they had to humor us. We got a live response from RapidForms on the East Coast. "We'd like to learn a little more," their CEO said to Price Waterhouse. He signed a confidentiality agreement and our accounting firm told him more.

I chatted up their executive vice president and kept it to a slow-paced mating ritual.

Another company, Rocky Mountain Banknote, became interested in Checks To-Go at the same time. Strangely, their interest came from wanting to get into PC supplies and had nothing to do with our efforts. But you never know. Any effort has some effect, and by being aggressive, you earn head nods instead of quizzical looks when someone asks someone about your business. Rocky Mountain Banknote had heard reports about the Checks To-Go resurgence but couldn't remember from where. When Rocky Mountain Banknote heard about RapidForms' interest, and vice versa, the fine art of starting a stampede with two cows began.

We expressed appropriate surprise, delight, and humility at being pursued, but in our best hard-to-get tone explained that life was quite good as is. Rocky Mountain Banknote couldn't stand it and made a cash offer that was a healthy multiple of earnings. We pretended our acceptance was reluctant.

Price Waterhouse probably doubled our sale price by finding another credible suitor without making us hang out a FOR SALE sign by advertising the business. Price Waterhouse's credibility helped. And they pocketed several years' worth of fees by doing the accounting work needed to close the deal. That's fair. You want them on your side.

CPAs are your best outside advisers. They've seen it all and they know your numbers and how you stack up to the world. You may not always like what your CPA reports, but its service is often your best way to win the race, and it often sees trouble before you.

Here's how to use your CPA firm better:

1. When a controller or CFO leaves, keep the position empty and bring your CPA firm in an extra three days to help close the books each month. It will cost you about half of the old salary and adds objectivity. You might discover something.

2. Before each annual audit, have your CPA's partner agree to spend extra time looking for a couple of extra things, such as possible cost reductions, or have the firm compare your management and operations with similar clients', reporting your relative strengths. Not overall, just tell them a couple areas you suspect are wobbly. They can crank up some comparisons in a few hours.

3. When selling a division or the company, use your CPA rather than a glossy investment banker. Your CPA understands your business better than an investment banker ever will, charges less, and has earned more credibility. CPAs are less prone to designer suspenders. And you don't look like you're for sale, which raises your value.

CHAPTER 44

INSURANCE STUPIDITY

S unrise Capital spent $80 million to buy Pacific Metals, and Warren Smith got a Ford, one fistful of cash, and a life insurance policy. Smith was happy.

He grew up in the business that his dad started and ran for forty years. He knew everything. He knew the cycles of metal prices. He knew how to negotiate commercial power rates and he knew where to find the best trucking prices by season and day of week. He swam in the veins of this business.

When Sunrise Capital's board, where I was director, agreed to buy Pacific Metals, part of the deal was to lease him a new car and take out a $5 million life insurance policy. Smith insisted on a maroon Town Car with a tape deck and the bigger engine. We agreed.

When we talked about the life insurance, Smith introduced us to his agent, who handled all his business and had for years. We smiled and later introduced Smith to our broker, J&H Marsh. With trepidation, Smith let us stick with Marsh.

The acquisition went through, and Smith got his new wheels. We took over his company under his supervision. A month later, Smith came in to talk to us about his insurance.

"I'm taking a loss on some real estate this year, so I would rather have the income than the insurance," he said. "Is it too late to change back?"

Our CFO, Bob Milliken, called Marsh, who reversed the contract without penalty and got the cash back. We sent the check for $180,000 to Smith.

A few days later, the phone rang and it was Smith, loudly protesting his payment. "Where's the rest of my cash?" he bellowed.

"That's all the policy cost," said Milliken.

"Nope. Nope. Nope," machine-gunned Smith. "I spent half a day with my New York Life agent. I saw the numbers. Hell, I still know 'em. That policy cost you a quarter mil, minimum."

Milliken took a deep breath. He started to explain. "We bought exactly what we agreed to contractually. You signed it. That's the coverage you had, with the same quality rating. The only difference is that we found it for $180,000. Marsh spotted ways to knock seventy grand off the premium without reducing your coverage anywhere."

"I don't believe it."

A delicate series of explanations and proof followed. Marsh managed our insurance. They bid every policy, were constantly in the market shopping for other clients, and always knew where the values were. Smith's premium expense had crept out of line over the years. It was the only leak in an otherwise tight ship. His view of insurance as a commodity, as opposed to a service that has all kinds of price variances, was costing him big-time. It was the only place in his business where he was not getting top value.

Smith never ever totally believed us. Part of his disbelief may have been frustration at the realization he had overpaid by so much for so many years. He never said as much. He refused to discuss it. For years afterward, he just kept mumbling that we conned him out of $70,000, which was easier for him to swallow than to realize his local insurance buddies had been sticking it to him for years. After all those golf games and fishing trips. How could they?

Of course, he ended up resigning prematurely from Pacific Metals. It was too bad, because he knew the business better than anyone. His ongoing input would have helped. But his outlook was jaundiced, so we parted.

Insurance is a lifeboat if and when you need it. The payments, though, are barnacles.

Here's how to gain protection without dragging in the water:

1. Use a broker who shops for insurance without getting paid commissions. There are values and rip-offs, just like any other product or service. The value of any coverage goes down as the commission rate and a regular agent's enthusiasm go up.
2. Buy less. Buy as little as you can. Companies with good coverage get sued more often for more money than those without heavy coverage. It's lawyer bait. Raise every deductible. Self-insure. Don't cover your company against the improbable accident, no matter how cheap. Always remember, insurance companies take in more from premiums than they pay back in damage payments. That's how they get their names on all those skyscrapers. That's their business, silly.

3. If, in a weak moment, you are struck by fear of losing some of your life's work due to an accident or lawsuit and therefore are considering raising your insurance, take a breath and consider setting up a more generous retirement plan outside your business instead. This survives a catastrophe in ways that no amount of insurance protection or lawyers can provide.

CHAPTER 45

CHALLENGE THE DO-GOODERS

In 1991, after a dramatic restructuring, a modest level of profitability was reached at Knight Protective and so the company added two community-oriented policies. Knight first added partial payment of wages for those employees called to jury duty. The second policy was to give the option of one paid day off a year to do charitable work of the employee's choice.

The rub was, nobody took the day off. We were trying to give something to the community in wages and workers and time, but nobody took an interest.

In the wake of the 1992 Los Angeles Rodney King incident, relief efforts were solicited daily. Still, no one raised a hand, so finally I called the Red Cross and volunteered for a day in the riot zone.

I went to their headquarters building in downtown Los Angeles. The people there were all social and sincere. They provided me with a map, a large coffee urn, 10 pounds of coffee, two cartons of Doritos, a case of Evian bottled water, two dozen boxes of Nabisco crackers, and a late-model station wagon to haul it in. I was given large Red Cross stickers—one each for the front and back of my shirt, I suppose, in part, so I wouldn't be shot, in part to score points for the Red Cross. Don't do good unless the cameras are rolling, you know.

They gave me directions to a relief outpost in a Methodist church in South-Central Los Angeles. It was a Hispanic-Korean neighborhood.

My job was to take the food and coffee in, set it up, and then hang around for a few hours. "Stick around and be seen," they advised.

The church was easy to find. A line of 300 or so people, and 99%

Korean, lined up in front. There was no shade at 10 A.M. and the sun blistered. The wait to get inside was two hours.

Once inside, they filled out forms in a process that somehow took another two hours. I found the manager for the Federal Emergency Management Agency (FEMA). He hadn't missed many meals and was a chain-smoking swell of neuroses.

"Get all that stuff in the back here," he said, almost surreptitiously. "We need to keep it away from the crowd. We don't want them just taking it."

I helped bring everything in because heaven forbid that people in need get things from a charity group that is there to give. I was there only a few hours. I figured they were full-timers.

I hung around as instructed. I talked with a relaxed psychological worker. She was sipping coffee and eating a Danish, sitting with three other volunteers who were also small-talking. The psychological worker explained to me that many of the people in the neighborhood, some of the 300 in line, had suffered stress and needed referrals for help.

She told me how tense the event was for everyone. She took a bite of her Danish. Then she told me that the four of them at that table had each worked 21 straight days. I was there for four hours, and they drank a lot of coffee in that time. Never in that time did one of them talk to a waiting person.

Two workers from the Fair Housing and Unemployment Agency set up an information table at one corner of the room. The woman worked on needlepoint and the man riffled through a dozen sports magazines. There was nothing else to do.

In the other corner, there were four workers from the Small Business Administration staffing a loan-application table. There was no one there, and the four sat telling dirty jokes. I heard a few. Not bad. But tax-paid.

At another table, there were 20 lines processing relief loan application forms. There were 20 volunteers, but only one line was moving. Apparently, only one of the volunteers understood the application forms enough to be efficient at processing them. In the time this one volunteer processed 10 completed forms, the other 19 volunteers did a total of three.

The setup astonished. It seemed that my coworkers would be giving more to society by working directly than by volunteering through agencies. Just as I was thinking this, an inspection team from Washington arrived.

Six well-groomed young bureaucrats marched to the FEMA manager's desk. Their intense leader got right to the point: "How many applicants do you have? How many are being processed? What can we do to help?"

The manager thanked the young bureaucrat and explained that he was stretched out, "but I have a fine group of volunteers and we can handle it."

"Well, we're proud of you," said the high-wattage Fed. "Please express our gratitude to all your wonderful helpers," he added at five decibels.

They shook hands and that was it.

This was only a one-day experience, but it was eye-opening and educational. If every employee did just one day a year, these charitable organizations just might start to get productive under the scrutiny, and for-profit employees would feel good about helping.

A little company-sponsored charity builds a more profitable attitude within the company by helping employees learn to live outside themselves and support others. Teamwork feeds on that.

Every profitable company should try some do-gooder stuff. You learn a lot by getting out into it every once in awhile and seeing more than the cameras and words of the media capture. Much "good work" is waste. Partly because the people doing it operate under a halo that avoids scrutiny. That can be fixed if taxpayers get involved.

Test your charities three ways:

1. Don't make cash contributions to any group. Instead, give time and effort. If they can't use your help but want your cash, you have to wonder.

2. When your company is profitable, pay employees enough for jury duty so they can do it with minimal sacrifice. Don't pay so well that they get free time off. Both of you should participate. Many business executives serve on the YMCA board, United Way, and school fundraisers, yet duck the real work of jury duty. That's why too many court decisions are made by the retired and the bored.

3. Create profits first. If you don't, you're not paying taxes and therefore are a parasite. Everybody uses public streets. Chances are some of your employees use public schools. This is not to suggest that those schools and streets are well-managed (that's another book), but if you're using them, you ought to help pay. The only way to do that is to make money to pay taxes. (And explain that the next time someone looks down their nose at you to say they're nonprofit. Ask if that means they evade taxes. Ask if they use schools or roads. Don't let the fraud continue.)

CHAPTER 46

BREAK LAWS CAREFULLY

In 1987, a group of Washington bureaucrats decided that all businesses could use some additional costs, so they created new hiring regulations.

One was a requirement that every employer have absolute proof of every employee's citizenship. It was quite unforgiving. An employer was subject to a hefty fine even if the employee had professionally created forgeries.

Of course, they designed new forms. This paperwork could be checked at random, and anybody found in violation could be fined $10,000.

It was a modest effort but it had the desired effect. It raised costs a little so businesses would have to raise prices a little, and it raised taxes so the government could hire more bureaucrats.

Life was grand, except for those who actually produced something. We had to live in regulatory purgatory, where the pain went up but there was little chance of salvation.

At Checks To-Go, our personnel files didn't meet the requirement. The problem was that these regulations were retroactive. All documentation was required for the past year.

We sent our controller, who was also our personnel director, to a $295 seminar explaining the new regulation. The controller was Cathy White.

At the seminar, Cathy saw several lawyers tsk-tsking about the unreasonableness of the new law, but warning of the severe dangers of noncompliance. Cathy also heard the lawyers offer further assistance outside the seminar. She just stayed and listened. What she heard was bad enough.

To follow the law literally, we had to add an item to the personnel file that shows proof of citizenship for all 20 employees hired for the previous year, with a copy of either their birth certificate or passport.

We followed this regulation and it took about 80 hours of work, but two months later Cathy came to me with a solitary problem. One employee, Don Silver, had been hired as a customer service representative eight months earlier, but it didn't work out and he left after two weeks.

When we checked our records and back with his former employers, we couldn't find proof of citizenship anywhere. Of course another set of laws prevented prior employers from providing anything that Don Silver, the phantom, didn't approve of in writing.

Cathy called one of the seminar experts. "You should hire a private investigator. That will at least show diligent effort if the question of this employee is raised," suggested this uneconomic being.

Cathy asked me. "Let it go, break the law, and we'll run the risk of a fine," I said. "This guy was on our payroll for two weeks many months before this law was passed. We've complied with the law concerning all the new hires, and besides, no one has ever followed up. Look, hiring an investigator to chase this down is ridiculous. What could be gained? Nothing. The only thing that changes is we spend less time working, which means we make less money and pay less taxes."

Cathy, who was a very responsible employee, reluctantly agreed.

We discussed it at length, and I explained it was always company policy to obey the law but sometimes there would be contradictions. Sometimes proper compliance merely reduces profits and raises costs, so prices go up and taxes paid go down. Everybody loses.

Do-nothing regulators are the best you can hope for. Do-something regulators end up requiring OSHA-mandated back-up sirens that also happen to violate municipal noise ordinances, or demanding documentation of the racial mix on your payroll in direct contradiction to laws against recording such information.

People have been writing laws in this country for more than 200 years. Sometimes they don't match up. Sometimes, the laws or regulations simply can't be met. When that is the case, tell the next manager up and break it. When lawbreaking is necessary, the CEO must bless it, or there will be anarchy.

To free your business from ruinous rules without creating chaos:

1. Never let anybody break a law or regulation without first discussing it with his or her superior and documenting it. The only reason to ever do this is when it is inherently impractical or contradictory to another law. That superior manager is responsible for letting his or her next

level up know. In other words, let the CEO decide. That's why CEOs make the big bucks.

2. Double your efforts to keep the spirit of that law. This is no defense, but it can't hurt, and sometimes, in a rare moment of rationality, it will be recognized as absence of malice. In an area of impossible record-keeping, don't display arrogance by never doing it. Create halfhearted records, but save your time for more worthwhile projects. This lets regulators save face. And should they check, you might get off with just a wrist slap.

3. If your company benefits economically by ignoring a law, you may be kidding yourself. Be triple careful. If noncompliance creates safety hazards for employees or some level of risk to your customers, don't break the law, just don't, or your mom (and millions of others) will watch you sweat on *60 Minutes*.

CHAPTER 47

THE TURNAROUND NEVER ENDS

I t's called "the dead cat bounce." Something rises. Not for long.

A good friend and great turnaround guy jumped into a wheel business. This outfit, an industry leader, never made real money. Losses one year, profits the next, averaging out to break-even over time with reasonable revenue growth but nothing to benefit the shareholders.

It took a year of $10 million in losses on $40 million of sales to jar the board into action. Craig took over.

He managed to generate about $15 million in profits over the next two years and pay back the owners their entire investment, something they'd not tasted or imagined in the prior fifteen years. Everybody's happy.

The third year this business lost $8 million and, being leveraged, defaulted on their loan covenants. My friend left.

The wisdom of hindsight suggests that the wheel business is a fashion business. Changes in metal technology swung away from the core business. And, there's always this problem of a turnaround guy staying too long and either rechanging the changes, needed or not, or moderating into a more disciplined mode which drives any agent of dramatic change nuts.

Craig Crisman's tales of Dynamark and Applied Magnetics also prove that if anything is smarter than a timely departure, it's coupling that to a new CEO to finish the package and then sell the business. Fundamentals change. Reinventing the business is risky.

Sometimes the momentum was real, but the participants celebrated prematurely. Or perhaps the turnaround manager overstayed, and continued changing things until that soaring business once again went into a power dive and was five feet off the ground.

When things go wrong the second time it's tougher to reassemble the spirit, unscramble the egg, or squeeze the toothpaste back into the tube. The second wind isn't there.

This happens more often than not. Once the fire is put out, stop spraying water. After the dent is pounded smooth, don't hammer the fender again. Now that you've removed the infected appendix, stop cutting.

Can you name a legendary coach who retired with a winning season? See the problem?

Once the losses stop, you've got to have the guts to change again. How? First remove the turnaround manager who fixed it. That's easy. Next replace with someone whose personality fits smaller changes, dialing in a click at a time instead of smashing the lock, doing a hundred things a little better instead of changing two or three things completely.

You'll have a tough time doing this.

The fix was a relief.

Editors call. Nobody asks investors for another check. No more threats from the bank. Vendors laugh at your jokes again. Employees feel there's a future. (Wrong. Nobody floats for long at break-even. Water is made of waves. You're rising or sinking.)

Changing the CEO when losses blossom is easy. Switching leaders when results have rebounded takes confidence. Think of the saved organizations that couldn't maintain the rebound. Penn Central. Chrysler. IBM. Montgomery Ward. Japan. Germany.

Any church except the Mormons. (Two years of compulsory recruiting, tithing, and the promise of rewards in the hereafter create a multilevel marketing deal for them that brings tears to Amway eyes.)

Okay, so this is bad news. Once you've turned the corner it's only the beginning, and needs yet another change at the top. Too bad. If you want a feel-good, easy book, go grab *The Sixty-Minute Manager* or one of the *Chicken Soup* books.

Victory is for the day, not tomorrow, and the same enemies are gathering to attack again. Your opponents are the same evil gang. Markets are changing. New competitors. Internal desires are now for a long nap. Belief that things are okay without understanding nothing stays the same, and the formulas that just saved you don't have a prayer of elevating you beyond subsistence.

This chapter is merely a reminder. A wakeup call. Don't get so pumped up as you manage the comeback that you forget to pace yourself.

Chapter 68 holds everything you need to convert this quick victory into a trend. No. Stop it. Don't jump ahead, just keep this primal fact in mind while you work through the rest of the turnaround chapters.

Then read the italicized sections, leading up to Chapter 68. That maintains it.

Until you've fixed cash flow, it's one step at a time.

CHAPTER 48

HOW IT FEELS

"**M**ilo, you know that talk we had about shutting down your department? I'm afraid it's time."

He got misty-eyed. We went through the numbers together. Milo wasn't a star performer or a poor performer but a good, shows-up-on-time-and-cares kind of employee that you need to treat fairly.

"How much time, Gary?"

"No reason to wait. If we know we're closing, we're being phony when we smile at our workers in the hallway. Let's go do it now." We did.

Milo deserved some help finding a job. I sent a few dozen letters and he missed one paycheck but landed a position twenty minutes closer to his home at comparable pay. The problem was that this new company had some problems, and didn't seem to be able to work around them.

Milo arranged that his new employer call me a year later. We visited. They recruited me to take it over, but I was trapped in the prior business, trying to wind down shareholder litigation. But it gratified, having a laid-off employee trying to recruit me to lead his next employer. And other laid-off employees, perhaps a fourth of them, returned to our company picnic for a couple of summers.

If you want to be a turnaround manager, the surprise is that you're a novelty, but not feared. If you want to scare people, become a minister or a cop or a parole officer. Hey, dentistry pays well.

There are two things about your upcoming life you need to know.

First is travel. The chances of finding a troubled business in your neighborhood, and the owners accepting you as a professional, are poor. You're required to come from a distance to be an expert. Not time zones away, although that does help, but as long as they haven't seen you in the supermarket struggling to figure out how to tear off those plastic bags in the produce section, well, then, you bring an air of competence that's needed. So the farther you travel, the higher your fees.

Second is the personality distortion risk. This isn't quite as bad as being a physician, with everybody looking at you with hopeful expressions. MD means My Deity. It's not nearly as artificial as a surgeon, where your power is so exalted that clients are certain that bathroom acts are somehow handled remotely for you. Your situation is nearly as bad as a purchasing agent's, where every suit walking through the door smiles broadly, asks about your kids by name, if you drop your guard for a moment, and could you find time for lunch?

What you must do, to avoid believing any of this is real, or to reduce the risk of suspecting 5% of it might approach a true evaluation of you as a person, is to spend equal time with customers and creditors.

Ahh! Now we understand what scumsuckers we truly are.

Now, even these folks will be gentler than they should, since you're the second person in the chair and not the one who caused the problem. Or, at least, not the one in the chair when the problem ignited. Same difference.

You can never care about the business. Only the money matters.

Yes, you are there to save it. But you cannot care. You won't be staying, so enjoy the people who turn out to be the pillars of the business, spend time developing them but don't get attached. You're leaving too soon. This jades you. Turns you into an asshole if you don't watch it.

And don't try to clone yourself with the replacement. You don't get to make that decision anyway, but if your compensation is proper, you'll benefit as much as anybody by finding the best, next leader. Don't trust yourself to do that well. There's self-worth involved, and the best of us sometimes enjoy seeing an operation wobble and fall after our irreplaceable self-absorbed charisma departs.

Ego beats the pocketbook.

To beat down that human tendency, remind yourself of its truth. Know that with time, your heritage is measured by others who possess more objectivity, and these temptations to prove only you could handle the situation becomes recorded in time as an unmanageable ego, one whose need to be superior makes you inferior.

Be outrageous to suckups. Humiliate them. Battle and enjoy those who challenge you. Do all this to encourage opinions. Then, and with supreme confidence, gather all managers together to announce decisions you make after hearing everybody and acknowledge the minority arguments . . . you are the sole majority . . . and ask all to support you in the directions chosen.

Dictatorship fails. Democracy fails. Leadership triumphs, and is more possible, ironically, in a trauma than in fat and happy moments.

If you're worried about how employees will greet you as a turnaround manager, stepping in to determine their fates, then don't even attempt one. You haven't the stomach. And, in the ultimate irony, the receptions are normally quite good. This doesn't matter; if you worry about that, you just aren't suitable. Do something else.

Those folks who will be best at turnarounds didn't finish this chapter. They could care less. Their confidence carries them. That works.

CHAPTER 49

DRESSING UP THE STIFF

The ultimate payback on a turnaround is an immediate sale.

Everybody loves that.

The shareholders and board fracture their wrists, trying to pat every square inch of their backs. Instead of watching the successes continue, which, if you think about it, reflects poorly on their prior efforts, they can legitimately celebrate their part of the victory if you sell at a nice profit. And they get financially rewarded. And many feel relief, since they don't believe the turnaround is real.

The new CEO celebrates, although his/her career may not blossom much further at this place, but if you recruited smartly the package accelerates the CEO's options upon change in control. That means the "permanent" CEO supports or may even have found the acquirer. The CEO's payback on time spent is terrific.

And you, sly devil, have made an immodest gain for boosting results quick. Do this a few times and start to realize how it compounds over time; when you do a sequence of turnarounds, geez, why would you ever take a conventional job or slave away at a startup, waiting decades for payback? Get real.

So, while pretending that we all want to hold onto this resurrected jewel forever, since that stance magnifies value, let's also talk boldly but quietly how we quickly unload the turkey before somebody discovers the bird doesn't fly that well.

(Others may more graciously talk about win-wins, and that's great when you spot one, but this focuses on a win. Period. For the shareholders. New owners beware.)

To weave the fabric, we'll trace through each of my sales. Some were significant investments. Others were acquisitions. But the interesting thing is that the process is the same.

Quaker Oats bought Fisher-Price Toys. Good move. Solid products with a great franchise. Fisher-Price Toys became a customer of our startup. We ended up developing an audiovisual category that became more and more critical to Fisher-Price Toys, a company that tended to develop everything internally. When they awakened one day and discovered that of their 130 items, we produced three of their top five sellers, it became time to talk marriage. They couldn't stand it.

Of course they couldn't acquire the spirit that created this, or own the intensity that made this happen, but that's the beauty of our system. Let the fat boys get fatter, do stuff they can't, bob and weave around and through them until they have to buy you. Yes, they'll screw up your concepts, but you'll be doing something else so it doesn't matter.

Anyway, we sold to Fisher-Price Toys and they did well with our stuff. But we licensed it to their competitors in Latin America, Southern Europe, Northern Europe, and Japan. I make those geographic distinctions since we set up a licensee in each. And those folks each did just fine, sending us a 7½% royalty check from their gross sales. (No, you can't trust them, so we designed one key part, an extremely small part but one that's difficult to tool, that we shipped them. They made the rest. But that critical part became a far more reliable audit tool than any accounting methods. And, just to make sure they didn't make the part themselves, we put a small blemish on one surface and I traveled to their markets and bought lots of toys every year and ripped them apart, checking out the parts to make sure we were the exclusive supplier of this little subassembly.)

Well, the interesting thing about the toy business was that you had to bet the company every year. And we did pretty well, with one exception. Fisher-Price Toys boomed, with average talent being swept along by a superb philosophy of good value, which happened to be unusual in that industry. So it worked.

Problem was, our client wasn't keeping up with the discipline required, and one day called and cancelled all orders for a year. It seems that in their mad scramble to add warehouses, they had one which wasn't on their IT system, and this particular one was where they were shelving all our shipments. So our magnificent annual sales growth was an illusion, merely a good rate, and they had product coming out their ears.

Of course, we had orders for more. And their ability to cancel was debatable. In a court, it would be a David vs. Goliath thing so we had some leverage.

Our company also had year after year's evidence of Fisher-Price's failure to sell our stuff to either Sears or Kmart or Penney's. After they failed for 90 days, we always had the right to sell them directly, and we did. Year after year. (This was way back when Kmart was viewed as a phenomenon, actually threatening to overtake Sears. Sam Walton was unknown.)

So the obvious solution was for Quaker Oats, the ultimate parent and awash in cash, to make a reasonable acquisition offer and settle the potential dispute amicably.

At Toy Fair that year, we made the rounds of possible suitors. Mattel's CEO, Ray Wagner, stopped in the lobby to talk, and seemed friendly and enthused as he explained to John Belden, our President, and myself why he couldn't consider an acquisition at this moment.

No problem. In fact, in one of those impossible-to-plan moments, Henry Coordes, the President of Fisher-Price Toys, happened to walk past as we talked with Wagner. Henry couldn't hear what was being said, good thing, but noticed Ray's head bobbing up and down with apparent enthusiasm as we talked and pumped hands as we left.

No investment bank in the world could boost value as much as that incident.

And two days later we had a similar moment while talking with Seymour Gartenberg, the CEO of Creative Playthings, a CBS subsidiary.

Days later Bob Stuart flew out from Chicago to visit. Bob was Chairman of Quaker Oats. An amiable guy, he visited, we demonstrated our stuff, and I drove him up to San Francisco where he was to meet Caspar Weinberger to recruit him for the Quaker board. I was the VP Marketing at our shop.

Our offices were in Mountain View. We had lunch at Chez Yvonne, a doubly decent place in Palo Alto. As was our habit for special occasions, we ordered a bottle of wine with the meal.

Bob Stuart, Quaker Oatmeal man that he was, nearly wearing a three-cornered hat, paled when the waiter popped the cork. We ate. The fish was nicely poached. He didn't touch his wine. I guzzled. When I noticed his full glass, I asked if he was going to drink it, he said not, so I asked if I could have it, he hesitated, nodded, I grabbed his glass and sucked it dry.

And, having consumed more alcohol before the sun began to tilt than is appropriate, I weaved through traffic on the 101 and dropped him at the city.

They bought us and paid a premium.

Now, you might be thinking that the lunch was the perfectly wrong way to behave at such a moment, and you would be perfectly wrong.

There were two factors at play here. First was that all large corporations screw up acquisitions, and the brighter you look to them the less likely they are to buy you. If you appear a little overwhelmed by your exploding business, or somewhat disoriented and not up to the task, their MBAs and staffers, who have never met a payroll, or more importantly have never missed a payroll, will roll their eyes and begin to imagine how much better things will be under their superior management. So looking too bright costs you money.

Second was the delight they took in having some entrepreneurial characters to spice up their organizational charts. This was in theory, of course, and it never lasted but it worked to close the deal. Quaker Oats thought I was trainable, asked me to move to Chicago and work alongside a board member's son at a subsidiary. Insiders whispered this was a fast ticket to the top of Quaker, but my read of the lad was that there were brighter blades in any drawer, and a fast ticket to the top of an oatmeal company didn't speed my breathing up that much. Next was the General Manager job for Canada, a slot that could've been fun but it was too close to Buffalo, Fisher-Price Toys headquarters. Several people visited daily, suggesting a level of control that might precipitate my coronary. Finally was the offer to take over a food business Quaker bought in Colombia, a country even then associated with foodstuffs that had more to do with pulse rates and hallucinations than nutrition, and drug lords who spit on judges. Sorry.

So the point is to not play their game, but be the wild card. It helps in a couple of ways. If they want to buy you, they'll rationalize your misfit personality as a needed accent for their blander management. They'll believe that their superior vision will accelerate your inspired but unsophisticated efforts further than you could have imagined. Maybe they'll be straighter about it, with themselves and you, and suggest you leave as part of the takeover. This is best. Saves you both the irritation of pretending to get along, all so briefly.

And they'll pay too much. This is the objective. Get them to pay too much. Don't start with that win-win stuff, please.

So they did.

Now that was the first time I'd been bought, and I was a bit player. But it was two lessons well learned.

Lesson one is to not beat your chest and brag about how you've done a Superman job. Let the business's numbers do the talking and allow the buyer to make their own projections.

Lesson two is to work hard at it. Those two hallway incidents, where our main partner, Fisher-Price Toys, thought they saw competitors wooing us, made the deal happen. Nothing makes the restaurant's food taste better than a long line at the door. The fact that both the apparent suitors were turning us down didn't matter, it looked like they were chasing us. And the bigger fact is that both these resulted from our working hard to find a buyer. We had dozens of other talks, none productive, at this Toy Fair because we had tired investors and needed to sell.

Our shareholders didn't want to experience another cycle.

It wasn't serendipitous that we were seen talking with two potential buyers. This was merely the result of hustling a lot of possibilities. If not those two hallway incidents, there inevitably would have been others.

It's a selling process. He who makes more calls wins.

Next was the printing group we started. I was CEO and had big options in the business. They didn't accelerate upon change of control, silly me, a move that cost me a bunch and delivered one lesson never to be forgotten.

The parent company, Intermark, already owned Arts & Crafts Press. They bought Franklin Press, which I took over and ran. We acquired Graphic Arts Center and consolidated financials for all three and later acquired Rush Press.

This pushed sales from an $8 million start with $300K net to just over $100 million and a net of $8 million in six years. The internal operating profit growth each year averaged about 30% while the overall grew at over a 75% annual rate. But we were so leveraged that one year might show a 200% boost while the next year would be a 50% decline. Keep those antacid tablets close by, please.

We nearly did an IPO, but Graphic Arts Center took a dive, so I scurried up, bid farewell to the CEO, and took operating control myself. We restored profits and doubled the prior profit record within the year and succumbed to an acquisition offer.

The acquiring company, Continental Graphics, was publicly held. So buying our earnings growth made theirs look even better. Our acquisitions were generally made in the middle of the year. This created an interesting stairstep effect on profit growth, with half of the boost coming in the first full year and all in the second. So just keep buying reasonably and the results seem to point to the sky.

Bear Stearns and Smith Barney each bid on the fairness opinion. The price was to be 32× our projected next-year earnings. That was, in fact, what the deal closed for. Bear Stearns wanted $280K for the opinion. Smith Barney asked for less, bidding $250K. The acquiring company went for the higher bid, since, in their chairman's words, "We're paying the highest premium this industry has seen, and if some shareholders sue to stop, I want that older banker on the witness stand instead of the kid."

This gives you a peek at how fairness opinions work.

Much of the allure was Wall Street's belief that US Press was on the cutting edge of graphic arts.

We helped the investment community arrive at that conclusion. The sales rates helped, of course. But the story behind it was an emphasis on growth areas. We did very little black and white. Our presentation showed how the world progressed to color. This included pointing out how few white shirts or black ties were in the room, while twenty years before they would have dominated. This meant pointing out, most briefly, the Henry Ford "any color as long as it's black" and the later Head Ski identical story while both were overwhelmed by color models from competitors. It mentioned the disappearance of black phones and asked if they slept on white sheets. Then we mentioned with surprise that our toothpaste that morning even squeezed out in color.

Cute. Compelling. But to buttress the examples, we then gave hard data about the long-term sales rates of pigments, proving the world's drumbeat, moving from blacks and whites to colors.

That made our first point.

Our second was sheer quality. So we talked about 45-rpm records going to hi-fi to stereo to CDs, and the shift from Dairy Queen to Baskin-Robbins and Häagen-Dazs, while cotton went from oxford weaves to tighter thread counts.

And the third point went to the categories we drove the businesses into, which were direct-mail printing, annual reports, and software manuals.

It made US Press a jewel. That's why we got a 32× valuation against projected earnings, at a time the industry was valued at 12× current earnings.

Were we unique?

Hardly. There must have been 200 other printers across the country who could have made the same presentation and proven that they were doing the same thing, many even further into it.

But none did. We got the value.

So take two more lessons from that. First, it pays to manage your earnings, without upsetting the fundamental business. In this case, our year-to-year numbers grew terrifically on average, but not smoothly enough for public investors. But they tucked nicely into a larger printing group quite well, where their effect was smoothed, and that acquirer could recoup the premium with a better story to their larger audience. Second, create a story. Make your business unique. And don't hesitate to build it around the place you intend to be instead of where you are. When shooting ducks, you always aim ahead of them. Same for positioning your company. It helps get you there faster.

A turnaround and sale of Checks To-Go came next. The turnaround took two months. (Sometimes the planets line up.) The sale took just over a year.

We talked to a few investment bankers. This business was too small, and it was a unique story, not the kind of thing any banker does well. So I hired our CPA's merger group, spoon-fed them the most likely competitors to acquire us, and drafted the offering letter.

Out of four possible partners, RapidForms of New Jersey, showed interest. Moore, Deluxe, and NEBs didn't respond. Bad. You never want one buyer.

So we talked, but suggested that a marriage in the future probably made sense, and went back to boosting our results. This, of course, increased RapidForms' interest. And out of the blue, Rocky Mountain Banknote called expressing interest. Perhaps it was out of the blue, more likely our aggression and growth caught somebody's interest and/or perhaps it was the activity with RapidForms.

So we invited Rocky Mountain Banknote out for a visit. And RapidForms the week after.

This made it possible to tell Rocky Mountain Banknote that a second bidder was coming in soon after them. We got their offer the following week, just as RapidForms called to cancel their visit.

It was a great price for the Checks To-Go shareholders and myself, and sad to say it didn't work out at all for Rocky Mountain Banknote.

The lessons here are: Work at it but not too hard, and expect the unexpected. If RapidForms visited when they first wanted to, we probably would have been looking at a pretty cheap offer, since there were no competitors. Luckily, Rocky Mountain Banknote knew RapidForms was visiting; I felt no obligation to update them when RapidForms cancelled and the deal happened at a good number.

Smiley Industries was next. Another quick turnaround, this one reversed itself in six months. We received an unsolicited probe from Precision Aerotech, a publicly traded parts manufacturer. I hired a broker to spin off the low-margin contracts and equipment, we got some decent money for that and, more important, an enhanced valuation on the rest since it was cleaner, a pure play.

The lesson here? In a schizoid business, break off and sell the parts. They add up to more than the whole.

Knight Protective sold to Protection One, an aggressive roll-up of burglar alarm accounts funded by Patricof Partners and Morgan Stanley. It took six months to shift Knight from four years of steep losses into positive cash flows. It took four more years to sell it. Details in Chapter 7, but the delay couldn't be beaten, major shareholders were in litigation.

Nobody wants to buy a lawsuit.

So as luck would have it, just as the suits began to settle, Protection One went public and raised lots of money dedicated to acquisitions. And over half of our accounts were scattered across California, where Protection One concentrated. (Less than half were scattered across 32 other states, making them more costly to serve than they were worth . . . that's another tragic story . . . and we had serious, debilitating product flaws . . . neither of these problems are problems, however, when you have an acquirer in heat.)

We had discussed the inevitability of this a year before, when Protection One had little money and Knight had lots of lawyers lurking. When the moment came, I hired ProFinance, an investment banking firm that specialized in the alarm industry.

ProFinance agreed that I had probably presold the business to Protection One, so we struck a commission deal that paid only half if that happened, but paid a full fee if anyone else acquired Knight. This paid ProFinance for presumably raising the price if Protection One acquired, by bringing other candidates. And the full fee was earned only for one of those others, so we could bet they'd waltz through.

Twelve did.

None made offers, by the way, and only two came back for a second visit. But Protection One heard about the visits. We had so many sniffing that my confidence showed.

For full disclosure, I let Protection One know about ProFinance's deal. Protection One wanted this acquisition so bad, they offered to pay the rest of ProFinance's fee so the bankers wouldn't try to urge us to take other deals.

There was an outfit in Chicago that was not only acquiring burglar alarm companies, it was just beginning to make inquiries on the West Coast. This move would threaten Protection One's franchise. Unfortunately, we could never quite get the Midwesterners to visit. So halfway through the process I flew to see them in Chicago. They cancelled. I had an advance excursion fare; we were gushing cash but still watching expenses, so I went to Chicago anyway. I did some work in my hotel room. I had dinner with a college buddy. I returned a couple of Protection One's calls, so they could see my 312 area code on the return number.

This drove them nuts.

We sold for 42 times monthly revenues. This was a record high for that time. Despite accounts scattered across thirty states, equipment that failed frequently and required way too much service, this was a high-water mark for the industry.

The lesson learned here is that there are moments that resonate in your favor, when the strategic fit is great and the cash is heavy on the other side.

At those times, it is your sacred duty to fan the flames, tease, pull away briefly, wink, and close for a premium price.

Timing is everything.

Since Knight recovered in my first year, my tenure wasn't stressful. I wrote a book. I cofounded Teledesic.

Now Teledesic wasn't a turnaround, but it was a ridiculously ambitious financing concept, so there's another lesson within it.

We got a first commitment from the Kinship Fund, a Midwest VC fund that liked Ed Tuck, the conceiver, ever since they invested in a prior idea he had named Magellan. That earlier effort was the first shirt-pocket GPS unit, and did quite well.

Ed's backer's money was contingent upon getting someone in the telecom world to also invest. So I called my classmate Craig McCaw, who was just then making bold moves out of cable TV and into this new thing called cellular phones.

Craig's guts, brains, and pocketbook seemed the perfect fit. He bugged me earlier for grand ideas and I'd never really come up with one, but Teledesic seemed perfect. So I called.

Craig agreed to meet Ed and me at the Beverly Wilshire where he would be attending Drexel Burnham's annual meeting, known to the media as the Predator's Ball.

Ed and I got all excited. We put together some budgets and slides. I drove up to Ed's office and we assembled the pitch.

"Craig McCaw's office called, Gary," a secretary said. Ed and I looked at each other. We were scheduled to meet Craig in two hours.

"We're not returning that call," I said. We packed up, drove Freeway 10 into the city, and hustled up the steps of the aging but grand hotel.

Craig spotted me in the lobby. The color drained from his face.

"Didn't you talk with my office?" he asked.

"No," I replied.

His eyes scanned the room. He stepped over to another banker, whispered something, and returned.

"I've just rearranged a meeting, let's go to my room and see if we can cover this in fifteen minutes."

We did just that. Except Craig drew it out to an hour. And talk about bright—three of his questions showed depth beyond mine, and I'd been studying the area.

"That's a long ways to transmit from a handheld receiver," he said. "How do you keep from frying everybody's brains?"

We stammered around a bit and promised to get some studies back to him.

"There were 18 fax machines in all of China just before the Tiananmen Square massacre last year. All 18 went dark the next day," Craig continued. "How do you expect countries like Bulgaria to receive your satellites flying over and beaming messages into their territories?"

There was something we hadn't thought of yet.

"What launch costs per pound are you budgeting for the satellites?" he asked.

Hey, one we knew, our budget assumed costs could hit $2,000 per pound, an aggressive figure, within ten years when the first birds launched. But it was a question nobody else had thought of to ask.

Now, there's a point here that applies to all financings and sales of businesses. This is a sales process. You cannot be timid. Making lots of calls, and making every call count, matters.

Within ten years Teledesic received $750 million from Motorola for a 26% share of the equity, following on the heels of AT&T's investment, Bill Gates, Boeing, the Crown Prince of Saudi Arabia, and others. On that day, in the Beverly Wilshire, Ed and I were hoping for $2 million in seed money.

In weeks we got it.

But if we had returned Craig's call, Teledesic would have never happened.

Sell hard.

My last example is financing again, not a sale of the entire business, but the principle's the same.

SkyDesk's first round came from three venture capitalists. The lead required that we get half from others. One fund acted interested, dragged, reengaged, asked a consultant for an opinion, met again, hired a second consultant, and dropped us. The first investor, seeing this, got edgy. Luckily another fund stepped up and closed fast, only after I looked them in the eye and said, "Listen, I've never lost money for an investor yet, and I don't intend to start with you."

"That's what I've been waiting to hear, Gary, we're in," he said.

Two quick lessons right there. First, don't keep pushing investors who are wavering. Pushing only makes them more nervous. They've got to come around of their own momentum after a couple of meetings. Second, don't hesitate to push hard after you've told them all they need to know. If you don't believe in the business, why should they? This is more relevant to financings than acquisitions. If they're investing in you, they need to see some fire. If they're buying your business, they need to see you reacting with cool.

Our next round came from a huge financial institution.

The first meeting was typical of a middle-management bully. In front of staff, he announced that they intended to create our service, and their only question was whether this would be with or without us.

This outfit seemed to have some natural fits mixed with too much bureaucracy, but on balance, we thought the credibility their money brought should be worth it.

They committed a bunch of money to market research, did some development with us, and had an option to buy shares at the end of a year. Their research underwhelmed them. They began objecting to some patent issues which were clearly conservative positions to the extreme. They asked for an extension on the option period. And, as part of the deal, they knew our monthly cash position and we were running out.

A prominent investment bank in New York asked to put in some private money.

We agreed.

They asked to talk to our partner, the institution. I prepared the institution for their call. The bankers couldn't run away fast enough afterward. So I flew to New York City and cried foul. Their attorneys agreed that they would close the financing.

Did this reputable outfit consciously drag their heels, raise bogus issues, wait until our cash dried up, and intentionally scare off another potential investor so they could buy us at any price?

I think not.

When you're dealing with any big corporation, each manager is incentivized to get a scalp or two, and I doubt that there was any overall scheme like that, simply because the liability is too great.

The lesson here: Don't let big companies bully you. They're more vulnerable than they are big. Their middle managers don't get that, but the uppers do, so when the middle overdoes it, jerk their chain.

Let's reflect a moment: We're talking about selling the business. In this last case, however, we're talking about a series of financings for a startup. It's all the same. With financings, you're merely selling the company a little bit at a time, showing progress as a business each step of the way, making the stock worth more with each round.

So about two hours after this institution invested, we started preparing for the next round. Sales take time when the price is fair. Only cheap sales happen fast. So the time to start is always now. Keep the business progressing or you won't have any luck at all, you'll just need to juggle both efforts.

At this stage, our earlier investors said that they were seeing a lot of eastern financial institutions showing an appetite for technology deals on the left coast, so we started hitting New York.

Months passed with only polite interest.

Our institutional investor suggested we try a company called CUC. Forbes just named them the largest Internet company in the country, so I mailed a copy of my earlier book to their CEO, suggesting we talk.

A book gets that letter past the secretary. You don't think I write these for the benefit of the literary world, do you?

He telephoned two days later, and set up an appointment with his acquisition team. I met them alone for one hour. We met a second time with our CFO for an hour. They offered us $4 to $6 million, and said somebody else should lead and set the price. We found a local investor with $700,000 who set the price at a noticeable step up in valuation, and closed that round.

CUC meanwhile merged with HFS, forming Cendant. Accounting fraud was uncovered, and their stock tanked. Everybody we dealt with was fired. I met our main contact a few months later.

"Boy, our CEO sure loved you," he said. We were walking the sidewalks of Stamford, Connecticut, headed for a pizza joint.

"Maybe I'll meet him someday," I replied.

"What?" he asked. He stopped walking and stared.

I repeated my comment.

"B-but you and he spent a whole day at his ranch," he said.

"Not me," I replied.

My contact became strangely silent, I didn't pursue it, but am convinced that the reason we got so much money so easily and so fast, on such favorable terms, was a case of mistaken identity. The CEO, whom I never met, encouraged his investment team to move fast with somebody whose name sounded like mine.

I can't prove that. But I'd bet on it.

We had something like $12 million in our bank account at that point, and began work on the next round. It seemed then that we needed more strategic partners. American Express, one of our investors, provided a list, including a few we didn't know.

There were three categories of potential investors. Telcos, data storage companies, and Internet service providers.

Now when I say strategic, recognize that like mergers, most of these alliances don't work. American Express found that their small business customer base were late adopters, so didn't take up our online back-up service with any noticeable success.

Cendant intended to market our service as another Internet offering, but the CUC claims to Internet dominance proved to come from their online auto sales service. They received something like a dollar or two for each transaction, but used the price of the entire car to build their claim of revenues. Hmm.

HFS, however, the other side of Cendant, eagerly planned to put our back-up service into their franchisees Howard Johnson, Ramada Inns, etc., which seemed truly a natural. They discovered the franchisees wanted no part of the franchisor near their data. That, and the colossal financial meltdown at Cendant, killed those prospects.

So always look at strategic investors or acquirers with hope, but recognize that the presumed fit may be more of a rationalization to invest than anything that will bear fruit as planned.

Telcos seemed a natural for the service, since we might round out their offering of services to small businesses. SkyDesk could be the missing piece of their puzzle. Online backup of data looked like a fit, using their lines at night when they're less busy.

Storage companies seemed a fit since we did the same thing, they with boxes and dedicated lines for big companies, and we over the Internet for smaller business, which is growing faster. We could be the parsley on their plate, enhancing their perceived value to investors. Makes a futuristic story for them.

Internet service providers were suffering from churn, and it seemed that bundling our service might keep customers from changing so often. We might add stickiness to their service.

It took about ten months, but two leading storage companies led this round, one a tape company and one a disc company, both public outfits and both glamorous, but neither having an Internet story. Until they invested in us.

We approached all the storage outfits the same way. I mailed the chairman of every storage company in the country a pound of parsley. A calligraphy note inside mentioned that we could become the parsley on their plate, making them far more attractive to investors. The result was $20 million of new money, from two industry leaders whose stock shot up afterward.

(We did the same to the telcos, mailing the chairman a puzzle piece, suggesting we were their missing feature. We likewise mailed all ISP chairmen, enclosing a superglue stick, talking about stickiness with our service. Obviously, the storage folks were more interested. Everybody responded, by the way, so sometimes getting attention is half the battle, and enclosing an item to get onto the chairman's desk doesn't hurt.)

From there, we headed toward the IPO.

A foreign investor called, unsolicited, asking to invest. We declined, explaining the IPO process required all our efforts, and we couldn't take time for diversions. This outfit was a high-flyer, listed by leading business publications as one of the world's top twenty-five tech outfits. Finally we relented, allowing them in at four times the prior price, in a round that brought in another $20 million of unneeded cash prior to the IPO. A couple of directors questioned whether we should accept the money. Management's stance was that when the geese cackle, you feed them, tomorrow's uncertain. Sure enough, the IPO market then died. But we had a pile of cash.

Anytime you're selling a company, be it an acquisition or a financing, the principals remain the same:

1. Position the business in ways that fit the acquirer's needs. Forget your own. Make it memorable without being too hokey. The parsley came close to excess, but made a memorable point. Ultimately, these decisions are approved by somebody totally unfamiliar with the deal; a parsley reminder can sway enough board votes to close the deal.

2. Some theatrics are required. There's nothing worse than having a single buyer. Two interested buyers are ten times as good. So create a bidding atmosphere, even if it's marginal. Going to Chicago to meet that other buyer, whether they want to see you or not, pays. Keeps the acquirer honest. No matter how smooth the deal is moving, remember, at the last moment, your acquirer has a fiscal obligation to beat down your price. Respect your buyers. Presume they're responsible. Therefore they must find last-minute reasons to toughen terms or drop price. With a second bidder, they'll be less aggressive.

3. Nothing substitutes for making more calls. This holds true for every sales process in the world, and selling a business is no different. But never let them see you sweat. The pursuit must seem to come unsolicited and be spontaneous. In one of the financing rounds, I crossed the United States, from Pacific City to Atlantic City, six times in one week. This, by the way, was a restful week, with all that airplane time isolating me from telephones. There's no substitute for hustle.

CHAPTER 50

PROMOTE OFFBEAT THINKING

O kay, my grade point average was 2.06. Since it took a 2.00 to get out of college, I viewed that as .06 of wasted effort. When I graduated in 1964 from Iowa State, I was not hotly pursued. Lennox hired me, and there was a quality to that outfit that taught me more than any institution before or since. Lennox was headquartered in Marshalltown, Iowa, about an hour of bean fields northeast of Des Moines. When I interviewed there, I stayed at the Hotel Tallcorn.

Lennox made furnaces. You bend some metal, weld it, wire it, and put some controls and a fan in it. That's all. No high tech, just solid manufacturing.

The workers at the Marshalltown factory, like those at the other two Lennox factories, did the job with less fuss than competitors in other parts of the country.

Every executive worked his or her way up. When I first started, I spent several weeks with a dealer. I knelt in spidery crawl spaces and climbed through cluttered basements. I was changing filters, lubricating pulleys, and installing sheet metal. I was dirty.

Then I did a stint on the draft table designing ductwork and layouts. I also learned how to calculate heating and cooling requirements.

This was real stuff! There were no junk-bond plays, no strategic analysis. Lennox was surrounded in reality and making money. This was American business surrounded by farms, an American Gothic company.

But that didn't mean it was slow. That year, Lennox invented the Direct Multizone System, a rooftop system that could heat 16 rooms individually.

It made flexible classrooms with movable walls possible so schools could transform with the changing enrollments and curricula.

They also invented a heat exchanger that didn't stress the metal and therefore didn't make those familiar annoying ticking noises.

These things happened because creative thinking was pursued, almost worshipped, in an environment that never got dreamy or out of touch.

They were always looking for a better way to do things, while continuing to do them.

Lennox also observed the effects of spray cans about 25 years before anybody thought about fluorocarbons. Their technicians noticed heat exchangers in beauty shops were corroding in years instead of decades, so Lennox developed a ceramic cover that protected the metal.

They were always looking for a better way to do things, while continuing to do them. This spread into marketing. Forrest Locey, the Columbus, Ohio, sales manager, discovered the industry's most economical way to sell air-conditioning. Roses.

It was the 1960s and every woman was a housewife, and every house in a neighborhood was occupied during the day. The marketing plan was this: Every time someone in Columbus bought a Lennox air conditioner, a florist delivered a vase to that customer on the day of installation. Then every day for the next five days the florist came and delivered another single rose.

Locey reasoned, and he was right, that by the sixth day the whole neighborhood would go crazy trying to figure it out. On that day, the florist delivered another rose in a vase to each of six adjoining homes in the neighborhood, two to each side and one in front and back. Each rose was accompanied by a simple Lennox card and a note about the pleasures of air-conditioned comfort.

Normally, a neighborhood sale followed within a week. Total cost: 11 roses that were volume-priced because deliveries were scheduled all over town every day.

John Norris, the president of Lennox, praised Locey publicly for being an original thinker and told the roses story to audiences with pride.

Twenty years later, his son, an MIT grad and later CEO, began pursuing a dicey technology that General Electric had but wasn't developing. The technology was called pulse combustion. It carefully controlled ignition so the expansion during combustion expelled the exhaust and almost all the heat could be wrung out of it. (Every conventional furnace puts about 30% of the heat out the chimney and into the atmosphere to carry the gases up and outside.) Waste was practically eliminated with pulse combustion, and pollution was slashed. The furnace cost more, but customers realized a payback in lower fuel bills.

Offbeat thinking gave Lennox a superior product, a commanding market position, lower fuel bills to customers, and cleaner air. In the stodgy old furnace business, yet.

Here's how to loosen thinking without going nuts:

1. Make sure every manager does some dirty field work. Handle customer complaints. Do a service call. Don't have planners. Let those who live with the plans make the plans. Make the sales crew spend time in the lab, and get the scientists out to meet customers. Transfer people between departments to keep walls from forming.
2. Once employees understand practical things, encourage unconventional thinking. Require managers to come up with better ways. Celebrate innovation: Write about it in the company newsletter, make half the stories about failures, and be sure to applaud those attempts.
3. Enhance this grounded attitude with outside ideas. Use your CPA firm to streamline your accounting. License ideas from others. Let the bank do your pension and payroll. Use reps instead of your own sales force. This outside contact brings in fresh air.

CHAPTER 51

CASH MAKES YOU STUPID

A cucorp started in 1989. It showed profits within the second year. By 1992, its sales passed $4 million. Dr. Pamela Coker, the founder and CEO of Acucorp, says part of the secret was remembering that cash makes you stupid and remaining tight, not getting giddy when the bank balance started to grow.

Their main product interacts with more than 500 other software platforms. Acucorp's business is built around COBOL, the most common software language in the world, yet the least trendy. All the competitors work on products directed at the newer languages, despite the fact that COBOL dominates the primary users. That's Acucorp's differentiation. You can make money zigging when the world zags.

"We make a profit every month," Coker explained one time. "And the funniest thing happens when you make a profit every month. You end up making a profit every year."

In the main office area, there is a large chart that is one of the most popular spots in the whole place. It's like the watercooler, only it means something. The chart, posted daily, shows cash collections for that day. It is looked at, checked, and talked about. So everybody gets what's important.

Receivables are viewed as nothing more than test market expenses until they are paid. There is no sale assumed, no customer satisfaction believed, and no commission paid until the money arrives.

Collecting for those sales fast at Acucobol serves two functions. It gets cash in the bank and it uncovers problems quicker. Aggressive collections work, and everyone, especially sales, gets involved.

In October 1992, Coker was having trouble collecting from her German distributor. She scheduled a conference for 200 European customers in Frankfurt and had all the bills sent to the partner. Her brinkmanship included a showdown at the hotel demanding $50,000 prepayment the night before the conference began. She arrived from America with no cash, so she couldn't pay the bills herself. Under pressure, the German managing director paid the $50,000 on the spot in order to avoid embarrassment. The story ended happily, with all the past-due bills paid before the conference ended. Future collections seemed faster, somehow.

Acucorp is a sinewy, taut company in a shrinking space with great margins after overhead, like all software. It encourages the 140 employees worldwide to examine and learn about the numbers in monthly financial statements. If an employee doesn't understand financial statements, Acucobol teaches the person how to interpret them.

Acucorp slammed into a wall in 1999 when all IT departments froze, waiting to see if the Y2K problem would be real. Then in 2000 the recession put revenues into a slump. But the company, being lean and quick to get leaner, survived thus far, while some comparable firms went toes-up. That's what watching the cash does for you. Profits don't pay rent. Cash does. In the long run, profits and cash match up, but day to day they don't, and that's how you lose a business.

Watch cash these ways:

1. Every bad debt starts out as a slow pay, so stay on top of collections. High receivables and high inventory are trouble signs. Yeah, the balance sheet calls them assets and that's wrong. They should be called liabilities, and they are for sure when they grow. Cash is an asset. You can buy groceries with it. Don't try to give Safeway your inventory or receivables when you're in the checkout line. That wouldn't be a pretty moment. Blossoming inventory or receivables is your first warning that the service or product is slipping while your income statement shows profits.

2. Have your payroll done outside so FICA payments are made automatically. This protects against the temptation to borrow from the government when cash tightens. Those who dip into the government's money end up living in the big house.

3. Never confuse borrowing with positive cash flow. Proper accounting says it is, but that's short-term thinking. Sales collected is the only true cash flow. All else is temporary or worse.

CHAPTER 52

DEMAND STRAIGHT TALK

I magine a CEO saying this to shareholders: "We had the worst absolute performance of my tenure, and, compared to the S&P, the worst relative performance as well."

This was in the second paragraph of a 1999 annual report. The first paragraph gave the numbers. Usually they bury those pleas for mercy in paragraph twenty after a page of talking about how bad the economy was, "but gee, it can't stay this way forever, can it now?" talk.

And slip the numbers, sandwiched between qualifying words, on page thirty.

But the chairman of this company went on in the third paragraph to say: "Even Inspector Clouseau could find last year's guilty party: your chairman."

You know how it normally goes. You invested in some stock. Didn't pay attention. When the annual report came you opened it, not having followed the stock during the year. The numbers are buried somewhere on page twenty but the management team is lined up for their photo on page three.

The chairman's message starts out: "2000 was a year of challenges . . . ," oh no, you think, ". . . yet a time for repositioning your company for the brighter opportunities ahead . . ." I better dump this turkey now, you mutter, "and before the nonrecurring charges . . ." you're slapping your head, knowing that nonrecurring charges recur every year, ". . . traditional accounting practices fail to disclose significant progress your executive team made . . ." it's the 'team' now, is it, and just how bad are the numbers, you wonder.

Berkshire Hathaway's 1999 annual report is the more honest example from above. Of course Warren Buffett, the chairman, was showing a profit even that year, and with his outstanding track record over time, some folksy confessions don't hurt so bad. He went on in the fourth paragraph to explain: "Our largest investees had disappointing operating results. It's no sure thing that they will quickly regain their stride."

Can't accuse Warren of hyping. He talks straight and highlights his errors. Here's the bad news and here's the worse news.

Truth eliminates many negatives. When people are straight, espionage budgets and efforts drop. The propaganda budget goes way down, and so does the ammunition budget. You no longer pay for second-guessers and checkers who check the checkers and slow everybody down, because when everybody talks straight, there's no need.

What goes up are profits. Saves money.

Buffett also knows how to talk about profits and risk. In his 1990 report, he predicted some bad results as well as some good results from a new business venture in supercatastrophic insurance. "We are not spreading this risk, we are concentrating it," he wrote. "We expect this to produce satisfactory results over, say, a decade, and we're sure it will produce absolutely terrible results in at least an occasional year, but I have always preferred a lumpy 15 percent to a smooth 12 percent."

This kind of straight talk has produced a company culture that operates many billions of dollars in business revenues with just a few people at headquarters in Omaha, Nebraska.

At Berkshire Hathaway, if you fail to perform, you are asked to explain. If you deceive, you are gone in an Omaha second. Turnover is low. The result is reduced operating costs because the staff is smaller and more attuned to business than to reading between the lines. This boosts profits.

Here's how to encourage straight talk:

1. Put some bad news in your employee and customer newspaper. Tell everybody a few of the things that are not going right. Readership will jump, the good news will be believed, and an air of trust will begin, but will grow only if you keep it up.

2. Deflate pomposity and puffery in meetings. Attack it. This is a threat to everyone's survival. If it ever becomes institutionalized, you will see the walls crumble, the numbers slip away, and never quite know what did it.

3. Terminate liars. Be rather public about it. Put this in your handbook as a company policy. Make sure you bounce an officer who lies sometime soon, a salesman who deceives a customer, a quality manager who bends the rules, and an engineer who tries to slip a technical misstatement past you. Deception is lethal. Bad news at least defines the problem. Lies hide problems and help them grow.

CHAPTER 53

CREATE REAL PLANS

No surprises. That was the mantra of the 1960s and 1970s among the corporate staffers at Honeywell who dreamed of a world where everything went according to plan. The personnel department (those are the folks called human resources today) put on full-day seminars on how planning could eliminate surprises.

Would you ever want to live in a world without surprises? Me neither. Fortunately, that world doesn't exist.

But they did their level best to create that world. Their large training staff taught everyone how to plan and how to plan to plan.

A cycle was organized, and each division was to present an annual report to the corporate office. The presentation took half a day and was attended by all the top officers. The plan was given to all in three-ring binders and then read, word by nonspontaneous word, by us managers. No whoopee cushions here. Just another zany group of hang-loose executives.

The plan was supposed to set out everything that would happen during the year. No further meetings would be necessary until the next year. If the plan was good, it would work and no changes would be necessary. All that was necessary, we were lectured, for the plan to be effective was for the planners to think hard and herniate our brains.

Our division imported Rollei cameras from Germany, Pentax cameras from Japan, Elmo movie equipment from Japan, distributed Nikor darkroom equipment and manufactured some items domestically, such as a slide projector and Honeywell Strobonar electronic flash units. We started with a product plan and competitive assumptions. We knew there would be a new

Pentax camera, and we assumed it would boost spring sales. We also knew two new compact flash units were coming, and we assumed those would also add sales. Just like that, product plans became sales assumptions.

It took only two months. At first, sales refused to commit unless prices were frozen and known, and production refused to give prices until sales were predicted. The balance was beautiful, if you're into that sort of thing. And it seemed we were.

The logjam finally broke when sales gave a forecast; then production relented and responded with cost estimates. Finally, there was some semblance of revenue and costs so the year came together.

Every brain herniated.

From this, departmental budgets were created, with great negotiations, as each department head pleaded for more people, equipment, and time to work on the plan.

Six months later, it was done and everybody understood and even semi-supported it. Our ad agency and our PR firm anxiously awaited it, so they could plan their year. This was the word according to Honeywell, and the Honeywell planners were happy.

Then, three days after the plan was submitted, Minolta announced a new camera at prices that were 30% below ours.

Golly. That wasn't part of the plan.

An intelligent response would have been to match the price with the new Pentax, but that wasn't in the document. Everyone had thought really hard on it, and then our thoughts became really hard. We decided to hang tough and see what would happen.

The inevitable happened. Minolta took the number one sales position. We reacted too late to stay in the lead. Vivitar, meanwhile, continued their steady takeover of the flash market, passed us by, and didn't look back or even wave. We had seen their threat years before, and even planned for it. We set up a Japanese manufacturing base to compete.

What a plan.

They, meanwhile, didn't set up any base but continued to shop all over Asia for the best pricing. Their plan was better, and their operating margins were 10% ahead of ours as a result. Their plan was better because it wasn't one, it was an attitude.

We planned again. This time we planned to sell more units in Japan, but it was too little too late. We had thought really hard about our plan. We wrote about it, talked about it, and at the time it seemed workable. In retrospect, that was the difference between us and Vivitar. They weren't talking only to each other, as we were. They were talking to customers and vendors. While we were still planning, they were living the plan and making adjustments.

Then, within six months President Nixon put in an (unplanned) price freeze, the yen made an (unplanned) devaluation, and suddenly gasoline was (unplanned) in short supply. Customers became nervous and stopped buying anything, which, of course, was unplanned.

Too many plans are written in this vacuum. They are so rigid that they are unreal and therefore unused. They become piles of paper.

Here is how to make plans work.

1. Make plans quickly. Don't let the process drag on. It doesn't get one bit better with more time. Avoid absolute predictions of where the economy, costs, markets, and competitors will be. Use broader philosophical statements of what changes will be made if the economy dives or soars. Those judgments are smarter when made in advance than during the trauma of radical change. If plans are realistic, they can be helpful. Base the strategies on your strengths and admitted weaknesses and assume some unexpected events.

2. Put in short-term monthly or quarterly checkpoints to alter the plan. If revenues don't hit a certain level by May, do not assume a hockey stick–shaped sales curve for June. Adapt to short-term results— monthly or quarterly. Markets affect you more than you affect markets.

3. Examine all the plans in your company. Kill a few. People should do more than plan. But planning is like escapism and reading fiction, untouched by reality. Find those plans that aren't really used for anything and bury them; plans are working documents, not credenza decor. There should be enough background in the plan that it is sometimes used just as reference material. It should also be used every month as a checkpoint on progress and to guide changes when results exceed or fall below the projection.

CHAPTER 54

GET ADVERTISING RESULTS

The dot-com debacle of 2001 began because nobody measured advertising results.

Consider this: Steve Ballmer was CEO of Microsoft, Steve Case was chairman of AOL, and Scott Cook was chairman of Intuit.

All three high-tech leaders, right?

Not so fast. All three came from the same company. Their first jobs were all in Cincinnati. You got it, Procter & Gamble, the biggest soap pusher in the world and the premier advertising firm.

And when everybody went nuts over the Web, these guys jumped into Web advertising, because advertising's something they knew cold, hands down, slam-dunk.

But wait, they didn't buy it. They sold it. Aha! They knew it didn't work.

So you've got all this 401(k) cash piling up, people dying to invest, and here comes the Internet. Now the Internet and the Web are real, very real phenomena that are altering the world. But not by as much as the stock prices suggested, not even 10%.

In the frenzy, everybody started advertising on the Web but nobody measured it. Rates were set at TV levels, the assumption being that if average programs on TV sold space for $50 per thousand viewers, then that's about where the average should fall for the Web, correct?

Billions and gazillions jumped on that faulty logic cuz nobody measured results.

Think about this for a bit. When you run a TV ad, you cover the entire screen. When you run a banner on a Web page, your ad is half the size of a postage stamp and surrounded by a dozen others. On TV you've got sound and animation with no distractions. On the Web you've got four or five words of type with jagged edges. On TV you've got passive viewers, relaxed, a receptive moment for ads. This is why the Sunday newspaper supplements have porcelain Shirley Temple dolls for only $39 per month and commemorative Korean War knives in limited editions, that limit being set by how much steel we can pound out in a thirty-day period, and actually sell the crap. But on the Web, the viewer is active, and that makes ads more irritating and clicked off easier. And on TV you've got thirty seconds. Web? Three or four seconds per page.

Nobody measured. Lots of folks got hosed. Measuring advertising is imperative if you do any. Always has been.

Honeywell Photographic had two new cameras to introduce in the fall of 1970. It was advertising manager Felix Pogliano's job to introduce both to the public.

The cameras were quite different. The Rollei 35 was the first pocket-sized 35mm camera. It was rugged. It had Zeiss lenses with a Compur shutter and a built-in light meter.

Felix knew a simple truth. Advertising efficiency can be enhanced more by simple measurements than by any other expense in business.

So he started with the assumption that this was an outdoor camera. You've got to test advertising, but you must start with a few assumptions. Felix placed introductory ads in *Sports Illustrated, Field & Stream,* and *Skiing*. Other ads were placed in *National Geographic* and *Time,* just to compare their response rates.

The next assumption about camera advertisements was that color cost 50% more back then but generated only 20% more inquiries. This response guess came from past history.

Every ad in every magazine was measured by its cost per inquiry, which ranged from $10 to $50. A word about that word "inquiry." We assumed that for every inquiry there were about another 100 people who read the entire ad but didn't respond. So the price per inquiry was really the price to reach 100 interested readers.

The first assumption proved right. The cost per inquiry in the active-sports media was about $28. The cost per inquiry for the newsmagazines and *National Geographic* was about $45. The assumption was proven, and the decision was made to go with the active-sports media. A number of ads were purchased, each using different headlines: "Big Pics; Little Camera" versus "Affordable Rollei Quality" versus "Great Action Photography from a Camera That Fits in Your Pocket," and so forth. Finally, we found ideas and words that dropped the cost down to $12 per inquiry. Now we were cooking.

Once the proper headline was found, Pogliano tested a full-page ad and quarter-page ads and reconfirmed suspicions that there was no reason to put a small camera on a big page.

After a year of testing and measuring, the ads were so effective that they were selling through retailers, with less than 4% of the sales going back into advertising. Every ad placed tested at least one element.

Honeywell then started advertising the Rollei 35 at different saturation levels in different parts of the country. They tried heavy Spring advertising in the Northeast and Southwest, without any Spring ads in the Northwest and Southeast. Warranty card returns were then measured by state against the dollars spent to see how much the heavy advertising actually increased sales. Budgets were then adjusted.

Eighteen months after introduction, the advertising budget dropped from $1 million to $150,000 per year. There was just as much product movement and $850,000 in additional profits. Advertising, in this case, worked. And as Pogliano tightened the advertising, Honeywell's profits grew.

But the other camera, the Spotmatic IIa, had a tougher time. A lot tougher. This was a conventional single-lens reflex 35mm camera, with a twist. Honeywell designed and Pentax built in a flash meter. Right into the camera. The flash meter always measured straight ahead, so the flash could be bounced off the ceiling for softer shadows or held out to the side to create more shadows across the subject, and the camera would still measure the light properly. When these effects were used, the camera compensated for reduced flash intensity.

The Spotmatic IIa had a tough time because it was hard to define. (We just used about 75 words to describe it.) The ads didn't do much better.

It was a new concept back then, and introductory ads were placed in *Popular Photography, Modern Photography,* and other fan magazines where the readers understood photography. Cost per inquiry in these publications typically ranged around $5. Readership was heavy, and readers were interested in photography and bought more than they needed. But the best we could do for our baby, the Spotmatic IIa, was $175 per inquiry. The message wasn't getting across, and our agency, Campbell-Mithun, was feeling the heat. (The fact that there may not have been a message was their problem. Who said business is fair?)

We invited Tracy-Locke, a competitor, to take a look. Their account executive reviewed what was happening, furrowed his brow, and left. One week later, he invited us to lunch, saying he thought his creative group had "cracked the code."

We couldn't wait. At lunch, the account executive, an upbeat Texan, eagerly showed us a proposed media schedule with several changes in advertising. "We're going to set new records for you. Your cost per inquiry will plummet," he purred, pouring a Sauvignon Blanc.

We were in a reserved side room of the restaurant, and the walls were lined with charts and graphs. He proved we would end up with eight to 10 times more inquiries if we inserted reply cards with every ad in the photo hobby magazines. This would work even if we ran half as many ads, he said, sure of himself. "We've done this for so many other clients."

He continued. If we expanded into consumer publications like *National Geographic, Time, Newsweek,* and the like, we could generate a larger response. The best thing to do was to put a coupon on the advertisement with the words "Free Brochure" on it in bold type.

We thanked them. We wouldn't let them pay for lunch and had no intention of even calling them for a few days. It was embarrassing.

Not for them, for us. Their ideas weren't bad, but our guidance was way off. Inquiries were never the goal. Sure, they could get us inquiries, but different kinds. Inquiries were merely an indicator of an ad's broader effectiveness.

At the same time, Campbell-Mithun held several focus groups with camera users to explain the features of the Spotmatic IIa. They got better and better at phrasing it, and they continually rewrote the ads. Results finally improved from disastrous all the way to merely awful. We quit trying.

The product died within six months. If you can't write the headline, kill the product. We lost $500,000 as professional explainers tried to explain an inexplicable product. The problem was the product. It couldn't be advertised effectively, and effective advertising proved that.

Chuck Taylor, the head of engineering for the electronics section, devised a product development program with me that we began using, and it killed a lot of dumb ideas. Before a single penny went into development, the champion had to show us the headline. There had to be a clear and unique benefit stated in twenty-five words. If you couldn't do that then, there was no product. If you can't do that today, there is no product.

Chuck went on to head product development for Sharper Image. Their new product process today starts with writing the headline.

These principles hold. An inquiry back then was an indicator, not a goal. On the Web today a click is an indicator, nothing more.

The choice of media is the most important advertising decision. Next is what you say. The least important, oddly, is how you say it. Creativity still counts, but it's not nearly as important as where you say it and what you say.

Here's how to get more for your advertising dollars:

1. Never run an ad that is not testing something. Start with media comparisons, where differences in effectiveness typically run from 10 to 1, strongest to weakest. Next, test the basic message. Different approaches vary in response by four times or more, best to worst. Test the size or length of ads and measure saturation levels.
2. Manage the agency tightly. They maximize their profits by running expensive ads a few times. You may do better with cheaper ads placed a thousand times.
3. Advertising has only one purpose: to sell more product. Image advertising is a waste; never fall into that trap. If selling more product won't help your image, why be in business? Advertising does not close the sale in most businesses, but that is no excuse for ignoring the sales objective.

CHAPTER 55

CUT COSTS BY RAISING QUALITY

Fisher-Price had a philosophy. It said toys must have lasting play value. That means that they cannot break and that kids must stay interested long after the newness wears off.

Durability was tested by drop testing and by endurance runs. Play value was stopwatched over a period of weeks in a private school run by Fisher-Price for local Buffalo kids. The kids chose from among 100 toys every day.

I joined the culture in 1976, when Fisher-Price bought Montron. I was marketing vice president at Montron. After the sale, I became managing director of AFI de Mexico, our manufacturing subsidiary, and general manager of Fisher-Price West Coast.

Fisher-Price and Montron developed a record player together. The design was difficult, and our new owners and we saw shortcomings in the other side.

"You guys don't have a clue how to design a knob for kids that is easy to use and will not break," sneered Tom, Fisher-Price's head of product development for the audiovisual category.

"God help you if you ever have to design something with more than 10 parts, or something that moves," I shot back. We were both right, and both myopic.

A truth was that Fisher-Price's philosophy elevated us. No matter how much smarter we thought we were, or how much Tom's taunts drove me nuts, we benefited from their philosophy of lasting play value.

Since Mattel bought Fisher-Price a couple years ago, I'm fascinated to see how they have evolved. Mattel was the marketeer. Fisher-Price just made good toys. At Toy Fair, a buyer would visit the Mattel showroom and look at the Gross Rating Points planned for a new item. (This is a measure of advertising exposure.) The buyer probably also looked at the new item's ad. And possibly even glanced at the toy. This is proof that the media exposure determines success most . . . the message second . . . the product least. For Mattel anyway.

Nobody goes to Toys R Us looking for a Mattel toy. They look for Barbie or some other Mattel item. But mothers do go to Toys R Us looking for a Fisher-Price toy. The brand has an earned reputation, and advertising doesn't matter much. So this marriage of oddfellows will be interesting to watch.

Anyway, way back in prehistoric times, just after Fisher-Price bought us, we designed a record player. Ours cost more because of the Fisher-Price philosophy, but it was unbreakable and couldn't scratch records nearly as easily as the competitors.

And then there were the solder joints. I knew a thing about solder joints. When in high school I interned at the Atomic Energy Commission, soldering cables used on a synchrotron particle accelerator. Fisher-Price's standards for solder joints, I discovered, were light years ahead of the Atomic Energy Commission's.

Standards like this gave Fisher-Price its reputation. When our record player came out, a dozen cheaper models were on the market. In the second year of the Fisher-Price record player, all 12 other players together sold about as many as we did. Ours became the top-selling record player of all time of any kind. At twice the price.

Quality leads to money. When buyers came to Toy Fair they bought whatever Fisher-Price had that was new, never asking about ad schedules. That saves marketing expense.

When parents shopped, it was the same. They might seek out a G.I. Joe and its accessories, but they would never know who made it. But they would go to the Fisher-Price section and find a toy they liked, even though they were unaware it existed minutes before.

This is trust, and it is based on quality. It saves advertising dollars, returned products, bad feelings, and the cost of redoing the entire product line every year.

While we at Montron were becoming successful, thanks to this guiding philosophy, another group of designers back in Buffalo were trying an improvement on another basic product, the Fisher-Price kite.

The kite was supposed to be a giant step forward, and it almost worked. All the consumer had to do was take it out of the box, slip two tubular struts into a Mylar-with-fiber wing, and it was ready to fly.

The kite was shaped like a bat. It had a retractable cord built in that served as a stabilizer, weighting down the bottom. To fly it you set the thing on the ground, grabbed the handle, and walked away. As you walked away, the kite's retractable cord played out the 60 feet of line until it hit the end. When it hit the end, the kite flipped up off the ground and, in a brisk wind, soared straight up.

The folks at Fisher-Price spent $500,000 to turn a great idea into the bat kite. And as they stood there in the brisk wind and watched the scalloped triangle swoop in the gusts off Lake Erie, they felt a winner.

But they tried to fly it one day when the breezes were only semibrisk. The kite wouldn't fly. It was too heavy. Yet this was a product that passed all the specific product quality tests. It didn't break when it was dropped. It didn't even rip if it was used as third base. It was durable, the colors didn't fade, and it was nontoxic. Heck, kids could teethe on it.

Somehow, the folks who dreamed up the bat kite missed the key ingredient to quality, which is functionality. It did not fly so hot. In light winds, when other kites were in the air, our bat kite sat fat on the ground, fluttering like a snare drum, wobbling like a penguin in need of Weight Watchers. The designers didn't get it. They saluted the rules without understanding the philosophy.

After three embarrassing months, and a half million painful dollars, Fisher-Price quietly pulled it off the market. The project manager on the bat kite understood the rules. The kite didn't fail the drop test, and it was nontoxic. But it didn't have the underlying thing the rules intended to protect, lasting play value. The record player passed the same drop test and was also nontoxic. It had lifetime solder joints and it couldn't scratch records; it worked and was enjoyable under normal play conditions.

Here's how to save money by boosting quality:

1. Quality needs to be pervasive because when quality improves, warranty expense drops, efficiency improves, and marketing costs go down. But quality must be more than just a statement, slogan, or rules. It must be a well-written companywide philosophy.
2. You can't inspect quality into anything. If you catch 10% bad, you're still shipping 1 percent faulty product, because inspection itself is an imperfect process. Help your quality department pursue causes of defects and correct them instead of just catching rejects.
3. Randomly pick one day a month when you visit and do nothing but check out quality in certain areas. Make the day different each month. Do nothing else that day; take no calls, see no outside people, and attend no meetings. When you go on a quality quest, spend all day quizzing the employees and customers. Ask what is happening and how it can be done better. Soon, your coworkers will pick up on this and do more. It becomes part of the culture.

CHAPTER 56

MANAGE FROM ONE PIECE OF PAPER

One sheet of paper. One. Three minus two. One, one, one. 8½ by 11 is okay. 3 by 5 is excellent.

Consider Robert Vlasic, who owned and managed an auto-leasing business, a nursing home, a real estate business, and a pickle company.

"I have a rule that one, and only one, piece of paper is submitted to me weekly from each business. This type of communication is critical," he said. His point is that there are just a few facts that count in every business. If those things are happening right, everything else falls into place.

His sheet for the pickle business shows the number of cases of pickles shipped that week, by category of pickle. It shows the dollar total, gross profit, and labor expense by plant. And it includes the number of hours paid by each plant for administration and labor plus overtime. It makes comparisons by the week and by the quarter.

The pickle business grew rapidly, and the others were steady. Rapid growth often leads to loss of control, but Vlasic refused to let it get complicated. Vlasic had a broad line with 73 items, including relishes, sauerkraut, peppers, and all varieties of pickles. By 1970, Vlasic had four plants and contracts with several growers of cucumbers. Still, Robert Vlasic wouldn't let it get complicated.

In 1962, Vlasic's first year, sales were $1.7 million with profits of $100,000. By 1971, sales had reached $27 million and profits were $1.8 million, not shabby for a commodity item. "Grow as fast as you want," Robert Vlasic said in 1971, "as long as we keep a 5 percent profit figure." At the time, sales were $27 million.

(In later years, two other changes proved principles mentioned in other chapters. Heinz dominated the pickle and relish business but moved into ketchup. If pickles and ketchup don't go together, what does? Well, they didn't. Heinz took over ketchup and lost the pickle business to Vlasic. So this pickle company with the funny name became glamorous, just enough that some fancy financiers took over, leveraged it with debt so they couldn't react to the smallest hiccup. A medium hiccup hit the industry and Vlasic went into restructuring, a fancy way to say the shareholders got stiffed and creditors half-stiffed. By then they were pushing over a billion dollars a year.)

Every plan the company made was exceeded by greater growth and profits. In 1971, the officers were projecting sales of $55 million by 1975. They hit $60 million.

It was easy. Vlasic was simply and directly managed and never let profits slip in pursuit of sales. Both came naturally, and key among Vlasic's principles was managing the entire business from one sheet of paper. It forced focus. It eliminated distraction. And everybody concentrated on the few things that counted: pickles shipped, overtime, and price.

You can run a business with financial statements, but that's like standing on the stern and telling the captain how many rocks you just missed.

If you want reports that look ahead, try this:

1. Put the management report on one piece of paper, dropping all detail that isn't critical. Include shipments, back orders, cancellations, and payroll expense as standard items. Most accounting data is historical. Add forward-looking data such as customer credit, returns, ad response, or number of inbound calls to get some sense of the market. Put in product development status. The idea is to keep one eye on the horizon.

2. Distribute this paper broadly each week so that everybody's critical number is seen by everybody else and there are no secrets. Highlight deviations, good and bad, so that everybody quickly sees what is happening.

3. Stick with it. Don't have time for other "interesting reports" created by those with idle time to enhance their status. Manage with one report and ignore all else. Schedule a meeting once a year to decide on revisions and subtractions to the report. When you revise it, don't let it grow. Each addition must mean a subtraction somewhere else. Use big type.

CHAPTER 57

INVEST SIMPLY

W hen Wall Street smelled some nickels and dimes in Forest City, Iowa, they grabbed their briefcases. They were players, after all, and turned up a new game piece in Forest City called Winnebago Industries.

In 1987 Forest City, population 4,100, boomed. Orders at Winnebago were strong and it looked as if a thousand motor homes a week could start rolling out of the factory by year's end. Dozens of citizens of Forest City became millionaire investors. None was richer than John K. Hanson, the 79-year-old, bombastic, contrary founder of Winnebago.

Hanson, who owned half the stock in the company, loved to try to out-smart the markets. In 1985, Winnebago placed a large order for Renault chassis to go inside the newest models. When he placed the order, it looked to Hanson as if the French franc were cheap, so he bought futures. As he bragged later, he was dead right. The franc increased so fast in value while he received, and was billed for, the Renault chassis that he ended up with, essentially, several thousand chassis for free.

Hanson showed a *Des Moines Register & Tribune* reporter the results. The company doubled profits, to $20 million, partially because of Hanson's savvy. Winnebago stock soared, and since he owned half of it, his personal net worth jumped by $80 million.

And the guys from Wall Street couldn't come fast enough. It didn't matter that there were only two ways to get to Forest City, either through Des Moines or Minneapolis. Or that both required long rent-a-car drives through flat farmland to reach it. The fruit hung low, and these pickers in suspenders and seven-piece suits were ready to snag some.

Winnebago met several bright money managers and investment advisers. "Last year," said Hanson of the new direction, "we made $13 million in the stock market and $9 million in the business."

The next year, Winnebago acquired some IBM mainframe leases in leveraged transactions. The casino was open as the advisers were lining up stock investments, straddles, bond plays, option trades, and all the other things financiers invent for bored people with cash.

A funny thing happened though, the house won. The bond deals were mediocre, the motor home market softened just after the factory was geared up, and the leases on the IBM mainframes were disasters. The company made only $3 million in 1988, and the stock price took a nose dive. In 1989, more investments soured and Winnebago lost $3 million.

Winnebago's major competitor, Fleetwood, didn't do any speculative investing. In 1987, they didn't do nearly as well as Winnebago did. The next year, they did quite a bit better. It was a smooth, straight investment road they followed. They didn't roll the dice; they put their extra money in CDs and treasury bills. Their returns were strong, not spectacular. The second year, their returns were still strong.

Fleetwood wasn't as distracted with fancy investments. Instead, they focused on their business and, over the years, soon saw Winnebago only in their rear-view mirrors. Some of it was plain old business hustle, but much of it (according to Wall Street analysts who follow the stock) was due to watching the business and not getting fancy. See how they seduce you first and then ridicule you for listening?

To prove cash makes you stupid, in the decade that followed, Fleetwood basked in success, relaxed a little, and Winnebago caught them, by a little each year, and now leads them. John K. Hanson died, professionals run Winnebago, and John V. Hanson, his son, sits on the board. The company's value has quadrupled in the last few years, in spite of a down market and rising fuel costs.

If you are not on Wall Street, don't visit. If you don't get information faster than outside investors, there is only one sure way to end up with a small fortune: Start with a large fortune.

Stick with what you know. Here's how:

1. Put excess cash in CDs, T-bills, and bonds. Then neither think that you are smart when you outperform everyone, nor belittle yourself when you don't. You are smart no matter what because you've minimized the effort and reduced distractions. In the long run, you will do better.
2. When you hire outside managers, use only a few. Pick them for the lowest management fee and most secure controls, and don't let

them stray from the philosophy in number one. Make part of their compensation a bonus for slightly outperforming the market. Don't give extra pay for an extremely good performance. That's a casino incentive.

3. Never review performance daily. If you do, you speculate. Soon, you are tempted to react. Invest in simple, nonspeculative uses and wait it out.

CHAPTER 58

NEGOTIATE FASTER

In 1973 at Honeywell, we needed new products.

For one thing, it looked as if Pentax would drop us as distributor for their cameras and sell direct in North America. That's exactly what happened. For another, Vivitar was killing us in electronic flash with Asian sourcing. American labor made us noncompetitive, and we lost that market. In addition, slide projectors, as well as movie cameras and projectors, were static and dominated by Kodak.

It was time to move. "How about AGFA?" somebody mused in a staff meeting. At the time, AGFA was the third-largest film company in the world—close to Fuji, while both lagged far behind Kodak.

I called AGFA.

"We've got 60 U.S. sales reps and six telemarketers," I told them. "Every photo dealer in the country hears from us at least every two weeks. Some of the bigger ones see us every day."

It was a seductive song. AGFA was struggling. They had 15 sales reps, and dealers often went months between calls. Instead of steady deliveries, AGFA dealers tended to be in heavy supply one week and out of stock the next.

Two weeks later, I was in New Jersey riding in a limousine with Bob Copenrath, AGFA's chairman, whose nickname was Mighty Mouth. Copenrath had a way with words.

"Mr. Sutton, we would like to give you this beautiful daughter of ours," said Copenrath, in reference to U.S. distribution of AGFA film. "But you understand that she has a tattoo on her tit."

That was his elegant way of saying that sales were flat and they were consistently losing money in the consumer division. We were only interested in the consumer division, so we decided to look closer at its blemished breast.

We talked about the possibility of increased sales if Honeywell distributed consumer products for AGFA. The strategy was for AGFA and Honeywell to combine sales forces using 65 of the 75 available salespeople. Dealers would see their Honeywell representative even more, and AGFA sales would be steadier. It wouldn't be pushed. Instead of dumping large orders, they would get more small ones. The sales rep would keep AGFA in a steadier inventory, as the last item discussed on their call. Dealers would never be overloaded and never out of stock. Our sales reps wouldn't be distracted, and we assumed sales would be better.

When I asked about their processing lab in Flushing, New York, I was hoping they would keep it. All we really wanted to do was distribute.

Copenrath responded as only he could. "We wouldn't sell our restaurant unless the buyer takes the kitchen with it," said Mighty Mouth. At least the analogy fit better and didn't give a visual that was as tough to forget as his first one.

It all made sense. AGFA was not making money with their sales level in the United States, and Honeywell needed a new product. Serious negotiations began two weeks later in Denver.

We laid the groundwork before we began. Up front, we told them maximum price targets we could accept on the products. We didn't pad it. Much. They later explained exactly what they needed in sales, and I don't think they padded it. Much.

We agreed to let AGFA help us set the sales figures, but only on the understanding that if their demands became frightening we would walk away and pursue other product possibilities. We had several others. None were competitive to film, and each would take considerable time to put together. But options existed.

It took three meetings. That's all. The price targets turned out to be reached comfortably. The sticking point was in how many items we would carry, but that was solved within 45 minutes in our second meeting as each side gave a little for common gain. The compromises were easy because both sides stated reasonable minimum needs at the beginning.

In the third meeting, we agreed to their sales targets, which were higher than what they had done previously, because the more we heard about their current distribution woes, the more the new strategy seemed to fit.

Two months later, it was signed. AGFA reduced their marketing cost and got a small sales increase. Honeywell added $5 million in sales and made some modest money on it. And it only took 60 days to put together.

You are not making money while you are negotiating. Prolonged negotiations build antagonism. Always go for a favorable result fast. Never try to maximize.

Here is how to make haggling more productive:

1. Know exactly what your minimum expectations are at the beginning. If the other side insists on something less, politely walk away. Start negotiations by expressing your best-hoped-for result, and then justify it. Give the other side reasons to accept your premise and understand your needs.

2. Never let anybody who loves negotiating do too much of it. If done well, there's some agony and sensitivity for both sides. Anyone who thrives on it is a bully or psychopath. Before agreeing to anything, set a deadline for a conclusion to the whole process and explain this is in both parties' interest. There are alternatives. If you don't have alternatives, this is not a negotiation.

3. Line up alternatives before entering a negotiation. You always negotiate better when you don't need to make a deal. The biggest mistake made is talking to only one possibility before finding the next. When you have several options, you don't become desperate. Therefore, you handle each one better.

CHAPTER 59

FLATTEN THAT PYRAMID

Smiley Industries was bleeding when I was hired as Chairman in November of 1988. Net losses hit 33% of revenues for that calendar year.

One-third of NATO's Apache helicopters were grounded due to the firm's inability to deliver a transmission casing to McDonnell Douglas. MX missile guidance systems' housings had been profitable until the peace broke out. Damn peace.

There were other troubles. Parker Hannafin was threatening to drop Smiley as a vendor for intricately machined hydraulic valves. Too many rejects.

Rohr threatened to take work away because of late deliveries. So did Lockheed. We had problems with Northrup too. We were putting out 120 quotes a month, but only winning an average of 10%, telling us we won only when we made our worst mistakes. (Later, when we specialized, we cut the quote rate to 40 a month and won half of them, doubling our profits.)

When I was brought in by the frustrated owners of Davis Industries, one of Detroit's leading metal stampers, losses were deep and accelerating. This aerospace manufacturer was in a supersonic power dive and five feet off the ground. There wasn't enough money for the next payroll. Hey, that meant me! I didn't have time to blink or it would all vaporize, including lots of jobs.

Quickly, we kneecapped some of our creditors, offering payments over time plus cash for any new orders. They agreed the better option was to go along. Then we renegotiated the McDonnell Douglas business and we had enough cash to meet three payrolls. The power dive leveled. Now we were flying several inches off the ground and praying for no trees ahead.

We looked at the operations. A huge rift split engineering and the factory. There were nine engineers but only two spent any regular time on the floor, and those two didn't spend any time engineering. The two floor engineers reported to one boss, who had no one else under him. The boss of the two engineers reported to his boss, who reported on up a level. Neither boss had anyone else reporting to him. An organizational chart would resemble a totem pole.

We changed the operations. We hired a new engineering manager who gave the nine engineers individual responsibility for about 20 projects each.

Chaos resulted. Engineers wandered the floor. It looked confusing.

But good signs emerged. The big aluminum coffee urn in the engineering area went from three batches a day to one-half. At the same time, the coffee vending machine by the factory floor suddenly needed to be refilled twice a week, instead of once.

Even though much of it still seemed uncontrolled, late deliveries went from 40% to 20% in three months. Rockwell restored our preferred-vendor status. The place had gone from tragedy to mediocrity, and the next challenge was to avoid premature rejoicing.

Once the organization was flattened, it became efficient. Davis Industries breathed a sigh of relief, accepted a multimillion-dollar acquisition offer for the business, and went back to the cushy business of making car parts.

Hierarchies make organizations sluggish. They isolate executives and create redundancies. Layers are filters and funnels. Get rid of layers and deal with them.

Here's how to speed up your company's reaction times:

1. Reorganize to eliminate a layer in the middle. Don't listen as everyone balks and complains about losing control. Layers create less control but the illusion of more.
2. Eliminate every management position that has four or fewer people reporting to it. That person doesn't have enough to do and therefore overmanages out of guilt. Take away unnecessary responsibility and give that person meaningful tasks.
3. Split your business. Forget the presumed efficiency of scale in large organizations. Larger means more layers, which means less responsive. Management becomes isolated with growth. Get rid of shared services; they become arrogant. Teamwork will return, and that beats the presumed efficiencies of size every time.

CHAPTER 60

WATCH FOR TROUBLE SIGNS

O̲ak Industries made burners for gas stoves. Honest, blue-collar work, but the executives craved more than the bowling alleys of Illinois to display their success. So in 1979 they picked up and moved the company to balmy Rancho Bernardo, California.

The official explanation for the move had to do with diversifications into cable television hardware and television stations. But there was more to it than the diversifications. You could see it in their arched Spanish building atop a California hill, in the elegant courtyard, and in the terrazzo tile of the parking lot. The folks at the top of Oak Industries wanted to go upscale.

They hired an interior decorator who was quite bothered that the new IBM typewriter casings didn't quite match the earthtone decor. Five dozen casings were removed and spray-painted terra cotta, mauve, and New Mexico blue.

Oak Industries acquired television station after television station all across the United States and amortized the excess prices paid over 40 years as goodwill. The expense of the move and building was capitalized over 10 years. The logo was redone into a contemporary angular shape from the old, fussy, 1950s design. Everything was lavish, even the description of the company in the annual report. Oak was "a thriving communications enterprise," it nonspecifically gloated.

For a while, the bankers bought it. They kept lending money since this "profitable" company seemed to deploy it well.

Wall Street jumped in too by selling numerous bonds to less-favored clients, so Oak could pay all the bills they were running up. The Wall Street firms didn't keep any for their own accounts, since that could be a conflict of interest. Neat, eh? After all, profits looked great. And then in 1984, what goes around came around. Oak Industries reported its first loss in years. "This is extraordinary," said a guy in red suspenders in Rancho Bernardo, trying to explain the loss. But it wasn't. This was merely the first shoe hitting the floor.

No one knew what happened until people looked, and then everyone knew. The investors' money had disappeared into a leather-lined, black hole.

The chairman resigned under pressure and then the board, amazed at what it had done, hired the exact wrong choice for the exact wrong reason. He was a glamorous failure. The new chairman was once chairman of a Michigan company called Wickes. This guy was just like the folks who ran Oak Industries in Illinois, he moved his company from the Midwest to southern California.

And then Wickes took over one of the tallest buildings in San Diego and put their name on it. Wickes pushed through reckless acquisitions until finally it all disintegrated and the company became the largest bankruptcy in American history for its time.

Oak shrunk and bled, reported loss after loss, until it got down to almost half the size it was as a stove burner business.

While these two companies trumpeted their San Diego arrival, there was a quieter outfit also starting in San Diego. You may remember reading about them earlier. As a refresher: "there is nothing fancy about Price Club, except for the bottom line." The company headquarters remains in an industrial building and the CEO still has a bookshelf made of concrete blocks and a board. But their 1991 bottom line was $129 million. The bottom line is the only appropriate place to flaunt wealth.

Everywhere else, you have to watch for trouble. Oak Industries didn't understand. Neither did Wickes. Both were flying high when they decided to "fix things," but they didn't understand that changing logos, redesigning offices, and moving are not cures for anything; they are merely proof of distraction. If you find yourself fixing logos and furniture, stop. Take a shower; go for a walk.

Diversifying usually doesn't work either. High-powered telephone systems cost plenty and never deliver a return.

There are plenty of places to find trouble before it shows up in financial statements. If you have empty parking lots at 7 P.M., you have trouble. If you have better relations with vendors and the press than with customers, something is wrong.

Watch for high salaries and low incentives, inventory growth, first-class travel, closed doors, new offices and old machinery, executive lunchrooms, and heavy trade association involvement. If there is grandiose publicity, heavy goodwill charges, capitalized R&D, and pride in size rather than profits, you've got problems.

Here's how to avoid this:

1. Never respond to downturns with logo changes, acquisitions in other fields, or changed accounting methods. Fix the real problems before touching cosmetics. Don't paint rotten wood.
2. Accounting says inventory, goodwill, and receivables are assets. They are not. If your local grocery store will accept any of these instead of cash, then they are assets. They are ugly, dangerous noncontributors until they are turned into cash. Earnings aren't up unless goodwill, receivables, and inventory are down.
3. There is no such thing as a perfect accounting period, or a perfect location, or perfect furniture. Changing these is guaranteed to cost money. Don't tamper with any of these cosmetics until you've had three years of true earnings growth. (Even then I wish you wouldn't.)

CHAPTER 61

SELL HARDER

In 1968, when Bob Hartley was 26 years old, he was hired to sell Learjets. He wanted to sell jets ever since he became an IBM typewriter salesman three years earlier. He first approached Gates Learjet when he was 23, and he kept coming back monthly until finally he was hired by the Dallas manager, Phil Lovett, who was impressed with Hartley's persistence.

Hartley joined a group of swaggering guys who lived and worked and wined and dined and took many rides high in the sky just to reach their annual sales quota of one. One plane at $1 million. It made for a gutsy year of all or nothing.

Hartley smiled and shook hands and went his way. The others snickered at him as they went golfing or to Las Vegas, sometimes both, on the expense account, to wine and dine prospective clients. Hartley had other ideas.

He put together a flip chart showing the economies of owning a Learjet. His chart showed the kinds of companies and travel patterns that made it a sensible purchase.

The chart also had glossy, adrenaline-charged photographs of gleaming Learjets in flight and on the ground with exotic backdrops. Hartley wasn't completely rational. He did demonstration flights like all the other salespeople, but unlike the others he prefaced the flights with a couple of hours of qualifying conversation. The other salespeople did the same talking, except that they did it on the demonstration, in the air. The information gathered during that initial conversation was essential: the person's opinion of Learjet, his or her travel patterns, and his or her financial status.

Hartley did even more preparation. He nurtured relationships with travel agencies and aircraft rental companies. Sometimes he was given information about which customers took the most flights. After a while, because he was there so much, he spotted prospects himself and then he ran a Dun & Bradstreet report to learn of the financial shape of that particular company.

He followed with a letter to the CEO. He introduced himself and Gates Learjet in a customized appeal to what he knew about the company. A few days later, he called requesting an appointment in a week. He was told someone would get back to him. He called again the next week. Each prospect received five calls. Ten new prospects were added each week.

He did this relentlessly. Told the story. Found the prospects. Every time, it was the same. Nothing happened.

Quiet chuckles greeted him at sales meetings when he told of how many presentations he was making and what he was doing to dig up new prospects. Some of the red-eyed salesmen pulled him aside and offered these one-sale-a-year words of wisdom: "You've got to drink with these guys. Golf with 'em, take them to Vegas. Use the expense account."

Phil Lovett stayed patient. He knew Hartley was working and he thought it might work. Sales came out of nowhere, from everywhere, anywhere, at anytime. Or maybe not for a while yet.

One thing in Hartley's favor was that he kept his expenses down. But Hartley was getting frustrated. Later, he confessed, "I was starting to see a giant career mistake. I was trying to sell million-dollar jets the way we sold $300 typewriters. There was no indication it would work and plenty of belief by others that it wouldn't."

In May 1969, C.K. Stillwagon, a wildcat driller in Houston, bought a Learjet from Bob Hartley. That one sale brought Hartley a $10,000 commission. His annual salary was $14,000. (Lighten up, readers, this was 1969 and you could purchase three decent cars with that commission.)

In June, Hartley sold another Learjet, and in July he did it again. He sold 11 Learjets in seven months and made more than $100,000. (Now we're talking a real full garage.) He also caused culture shock in the Gates Learjet sales department where suddenly work occurred in places besides Las Vegas.

Selling is like every other career. A quick wit and great pitch don't hurt, but qualifying prospects and calling on lots of them wins.

In 2001 and 2010, check the top sales producers. Now check who makes the most calls. Same names, no matter what the industry, right?

Here's how to make sales more efficient:

1. Emphasize prospecting. Teach new salespeople how. Make prospecting a topic at your sales meetings. Have your top salespeople share their knowledge.

2. Display the number of calls each salesperson makes next to his or her sales results. Count letters and phone calls as equal to personal visits. Metro people can manage a half dozen calls out of one elevator. Rural folks must use more mail and telephone work.

3. Have contests with small prizes to see who knows the most about his or her customers. Who signs the check? Who approves the purchase order? Are their sales up or down? Do they always get bids, and how many? Does the low bid always win? This is how to ensure that your salespeople are asking questions and not just talking.

CHAPTER 62

RAISE ETHICS, RAISE PROFITS

When the governor of Baja came to cut the ribbon at the new Fisher-Price factory in Tijuana, we still didn't have telephones. The phone company couldn't hook us up for another 30 months. We didn't even think about having a ribbon ceremony until the contractor mentioned it.

This wasn't a big building, just 160,000 square feet. The contractor put it up from our designs in three months, paving over a street that used to run between city blocks. There were only two builders in town and one wouldn't bid. But, when our contractor quoted eleven cents per square foot, well, are you going to shake your fist at the sky?

When he finished he asked if I'd care to have the governor attend the ceremony. I said that would be nice.

"When do you want him here and what do you want him to say?" he asked. Ah, yes. That is how it works. But we remained hobbled since we couldn't coordinate truck crossings with the U.S. without phones.

And so we had our ceremony, complete with mariachis, free tortillas, and fruit. After the brief ceremony, everyone stood on the gravel street in front and looked at the building while kids played soccer with a can and dogs barked at the activity. The governor assured us that he could take care of our telephone problem as he winked and roared off in his chromed pickup with oversized tires.

At the same site two days later, our contractor pulled me aside. "The governor's office called today and gave me the name of a consulting firm. They said you would know what to do with it."

I called the consultant. An agent for the consulting firm came by with a prepared offer, guaranteeing a phone line within six weeks for a mere $10,000. He smiled and told me that his firm had expertise in cutting through red tape. "We'll take half now, and half when the phones are up," he said.

He held out a brochure. I took it and at his urging opened to the page that listed the board of the consulting firm. I recognized five names. Four were top officials with the phone company. The fifth was our ribbon-cutting governor.

Hmm.

I worked for a company, Montron, that had been acquired a year earlier by Quaker Oats and combined with their Fisher-Price toy division. Before I took over the Mexican operation, Quaker Oats required I sign a statement regarding improper actions. The same statement required a new signature every year. It said: "I will make no payments that are questionable, or that I have reason to believe are questionable, either by the standards of the country I am in or by the accepted standards in the U.S. If doubtful, I will not do it even if it makes business more difficult and less profitable. In gray areas, I will try to imagine how the transaction would look if described on the front page of my hometown newspaper, where my neighbors, high school teachers, and parents would read about it."

The guideline saved time and energy, since opportunities abounded for making creative payments at the border.

The strict rules actually made life easier. We didn't have to think about it. Forced ethics.

I told them I had no authority to make a $10,000 payment to this type of consulting firm. They smiled and said, "Be that way."

And so there we were, squeaky-clean, feeling most ethical, and quite telephoneless. It was some fix for a new factory.

We found a woman near the border who operated a ham radio. Maria Concepcion Gonzales lived in a single-story wood-frame house, tarpaper roof, two cardboard windows, and one glass. It was about 300 yards from the barbed-wire fence separating the United States and Mexico, and we hired her while she was boiling field corn in a washtub out front. We paid Maria Concepcion $75 a month to send messages two to three times a day to an operator on the other side, who would then telephone our engineering and transportation group in San Diego for $5 per message. It was clumsy, slow, and confusing, but it was legal and cheaper than $10,000.

Fortunately, profits and ethics are often compatible. Even more fortunately, sometimes they are not. If it were always easy, ethics wouldn't mean so much. The foundation of your business must be ethical or you will not last long.

To create an ethical base for your employees, do this:

1. In clear, specific, unmistakable language, put limits on entertainment of clients. This is especially important in dealing with governments. Spell out exactly what kind of donations are permissible and what kind are not.
2. Rotate your buyers and don't allow any lunches, fishing trips, entertainment, or gifts. Never let buyers give last looks to any vendor when taking bids; that merely guarantees you get a meaningless first bid.
3. Pay your bills on time. Don't take prompt-pay discounts for late payments unless you say up front that this is part of your deal. If your controller has nothing better to do than add a day's float by issuing checks from distant banks, tell vendors where the checks will come from and in what time zone before they quote. Stealing pennies like that takes time and loses dollars in spirit.

CHAPTER 63

RIDE THE BIG WAVE

Every long-distance phone company is obsolete," declared my pal, Ed Tuck. He wore a crewneck blue wool sweater and chomped on ham and eggs and grits with cheese. That's Ed, always taking the big bite.

In this case, in October 1989, it was beating the international phone companies. He chatted in reasonable-sounding comments between swallows at the Holiday Inn next to San Diego's Montgomery Field, and while reasonable-sounding, he was, uh, talking about challenging the largest companies in the world.

"It costs every phone company in the world almost $2,000 to hook up a single new subscriber," he said in a preface to how he proposed we start this multibillion-dollar company. "By 1995, there may be upwards of 140 million people worldwide who want phone service, can afford it, but can't get it. That's the market."

Pretty outrageous. Tuck explained that phone company hookup costs have continually risen over the years and that there is no way for the phone company to avoid even higher costs. "It's inevitable," he said.

That was the moment. Even before he explained his concept of a dense geodesic pattern of low-flying microsatellites, my head was nodding.

It wasn't boring or confusing, as much technical talk is to outsiders. What he said was enthralling. His dream was "a long-distance network that covers the world, especially remote areas, and hooks up customers at a fraction of the normal cost."

Time for lithium? Naah. Tuck's not your normal 70-year-old—he drag-races a Corvette, drives a cycle at speeds way, way into three figures, and alternates between a hot plane and his new helicopter, a spooky Notar version without any tail rotor.

I met Tuck in 1986 when he described his vision for a handheld navigator. The idea was to create something like an oversized calculator that would take readings off satellites and tell users exactly, within a few feet, where they were anywhere in the world. The proposed satellite system, dubbed GPS, wasn't yet proven.

Well he did it. It worked. By the time of the Gulf War it was an indispensable military tool. Boat dealers were buying them by the truckload. And now GPS is part of our language and installed in more cars every year.

When Tuck first explained over breakfast his idea of taking on the phone companies of the world, it felt like that same moment from decades before when Dean Peterson got a little wide-eyed, telling me about the possibility of autofocus.

Proven people both times, careful logic, and outrageous business potential. When the planets line up like this, you pay attention. If they line up for you every day, get some medication.

I jumped. With Tuck leading, we started Teledesic.

First, we needed money. Ed put together a simple presentation. We compiled a list of the 100 most likely investors and sent each a one-page description of the project. We wanted $1 million for a feasibility study, which would take a year. We called each potential investor.

About 20 potential investors reluctantly agreed to sit down and listen for an hour. Our strategy was simple: If all 20 said no way, we would kill it and get on with life. But if we got just one or two to merely think about it for a moment, then we would expand the effort and hustle all 100. These first 20 were our sanity test.

We would rewrite and rehearse each time, all the while making it better.

In the first week, though, we were stunned. Our first three potential investors said yes. They wanted to give us money.

Teledesic was born in May 1990. It was funded half by the G.D. Searle family trust and half by Craig McCaw. We had to turn the other money down. That is a process for which I had no prior experience.

A dozen expert consultants were scouted out and then contracted to design satellites, do market studies, antennas, rockets, switching, patents, regulatory laws, and constellation design. They were paid less than they normally made but got stock in the company, and it could be a handsome payback one day.

They have made tremendous advances and, as of press time in 2001, have several hundred million in the bank and a valuation of $3 billion. So this idea grew by $3 billion in one decade.

In a book I wrote in 1993 I chronicled this startup, and said this is how you do it. I mentioned a competitor called Iridium and predicted its failure, due to sheer economics, and suggested another competitor called Globalstar might be the stronger competitor for us. Motorola, the primary backer of Iridium, began hedging away from Iridium and toward Teledesic financially, and today owns about one-fourth of Teledesic.

In the years and billions of dollars spent since, Iridium went bankrupt but was bailed out by the military for their own purposes. Globalstar is wobbling at press time, and Teledesic has watched them and taken some major shifts in direction.

Teledesic is a Wal-Mart sort of phone company, with growth potential in sparsely populated areas where phone lines aren't practical, and is particularly appropriate for data, which is the fastest growing area of telecom.

AT&T invested, Bill Gates invested, Motorola invested, the Crown Prince of Saudi Arabia invested, Boeing invested. This puppy got big. Will it work?

Time will tell. And we're talking months, not decades. Teledesic may change the world a bit, create 30,000 new jobs, save a dozen lives daily, create knowledge-based jobs in rural areas, and help the balance of payments. Or it may quietly go toes-up. At least we'll know. The point in dreaming is to recognize the big one, to swing for the fences with a Babe Ruth swagger. It's therapeutic. To try is to succeed. Nothing feels more hollow than wondering what might have been.

Here's how to guide your group through the big dream:

1. Hold back nothing once a huge opportunity seems sensible. Half-hearted effort kills the best of ideas. Spend heavy and fast if the market seems big, knowing some is waste. Getting there quicker pays for these errors. In a way, much of the good business you've done is building your strength for this moment.
2. Don't try to own exclusively, or control it. Bring in, quickly, as much smart money as you can. Solos never capture a market.
3. Keep your senses open while running the business tight. When that inner voice pushes you toward risk, listen.

CHAPTER 64

SEED YOUR CULTURE WITH THE EMPLOYEE MANUAL

Alot of business books talk about company culture. This has little to do with yogurt. But while they espouse it, they don't tell you how to create it. Yeah, company picnics are great, yawn, but if management doesn't "get it," that picnic just alienates employees from their leader buffoons even more.

The whole deal about culture is to have an attitude about what you want for your business and to have the guts to talk about it. Specifically.

And there's one moment, a best moment you have with every employee to help create that attitude. When they start. Or are almost ready to join.

They're curious. Eager. And that's why the employee manual is key.

You, the CEO, should write it. Don't let HR or legal write it, that's a perfectly crummy way to start out an employee. Here's the manual I first wrote for SkyDesk in 1997, and then revised a year later when we were approaching 100 employees.

Thanks for joining SkyDesk!
This tells what we think SkyDesk is all about. A quick reading may answer some of your questions in advance. We dated this, since we work in booming markets and technologies, with user desires that shift quickly. So, some of this will shift and a few areas may be laughably wrong by 2001.

And, hopefully, we'll be busy capturing new customers and conceiving breakthrough services. That means this employee manual won't always be up-to-the-minute. We don't have that kind of time.

What should stick will be the philosophies and attitudes. And there are sections, where a couple of policies are described, that you really must read and agree with. Sorry. But one of the great things about being a new business is that there are really only a few that matter: (1) terms of employment, (2) intellectual property rights, and (3) confidentiality.

SkyDesk is the leading provider of data protection, collaboration, and migration services. That may not be true three and a half hours from now, but at this instant it is a blissful fact.

Sure, there are pesky competitors which we'll disparage in a moment, but none quite deliver the services SkyDesk offers or plans.

First, let's look at those services: @Backup, SkyFiler, and SmartClone.

@Backup is the online backup service, the genesis of our business and cornerstone of SkyDesk technology. It's the best. The service was launched in 1998; we're doing hundreds of restores daily and haven't yet, to our knowledge, lost a bit, byte, or gig of any customer's data. More importantly, we constantly make it easier to use, which is the first thing that matters in the market. Hey, these folks have lives, they love having their data protected but simply don't want to work at it or think about it.

@Backup sells well on the Web, since that's where those folks are who are comfortable online, but doesn't scale up into a huge business there. Our partnerships, however, where the service is tightly bundled or is even a nonoption, will hopefully generate millions of users. Some of our partners think so and we've got our fingers crossed.

Those two sales methods mentioned also reveal a larger truth about @Backup. It must be preinstalled or easily purchased with a click, or the sale is lost. We're talking dental floss mentality here; yes, we all know we should, but few bother. Make it quick and easy, and a valuable business is born.

Let's put it another way: Drive the streets of San Diego and you won't find an insurance store anywhere. Ditto for other cities. (Stick with this, there is a point coming that matters.) Try to recruit employees without an insurance plan, and you'll be very lonely. The first fact, no insurance stores, proves that nobody goes out to buy insurance. It's a service that's sold, not bought. @Backup is insurance. The second fact, new employees expect and demand that insurance be part of the employment package. So people want insurance. They feel uncomfortable without it. But they want it bundled and packaged and they don't voluntarily buy it very often. This is the @Backup story.

We currently sell a year of service for $99. Quite a bargain—unlimited restores, backup as often as you want with up to 100MB of critical data. Fewer than 1% exceed that. Most stuff on a drive is software [which is replaceable and probably obsolete, so there's no desire to replace it after a crash] and downloaded materials, which are obviously replaceable. Drives are getting huge, to accommodate these other uses, but the unique and generated data amounts are a smaller part of this mix.

Unique data is that stuff entered through the keyboard. Lose that and you've lost it. And typing speeds seem to stay the same, year after year, so the amount of critical data created daily stays the same. Fortunately, that critical information accumulates and, unlike the PCs and servers holding it, the value of the data grows with time.

@Backup is a sweet business. A terrific value. Saves people lots of confusion, heartaches, and losses. Still marketing-intense, but as folks hear more about it and we get smarter about making @Backup simpler, sales accelerate noticeably each month.

@Backup faces four nasty, brutish competitors.

First is lethargy, and this is the worst. People don't get around to it; they say they will, mean to, feel better when they are backed up, but it's just one of those things that doesn't get done, even with the best of intentions. @Backup solves that, it's totally automatic, if we can just get them online to try.

Second is the Zip Drive, a mechanical substitute for our service. Many prefer the tangible feel, despite proven undependability of most popular tape and disk systems, just as many bank depositors still want a passbook. It takes time for habits to fade.

Third is Connected, the only survivor of five online backup services that jumped into the business in 1996 and 1997. (X-Act Labs led the way, underwent surgery, and emerged as Atrieva, just finished another switcharoo and is now Driveway . . . no longer a backup service, but an online storage service. Connected was next and now sells their software to corporations who want to run the service for themselves, and have withdrawn, for the second time, from aggressively offering a service as we do. Then SureFind, tuneup.com, and SafeGuard all jumped in, and all three died in 1998.)

Fourth are the storage services like Driveway. This area saw X-Drive, I-Drive, Driveway, NetDrive, FreeDrive, and Visto all pop up and get huge funding in the last year. They don't quite compete with @Backup because they are storage and access, light on security, manual and free, so serious users won't go there, but some bottom-end erosion of our business market will likely happen. Would you buy a padlock from Mattel?

Keep your eye on the CD-RW discs and drives coming, since there's another threat to @Backup. These new discs drop the cost another magnitude. They don't store the data offsite, and they don't encrypt it, and since they're a product, they are a chore, not an automatic service. But they'll be an option. Just like answering machines were killed by the voice messaging services, we still believe customers prefer the service over a box with wires and moving parts, and for good reason.

@Backup is the first of three Internet storage services SkyDesk will offer business users.

SkyFiler is the second. This essentially is an industrial-strength version of Internet storage, making it possible to access and work on your data from any Web browser. This service faces three competitors, none head-on.

First is the laptop or notebook device. SkyFiler is a reasonable substitute for these boxes in many situations. Second will be that group of free storage services just mentioned; however, their features and gaping holes in their security mean, again, they'll only get the more casual and non-business users. Third is Lotus Notes, a viable competitor in the larger corporations, but a far more complicated and expensive service. It also has many features beyond collaboration. But ours, thanks to some smart thinking and the acquisition of Shared Planet, goes beyond them all.

Notice here we say no more about SkyFiler. It's a work in process, with uncertain final features, so a little stealth is in order. Just know that it will be more businesslike than what's on the market today. We think we'll come up with a friendlier name, too, by the time it's debugged and ready for the world.

Finally comes SkyDesk's third offering, SmartClone. This service concept will make migrating data from an old PC to a newer model easy. There's a lot of heartache and frustration in this process, and we think anything that eases the experience will be applauded. Several leading PC makers agree. Again, as a plan that's not yet born, we'll stay a bit tight-lipped on SmartClone until it's closer to launch. What we can say is that there are immediate solutions that involve cable connections, which we think are great for today. But for those who can see around the next corner, modems are getting faster and pipes are getting fatter, which suggests an Internet solution isn't too far away. And we've got huge technology and patent advantages for that inevitable moment.

SkyDesk is the only business-to-business Internet storage service. The lightweight and free services aren't suitable for business. Connected sells a product, not a service. We have both a unique niche and indirect competition.

That covers the services planned for the immediate future. Now let's discuss how we get there.

To create these services, our engineering department is growing and will keep growing, recruiting mostly senior engineers and few, if any, that are fresh out of school. We avoid "feature creep" during development, since release dates in this accelerating market are one of the key features, and will sacrifice other bells and whistles to be timely.

Our product management department, newly created, has the delicate task of watching this, contributing to feature list priorities, and putting together cosmetics and sites that optimize sales.

We're still learning. The biggest weakness SkyDesk has is a group of employees that are so technically competent that we sometimes forget that the world needs simplicity. AOL didn't win by being technically superior to

Prodigy. Microsoft wasn't built on bug-free releases. If you owned shares from the beginning of either of those companies . . . sorry . . . scratch that, had you bought them you wouldn't be working now . . . simplicity sells. The fewer the clicks the better.

We must get to where every new service isn't even begun until somebody has written the description that tells what the unique user benefit is, and does so in twenty words or less. If you can't do that, it's not a viable offer to the world.

One area where we lagged, and were lucky not to embarrass ourselves, was in testing. Now that department is in place, and new services and sites that are released will have been wrung out and most major bugs found and squashed. We were overdue for this capacity. Kind of like doing a backup, we just didn't get around to it as fast as we should have, but feel a lot better now.

Direct Web marketing strives for 20% monthly sales growth with flat budgets, a daunting task made more achievable by the download and installation getting friendlier and easier, the market accepting the concept more every day, and a longer-term downward trend for Web ad rates. This trend is all of a couple years old, which is an Internet lifetime, but for this instant seems to have flattened. Stay tuned. We expect to maintain this effort, even spending more should the response rates improve. While partnership marketing should grow huge, it's this direct Web marketing that teaches us what works, so we can guide our partners.

Partnership marketing is just beginning, starting with Dell. We've signed every PC maker that counts in recent months, have the three largest DSL providers, both high-speed cable modem outfits, and are working on the ISPs. So the challenge now changes for partnership marketing. We don't need to get 'em. We got 'em. Now we have to make them work and, in so doing, establish SkyDesk services as the standard. We suspect one or two will lead the way, those who integrate more aggressively, and the others should follow within a year, after we've proven the new businesses with others.

Our accounting and finance group face two challenges. One is simply keeping track of how many paying subscribers we have. This seemingly simple chore gets complicated by the expanding number of partners, different kinds of trial offers, and churn rates. This is a question we always need to answer accurately, since it is the way most of the outside world measures us. We all know AOL has twenty-three million subscribers, but none of us can guess what their revenues or profits were last year, right? So making sure that yardstick has integrity is key. Today we have 62,000 users that have given us their credit card, or whose service has been paid for by one of our partners. Some of those are still in their thirty-day free trial, but we know that 44% of those who sample @Backup will convert and pay, and this is a percentage that is growing higher. (We're not yet selling SkyFiler or SmartClone, but do have a group of beta testers with Sky-Filer.) Paying subscribers are all that count. The second chore for this group is the no-end-in-sight need for new investment. The reason for continued financing will be covered in a minute, but for now, file that as a critical chore that this group stays focused on.

Operations is where some of this money goes, as we hope to add users at increasing rates; it begins to make more sense to have a dedicated backend that we control. In the beginning, we were able to rent this capacity. It's approaching cost-effectiveness to do more ourselves, which is a weak excuse for insourcing. The better reason is that we can give faster and more consistent service, which is all that matters for capturing and keeping subscribers. (When you see somebody walking the hallways and talking into a cell phone, that's ops.)

Keeping subscribers, of course, is critical. This is where customer care is a fundamental backbone of the business. The rest of the company must make their jobs manageable by making the services idiot-proof and reassuring to use, with billing that's effortless and sold without undeliverable promises. And, it behooves us all to ask customer care from time to time about what's happening and what our users are saying to them, so we know where we're coming up short and can fix it. Keeping subscribers means keeping payers. Those who don't pay are not subscribers. Therefore, we keep subscribers with better service and choose not to give lesser service, compensating with excessive free periods. That's a greased slide toward sloppiness.

So that's how each area fits. There's another aspect to this business and our times. That's an unprecedented need for speed and risk. By that, we recognize that there's a bunch of investment money out there today, backing outrageous ideas, and the most certain way to become roadkill on the information highway is to be cautious.

As that guy with bad hair, Albert Einstein, once said, "If at first the idea is not absurd, then there is no hope for it." He made that observation when there was less research money around than there is today. It's all the more true now.

SkyDesk always wants its services to be better than the others. Better means that they work, of course, but it also means they are the easiest to use. The fewer the clicks and the fewer the screens, the crisper the language the better. Make it so your mom can use it, or Uncle Harry, and we've got a business that will soar. Yes, we have many business customers, but nobody anywhere is offended by simplicity. It remains the major catalyst for widespread use.

Given those thoughts, it also is the ultimate in naiveté to try to release a perfect product. It is not possible. Our world today offers up too many machine variations, application quirks, and user habits. Graduated releases, on time, that allow for follow-on work that can drive toward perfection, deliver better services to more users than any other approach. So we do. And we test plenty along the way.

We will finance with debt where we can, increasing risk, because selling too many shares reduces the returns to employees on their options and shareholders. It also increases the downside, no free lunch there, but a compelling reason for walking on these wilder sides with most options is that there are competitors emerging all around us, and it would be tragic to lose the race to a more adventurous startup with a mediocre line of services.

Operations and the backend will be less cavalier. Where dependability of service is balanced against costs, our choice will be to pay extra for the reliability.

Marketing will take risks, fail, and do many things during this year that are uneconomical in the short term. (This is calculated against the probable growth rate of these markets, and sheer guesswork at when the business masses will be comfortable with their data hosted and accessible online.) The direct Web marketing seems destined to improve every month, as they've been doing for two years. But we do hit a ceiling each time we try to dramatically expand the Web marketing, and that's caused a couple moments of pain. Our partnerships will be sporadic, a few great ones, some good, and several disasters. We cannot yet know which will be which, but ought to be smarter in a year. Our services seem inherently incidental to other offerings at this moment, so we suspect a few partners with strategic motivations will drive our numbers.

Those motivations can be more margins (PCs, ISPs, DSLs). It may be increased loyalty (PCs, ISPs, DSLs). Or it is sometimes reduced risk (ASPs, other online data services). It can be differentiation, for a brief time (ISPs). Hard to know which channel will warm to which approach, and they'll never all see it the same way. They all, however, will not allow themselves to be distracted from their core businesses for our sake, any more than we would, so we've got to know our place and enhance their offerings without disrupting them.

Earlier in this sermon we threatened you with a couple of rules, so let's get to that.

Perhaps you were expecting a dress code? Sorry. We have none.

Hours of work. Sorry again. But somebody has put together a holiday schedule, and you can see that on the Intranet.

Since everybody is a shareholder, it seems to work out without those kinds of rules, at least so far. You'll note that most SkyDesk employees chuckle when an eight-hour day is mentioned, a thing that is viewed as a charming relic of times past. You'll see a few folks in on weekends, one or two manic moments when somebody pulls an overnighter, and emails ricocheting around in the wee hours. It's hard to be different when the business has some excitement and promise.

We tend to have daily or weekly conversations, hopefully two-way, instead of annual reviews. And in the hallway bantering, we hope employees all challenge higher-ranking or more senior people and attitudes . . . we hope those arguments have a chance of going either way . . . and we hope all sides possess the maturity to support the conclusion, once opinions are aired.

This takes work. It's easy to nod while reading this. But we all need to remember it later, when that confrontation occurs, and this theory starts to matter.

When something goes wrong, it helps us all if you are sure to always cough up bad news the instant you see it. This makes a healthy organization. Celebrating victories happens automatically. Looking away from problems turns pain into tragedy. Not easy. Try.

There is an org chart. Somewhere. More importantly, everybody knows what they're supposed to get done in the weeks ahead, and when you don't, embarrass your boss by asking. (Yes, we do have bosses and we are all employees. "Associates" might be the fuzzy-wuzzy label du jour, but while we're trying to build a democracy here, we can't jeopardize things by confusing that with chaos.)

Our salary policy is that we hope you are slightly beyond comfortable, but buy into the collective dream of making your stock value into a life-altering phenomenon.

We have no secretaries. Do your own. We have office management to handle all that implies, plus HR things.

We spend money where it relates to revenues and new products, and remain a bit cheap elsewhere when we can. Advance discount fares when practical, no first class except with coupons, kind of a Marriott time, which feels posh after our earlier Travelodge years.

It's too soon to go for profits. Seizing share of a new market is cheap early on and expensive or impossible later. For that reason, profits aren't the goal for a long while. We don't buy into the Amazon model thus far, because they show no signs of approaching profitability, but perhaps there's an unplayed card up their sleeve. We're headed for big earnings, but not for something like eighteen months to two years.

Everybody has shares of stock, so we're wed that way, and the question is how to turn those shares into some real value. You know, paper that Safeway accepts for groceries. Well, there are several ways. An IPO, or merger with a strategic partner who needs our technology, for instance, are the most probable ways. The IPO market is obviously unpredictable. However, the large corporate interests seem to always be around, and several have invested and others want more. When the time is right, that will happen and we'll all profit. But we have to do something for that benefit. That is to create some superb new services, ones that others cannot deliver. That makes our value higher. And the new investors profit.

In recent years, we've encouraged a couple of brilliant people to leave. One worked very hard, the other reasonably. In both cases, they couldn't accept any consensus that didn't go their way. It would have been fine if they just picked up their ball and went home. But they stayed and pouted. So departures were gracefully encouraged. This happens. We're embarrassed by it, and never certain if much of the failing isn't ours. But we can't live with prima donnas, whatever the cause. Skill and hard work are expected. That's what we hire and hope to maintain.

But no matter how good, any attitude that corrodes the SkyDesk spirit needs correction. We neither enjoy facing these situations nor do we avoid them.

Okay, we're finally down to the three absolute, no-quibbling policies.

The first is that SkyDesk is an at-will employer. This means when you join, you understand there are no contracts, implied or real, for your employment and you may be fired at any time for any reason. Period. Now that sounds harsh, but with the strange employment rules our lawmakers invent, this is simply the way it must be and your joining SkyDesk means absolute acceptance.

The second covers intellectual property rights. Everything you conceive and create involving data storage or management, while employed by SkyDesk, belongs to SkyDesk. That's what those skimpy paychecks cover.

Finally, you understand that in a highly competitive field such as ours, where competitors will solicit business plans through a friendly financier and pretend to be interested in merging to learn more about how SkyDesk is doing (both real and recent events), everything we do in design, marketing, and running our business, including the plans discussed in this, are confidential. Relatives, school chums, and media simply need not know until and when it suits our business purposes. Loss of trade secrets hurts us all. Be careful.

So that's it. We're glad you're here, and your signature on the next page is proof you've read this and agree.

I have read the SkyDesk Employee Manual. I accept the philosophies and rules as a part of joining SkyDesk.

Dated: _____

_____
Signature

_____
Name (Type or Print)

Some exceptions I would like to discuss in this manual are:_____

_____

_____

_____

_____

Okay, a little heavy on technobabble at first, but this was a techie business and necessary for employees, if not you, to grasp overall. Years have passed since writing that manual, so publishing here doesn't divulge anything the public doesn't know. Except, perhaps, the attitude.

But think over the last sections. This sets a tone for a work ethic. It gets pretty clear that there will be no stars or excessive salaries, but if the business does well, we all make out on our stock options.

And, in fact, we had an employee who abused the company secrets. Our expensive attorneys (pardon the redundant phrase) had suggested for years it would be a good thing for them to write our employee manual. Can you imagine how inspirational that would be?

Well, the point is our lawyers came around to saying, when they had to prosecute, that the wording in this made their case easier than anything they would have drafted.

This was understandable. A jury could get it. And it did make the case with reasons for the need for secrecy, in a tone that wasn't harsh or punitive. So we did just fine.

But there's a larger point and a more compelling reason for an employee manual. And you, as the CEO, should write it.

This sets the company direction. It establishes the philosophies. The specifics will change, they always do, but the broader directions remain. And you, CEO, must do that yourself. This is one chore that cannot and should not and must not be delegated. If you are incapable of expressing it, another career is a real good idea.

Even if you're not quick with a phrase or clever with words, you do it. This forces you to get precise yourself. It makes you focus. And you'll come out of the agony of drafting it with a sharper resolve yourself about where the company is headed and how it will get there and what everybody needs to do to help.

This is good.

Start writing.

CHAPTER 65

ELEPHANT HUNTING

ere's how to recruit the "permanent" CEO.

It's a different hunt. This is the most important chapter of the whole book, so I'll try to write well so you can read and then reread without tiring.

First of all, we never clone the turnaround manager. Now the business is healthy so another turnaround is exactly what's not needed.

The turnaround guy enjoyed reading, skiing, woodworking, or photography. The next CEO belongs to a book club, plays tennis or golf, sails, and plays bridge. One's a loner and the other's more social.

Take another pass through Chapter 1. That tells you more about where successful CEOs come from than any recruiter could dream of. If you cheated and peeked at Chapter 16's comments on interviewing, forget about most of that. CEOs have tighter schedules and you can't bring them in for a beauty parade. They've also got a bit more ego than that (sorry, I am one) and would head for the airport if they sensed you controlling the situation like that.

Nothing you do for a turnaround is as important as selecting the right CEO to carry the business into the next level. This is obvious, so I'll try to not say it again.

Now, assign a selection committee from the board. Make most of them CEOs or former CEOs. Keep this committee down to two or three, and make them individuals the rest of the board respects. Having had P&L experience is critical. It lets them banter comfortably with the candidates and compare war stories.

Select the search firm. Do all the steps outlined in Chapter 1. Remember there are no search firms that have ever filled 90% of their searches successfully and there are few that fail at over 80%. Superstar firms and total losers do not exist, but the management of the firm makes a huge difference. That means your management, not theirs.

So spend more time laying out the requirements for the search and less on talking to a bunch of them. You'll sense by their responses which are currently overloaded and which are hungry. This changes from week to week, which is another reason to rid yourself of any idea that the perfect firm exists.

Get one member of the selection committee committed to meet weekly with the search firm, at least by phone. Let's call this person our Chief Recruiting Officer. This CRO must also be ready to interview four to six candidates during the process and bring it down to two or three for the committee. The CRO will travel for most of these interviews.

The search firm will screen twenty candidates by phone and interview a dozen personally.

The turnaround CEO should not be the CRO, but should participate in the interviews. Turnaround CEOs and second-stage CEOs are oil and water, energy vs. discipline, "change something big immediately" types as opposed to "dial it in a click at a time" personalities.

Don't even consider using an industrial psychologist to screen finalists. If you do, reject anybody that agrees to undergo this—they have too little pride.

However, getting inside each candidate's head is critical. Here's what the CRO must do to have a meaningful interview:

1. First, we assume the company description sang, and has enchanted the candidates while giving them a true picture of the challenges. The search firm's enthusiasm should have accented this.

2. In the CRO's first meeting with the candidate, get isolated. Make it in a hotel room or private conference area of the airport. No cell phones. One legal pad for notes. No public visibility. Take more brochures and annual reports and material to give the candidate.

3. Take the lead and spend a few minutes giving more background. Add some new detail. Tell the candidate why the board is fascinated by his background and the possible fit, but keep this short. What you're doing is merely polite, giving some information before extracting more from the candidate.

4. Now we're in the interview, and ask if it's okay to take notes. Don't put the candidate's name on top of the page, use a code. Keep the candidate relaxed.

5. Tell the candidate what your parents' jobs were, briefly. Then ask what the candidate's mother and father did. Ask if it was a happy family.

   Jot down notes. Later you can think over the responses, just get enough detail so you can recall and cough it up for others. You're getting two things with this simple question. First, you're seeing if the candidate came from privilege or the working class or somewhere in between. Second, you're getting a first glimpse of his/her abilities to communicate.

   A wealthy background might mean this candidate has a broader vision for the future and bigger aspirations than others. It may also show that the person presumes success comes easily and relies excessively on others. This is neither good or bad but gives you things to watch for and think over later. A more humble background could show higher incentive and intent to struggle for results, or it could mean the candidate has passed his or her comfort level already.

6. In one sentence, tell the candidate where you went to school and what it was like. Then say "I see you went to ____ and ____. How were they?"

   Again, no good answers and no bad answers here. If they went to Harvard or Stanford, their intellect will be just fine but you can't measure their judgment. If they went to Mid-State University, that's okay, some great work ethics come from those places and you'll notice them more eager for the challenge, while the more polished diplomas expect you to defer more to them. Neither school level makes that much difference, but see if they changed majors more than once or didn't quite finish. That's worth pondering. We get more directional with age and pick up some tenacity, but those who start out with less must improve more.

7. Tell him what your favorite thing is about work. Then ask for his/hers.

8. Tell the candidate what you do in your spare time. Embellish with a few sentences. Then ask about their hobbies.

   This is the window into the real person. If they have no outside interests, well, you know that certainly doesn't disqualify them. The tempo might pick up a bit in your office with that person in there seven days a week. If they love to attend PTA, go to trade association seminars, speak to the Chamber of Commerce, and sit on several boards, well, you may have a problem. Your best CEOs aren't balanced and in tune with the karma of the world; they're fixated on their business.

Their outside activity, if any, tells you if they're inherently social or loners, active or passive, creative or traditional.

9. Tell them what you dislike most about work. Ask for their least favorite thing. While you're keeping notes, be consistent. If they talk a lot, take a lot of notes. Where they are brief, be short. One thing you'll be interested in is to remember how long they talked about their most joyous task vs. the most despised aspect of their job. Besides getting a good reading on what they'll concentrate on in the job, the length and intensity of each answer shows how positive and how negative the person can be.

10. Now break away from the list and tell them more about the business, field their questions as best you can, and write down what they ask about. This tells you where their focus will be.

11. Cater to the candidate, keep it directed but not too mechanical. Get a refill for his/her coffee. Or water or juice.

12. Next ask their advice. Prepare for this one, and have real examples from the company. Somewhere there's a marginal executive, whom you should describe; and give details. Ask the candidate what they'd recommend doing.

If they say fire him, this is the wrong candidate. The turnaround is over.

If they say warn the employee specifically, and have a review in two weeks or a month, this may be a keeper, a manager.

If they say watch him, pass. You want activity, not an observer, but one who acts judiciously.

Ask their advice again. This time describe a new plant possibility, with an Industrial Revenue Bond, or an office lease coming up next door; give the numbers for a reaction. If neither situation exists, give a lease or buy situation with a piece of equipment with the numbers and ask which way they'd go.

13–19. Seven more questions for counsel . . . tell about an auditor negotiation, see what he or she recommends, a troubled customer situation, a possible strategic shift in products or pricing or services, a road show for investors, an operations problem, a speech opportunity, and a reorganization of engineering. Make all of these real and pay attention to the responses.

You'll learn something about candidates and your business here. If they're fuzzy with answers, leave them as politely and as quickly as possible. Note which of the above situations they tend to dig into and which they gloss over. Half are insider questions and half are outsider, and you need to know where their balance lies.

20. Through all of this, jot down each question they ask. You need to see where their curiosity is.

21. Ask how their spouse feels about the possible move. If they haven't discussed it, they are either domineering types or aren't serious about your possible offer. Note if this is their first, second, or third marriage. One or two ceremonies are okay, people do change and performers stress their home life. Three marriages is where you need to back away, either the person has bad judgment or is incapable of accommodation. Get out the gong.

Use this same sequence with all four to six folks you interview and keep notes the same way with each. At the end you'll be able to stack them up and discover some differences in each that weren't evident when you were talking. Yet by doing it as outlined, it's not artificial feeling or cumbersome.

Next get a report to the board on all four to six, giving emphasis to the two you favor, and have the other member or two members of the selection committee talk with the candidates in an unstructured conversation. They already know most of what they need to know from your report, so these can be more fun and frees candidates up to sell. Pitch the upside. Confirm the candidate's probability of success. Have them probe further into salary vs. incentive and start making your case for much of the latter and little of the former.

While they're doing that, the CRO (remember?) checks references. This is sensitive to the max. Don't bother with any provided by the candidates, simply note whether they tended to provide recent or dated ones, peers or bosses or subordinates, and from which companies.

Your job here is to get reliable background checks without blowing the candidate's cover and there's no other way to do it than to lie. Well, let's call this extremely deceptive.

Call peers, vendors, and customers at places the prospect has worked.

Describe your company without naming it, and say you're looking for someone to fit a board seat. This is true, but splitting hairs. It's a way to get some unvarnished truth without jeopardizing your candidate's status. Describe your candidate's background as being the profile wanted. See how many offer up his or her name. When they do, dig in.

If they don't mention his/her name, along with another name or two, then give your candidate's name casually, and ask if he/she might also be a good candidate, and ask why or why not. Make this an offhand, last-minute question, to protect your candidate. You'll get closer to the truth that way, since they'll not think you're serious.

First of all, you run a credit check, traffic and criminal, confirm educational and employment claims of all six candidates. Get their approval, you've got to have that, then let Equifax or some other service run each of them. Ask your search firm for a good one. Never let the search firm do it.

Now, here's a kick in the pants, but with these six finalists you are going to catch one who lied about tenure on a job or education. Automatic disqualifier, of course, and shocking but that's our world today. It's unlikely you'll hit a criminal record but you can't afford to assume so. Check that.

If you uncover a bunch of lawsuits pending, pass on by and don't go back to that person, whether he's the plaintiff or defendant. Something's wrong. If there's a history of traffic violations, you've found a sociopath and need to let another company suffer. Bad credit? Pass, he's irresponsible.

You're now in the dangerous position of being down to three candidates total and need to keep moving them each along; start with an offer to your favorite, while sending a truckload of flowers to the spouses. One of the two favored ones will drop out, so you must keep dancing with them all.

Make sure the board is prepared for what you've got to offer and is kept up to speed on the offer and any dropouts. They need to understand the position isn't being jumped at by everybody, so they'll support the process more.

Allow me to repeat, mucho incentive and poco salary make for bueno future earnings. Fade away from those who escalate salary needs as the closing moments approach. They're showing good technique, which you want, but a bad heart, which you don't.

Do all the above, plus the hints from Chapter 1, and 80% of the time you'll land a CEO who will flourish and make everybody's lives better. Should that other 20% situation occur, promote the person inside whom you had in the back of your mind, but didn't want to tease with the possibility; tell them they should be flattered by knowing they looked better and better the more you searched and put them in the job. If this internal candidate is truly a bit green, create a chairman's job for a year, only, with the promise that this person goes away at the end of twelve months and meets with only your new CEO on a monthly basis for a brief chat before the entire board meets.

CHAPTER 66

BOARDS SUCK. HERE'S HOW TO COPE

Any resemblance between people described in this chapter and living persons is purely coincidental. The moon is made of blue cheese.

Okay, if you're any good at turnarounds, that suggests you're not the most social or collaborative person in the world. You don't do well on committees. As a politician, you'd fail fast. And the problem is, when turning around a business, you've got to deal with a board of directors that's sometimes nearly as jumpy as they should be.

This can blow everything. Easily.

Never forget that boards are inherently political. One director, one vote. They're a group that can fire the CEO at any time, presumably, yet they are all equal with the CEO. But if there are five directors, there will be five agendas; with seven, seven.

Turnarounds require dictators. There must be momentary independence from the directors. To understand this, let's consider how a board operates in normal times.

Boards make three decisions. Only.

First is firing the CEO. Second is hiring the next CEO. Third is approving budgets, executive pay, mergers, and divestitures.

When a board decides more than that, there's no CEO. If there's no CEO, the board has failed. So.

Now the problem with this is that the directors cannot make these decisions intelligently without knowing a few customers, talking with some employees from time to time, possibly a competitor, plus checking with the auditors. Activity well beyond those few decisive moments is mandatory.

And that's why the CEO and the directors talk and consult with each other from time to time. But the CEO decides.

The care and feeding of a board means you've got to find some social maturity within yourself that doesn't normally show in a turnaround guy, and manage the politics. Now, now, stop. Don't start. Don't go saying you can't be political. You do shareholders an extreme disservice by not being political. And I hope you're a shareholder. So don't shoot your toes off and remember, one director, one vote. This is just the way it is at the very top.

Two tales of companies, neither turnarounds, shows this nature of boards and my below-average ability to deal with them.

It was my first CEO job, and wow, one director seemed a little weird. As time went on, it proved out that a reason he seemed a touch weird was that he was weird to the core. Weird squared. Okay.

My other board members behaved rationally. But this one director was given to tantrums and shouting.

He had an obsession with the PC, feeling he mastered the universe because he operated one in the early 1980s. His position on the staff of a holding company that owned us, alongside a couple dozen other businesses, put him in touch with all the other CEOs. One July afternoon, when the economy swooned and almost every company underperformed, he put each company's financial results into a program he wrote that automatically typed letters chastising every CEO, mentioning their abysmal results specifically.

Automated whippings.

In four blistering paragraphs, every CEO's letter ripped them apart for modest sales gains or reductions and screamed at their declining profits or losses.

There was one problem with my letter. Our sales, luckily, happened to be up and our profits doubled the prior year. No, it wasn't always so. Just at this moment. So I looked at this bizarre letter, my first formal communication from the holding company, on their letterhead, almost using profanity for doubling profits over the prior year. The parent company was consolidating into a growing loss.

Beyond weird. Some letter. My leaders. This is the kind of inspired direction that makes it real hard to click your heels together and salute.

Two years later, when I brought in the acquisition of a northwestern business, this psycho-director screamed so loudly against it that managers from down the hallway scurried up to the boardroom to see if there was an emergency.

Well, we bought it anyway, and this turned out to be one of the best investments the company ever made, from a cash flow standpoint. As if anything else mattered.

Now psycho-director wanted to run it. He asked if he could be CEO.

I said no. "Robert, you're mentally unstable. That's not a desirable CEO trait, especially for a business with 700 employees."

Not a good comment, politically. A great comment factually. He saw a psychiatrist weekly, sometimes daily, boosting the parent company's medical premium by a noticeable amount. He also was conducting several email affairs with persons, presumably women, who would spend an hour or two each day typing nasty little suggestions to each other over this newly discovered thing called the Internet.

In time, another holding company wanted our group.

My unbalanced director handled the negotiations but neglected to tell me they were occurring. Before I knew it we had an offer, and part of it was that my strangest board member was to become CEO of the northwest company.

My stock was acquired in the deal, so any pain was anesthetized with cash, but the folks in the northwest had to suffer through this guy's temperament. Finally he hit a moment where some "accounting irregularities" popped up and he was put on the street. But that was two years later.

That incident needn't have happened. It was my fault. Instead of handling his strangeness directly, I should have been political and mentioned it to the other directors. Then his little side campaign to get the job he wanted wouldn't have gone anywhere, or distracted from his negotiations, which probably cost unknowable millions in valuation. Even the new owners suffered.

I should've undercut him. Quietly. Machiavellian? Yes. Best for the shareholders? Yes. And we all work for the shareholders, so suppress those pristine thoughts of straightforward activity. I'm not saying often, that's not necessary or healthy, just recognize those moments when being sensitive to directors and their one-step-removed positions sometimes need and deserve a little extra coaching.

The board is inherently political. It's a voting body. Your behavior needs to change. I'm sorry. You must lobby your board. Work the votes. They should be predetermined before meetings. And get rid of disruptive directors when you can. If you can't, make sure their influence withers or they'll seize opportunity for themselves in times of turbulence.

This described the care and feeding of a board in normal moments. In abnormal times, like a turnaround, you cannot afford to nurture directors. There's no time. That's why it's absolutely necessary that your power be defined clearly in the contract before you begin. Never, ever, not in this ice age, agree to set terms later. Period.

But in your deal, let the board fire you any time they want without reason. They won't prematurely, since they're horrified with the mess anyway, and they'll be relieved later, but not confident enough even then to assume control, as long as you have a contract. Don't change the board either. Maybe a couple of seats. But you gotta have a few directors who remember how bad it was so a semblance of gratitude will come your way with the fix. It'll look entirely too easy to new directors.

Don't have any board meetings at first, just assign one director to talk with for an hour or less each week through the first month. Perhaps meet with several directors for a couple of hours each month after that in a highly informal conversation, so you don't end up spending valuable time preparing instead of fixing.

Normal board governance is a great thing for normal times. But in rough times, you can't have that many hands on the steering wheel. How many committees can you name in history, private or public, who accomplished great things? Got that?

Have you ever heard of a great board, when people talk about what made an outstanding company outstanding? See?

Oversight is bad when the battle's on. Jimmy Carter became famous for his management of detail. This hit a height when he was in direct contact with the mission leader in Iran, attempting the hostage rescue. That disaster needn't have been. Ronald Reagan was criticized for sleeping through an air battle between our pilots and the Libyans. But the result was zero casualties for our side and an aluminum shower over the Mediterranean.

Making that point one more way, consider that before America had a Joint Chiefs of Staff and a Secretary of Defense, it never lost a war. Since creating these oversight groups, we had a stalemate in Korea, a defeat in Vietnam, and a victory in the Gulf War, if a thirty-day skirmish counts.

Just so you understand the potential for problems a bad director creates, let's consider another situation. This was a startup, not a turnaround. I was CEO.

Six financings brought in about $60 million. The valuation was $1.3 million in the first round and steadily stair-stepped up to $240 million through these five years. Not shabby.

In the third round, a giddy NYSE company offered us $6 million, provided someone else lead that round and set terms. The $6 million would match any price. A Boston firm we liked offered to lead the round at a modest boost and would also put in $6 million. Value up, and a lot of money.

Our board met in a private session, excluding insiders, and selected an offer from another firm which only offered less than a million, but at a slightly higher valuation.

This boosted the value of everybody's holdings, but also meant we'd be back looking for more cash sooner. It also kept the Boston firm out of our investors' backyard, which may have been a side agenda. I don't know, I wasn't part of that private discussion.

So we took the under one million as a lead and pulled in the $6,000,000 at the slightly higher price.

The firm giving us the pittance of lead money wanted a seat on the board, although their total shares would be well below all other directors' holdings. The firm's general partner, I'll call him Mike Adams (not his name, but an acronym), also liked a subsidiary we were shepherding more than our basic business.

Mike Adams, after our second board meeting, privately encouraged me to merge with another company. He set up a meeting with an investment bank that he knew. This bank, not a household name, ranked several brackets below anyone we had dealt with. Their officers wore gold chains and pinky rings. Mike Adams (not his real name) assured me that the merger partner was approaching break-even cash flow. His classless investment bank said the public would lap up our stock after merging.

Mike Adams introduced me to the CEO of the proposed merger. This gentleman turned out to be a friend of Adams'. And it seems Mike had some financial connection in our proposed merger partner.

I declined the merger. The proposed partner entered bankruptcy 70 days later.

Okay, fiscal malfeasance. Slam dunk. Near fraud. One ticket to the Graybar Hotel's white-collar wing. Except Mike Adams had been smart enough to lobby me directly, and relentlessly, without mentioning a word to anybody else on the board. He wanted this merger to be my idea if it happened.

I had been stupid enough to kill the idea, without exposing Mike Adams' behavior to his fellow directors, those who would have suffered while he gained. Dumber yet, I never mentioned it later to any board members. They took their monthly seats alongside this reptile, unbeknownst.

Repeat after me, boards of directors are political. Totally. I thought handling this issue directly with Mike Adams was the thing to do. Wrong. Naiveté is not blessed. Pure and direct actions breed toxic results in a political environment. Mother Teresa would have made a lousy cop and you wouldn't want to live on her beat. Great lady. Bad cop.

Soon after, Mike Adams agreed to become chairman of our subsidiary that he liked so much, in exchange for 5% of its stock.

This was proposed in a board meeting by one of the directors who had promoted taking Mike's smaller amount at the higher price, thereby pulling in the eastern money at a premium valuation. Hmm.

I watched that happen in a board meeting that I ran. It didn't strike me until two years later that perhaps these folks chatted ahead of time, and perhaps a quid pro quo took place, and was formalized right under my gavel. Maybe, maybe not.

So Adams chaired the subsidiary and requested I stay hands-off for several months. His new CEO moved headquarters, hired two ad agencies, leased pricey space in three cities, while a large majority of the staff quit in his abrasive first two months and were replaced by higher-priced talent.

But it seemed okay since Mike Adams told the board we would get an offer from a midwestern firm to invest in this subsidiary at a valuation roughly 10× our investment. Soon. Happy days.

It never happened. The service being oversold wasn't working. I asked Adams to step aside, fired the CEO, and stripped back the expenses. We limped along and sold the business a year later for less than one half of a poorly written song, never quite escaping its tarnished history.

Oh, by the way, a few companies who survived this same space were selling for 20× what we got within a year. Premature ejaculation from our adolescent director.

Meanwhile, since we didn't have the planned funding for the main business, cash was drawing low. My managers asked if they could work without pay in exchange for more stock options. Good idea. Great attitudes.

I put together a package for our two-man compensation committee to consider. They approved it the same day, one by email reply and the other with a signed fax.

The financing got closer. Management went without pay for a couple of months. We received a term sheet.

I turned over the next board meeting to our CFO to run, the only meeting I missed in five years, so I could close a final investment that day on the east coast.

Mistake. Mike Adams disrupted the meeting, shouting about management's abuse of the investors, among other things. Remember, now, that his shares were jumping in value, including the dilution caused by management options, which barely affected the increase. His shares grew in paper value by 5× in two years.

So Mike Adams seized the moment. The compensation committee actually backed down and promised to renegotiate management's option with me when I returned. This compensation committee, of course, were two of the same three directors that decided to take his teeny investment at the higher price, forcing us to raise money prematurely.

I declined the compensation committee's suggestion that we give up our options, but reminded them that the board enjoyed the complete freedom to fire one or any of us anytime they felt we were overpaid or underdelivering, and that we wouldn't respect them unless they did so.

Testy moment.

And you see, if I had allowed the stink around Adams to waft across the other directors' nostrils, ahead of time, for his secret attempt to merge with his dying company, and for later trying to divert our cash to the subsidiary that he was granted more ownership of, well, his attempts to rile the board would have met with quizzical smiles and mutely arched eyebrows. I should've done that. And the act would have been best done without his knowing I did it, so open hostility didn't make the board dysfunctional. Better it be mute smiles and quizzical eyebrows voting him down without his understanding why.

But this is how boards work. And like democracy, a board is a terribly cumbersome system that merely happens to be better than any alternative, so recognize what they are, not that ideal that they could never really be anyway. So we closed the round at a healthy increase in value and management kept their options.

Wouldn't you know it, a neighboring company's CEO approached me almost immediately with a suggestion that we merge. There was no fit. Nada. This neighboring CEO, however, was funded by, you guessed it, Mike Adams. It seems Adams held a larger percent of this other outfit. And it seemed the instant we got a nickel, Mike devised a scheme to get at it. The merger proposal was such a misfit I didn't even bring it up to the board, and neither did the neighboring CEO. In a supremely naive nonaction, I didn't mention this transgression of Mike Adams' to the board, but just told him to knock it off or I would.

At this same moment, the public markets heated. DLJ, Salomon Smith Barney, and Bear Stearns teamed to take us public and we filed with the SEC.

Along the way, two new investors surfaced, spontaneously, and asked to put in $20 million at yet a higher price. We said yes. One of them requested that I get a Key Man Life Insurance Policy to protect their investment.

I failed the physical. Seven-day weeks had pumped up my blood pressure, so I took some medication to normalize it. Problem was, that made me woozy. But that made me insurable, at a premium price, so we bought that policy and deposited their $20 million.

In the longest library list of desired characteristics for a CEO, however, woozy just never makes it. It was time to go.

The IPO market tanked meanwhile, but we had an unbelievable pile of cash so it hardly mattered. I hired a search firm and told the board to replace me.

In preparing for the IPO, several inside directors were asked to resign and did. We recruited some terrific outside talent. I asked Mike Adams to leave as part of this changeover, but he was the only one who refused. The others held much larger blocs of stock, but agreed that it was in the company's interest to recruit outside directors with less self-interested resumes.

And other than Mike Adams, we looked terrific as a board. All of them except Adams were of greater professional accomplishment, educational backgrounds, and self-generated wealth than myself. And I am hardly prone to modesty.

So we were wallowing in cash, I was unfit for battle, and, in a significant problem, some marketing partnerships we signed up were failing. Time for a quick shift.

Now, Mike Adams had seen our management plunge through this before. In a carbon-copy moment, two years earlier, just after he invested, a series of channel contracts failed to produce. Tough moment. So we laid off 30% of the payroll and redirected the business. Cancelled a bunch of contracts. This took all of sixty days. And the stock became worth more the following year and 5× more the next year. Stumble. Recovery. Part of a startup.

One difference this time, however, was that the financial markets were collapsing, bad news, but the company had a pile of cash, good news. My blood pressure problem was the wild card, since the new board joined for options with me as the CEO and the presumption of an IPO. And the new board didn't have the history of seeing the company hit a wall like this and rebound.

They were ready to panic. Another problem, ironically, was this board was so good that they were all focused by bigger things in their other lives than our business, and didn't want to be distracted.

So Mike Adams' next activity was to agitate the board for my earliest departure.

This was fair. More than fair, barely arguable, I'd say, except it left only two directors with over a year's time with the business, Mike Adams and an original investor, neither with operating experience but both with time on their hands. And this Chief Woozy Officer had a physical problem and wasn't battle-ready.

What wasn't so bright was that Mike Adams didn't just lobby the directors, he sent blind carbon copies to major investors who weren't on the board. This upset them and they tipped me off.

Rather disruptive, that.

About blind carbon copies, I've not yet sent one in this lifetime and don't plan to in the next. A blind carbon copy seems to reveal more about the character of the sender than anything the content could ever reveal, don't you think?

Anyway, what also happens here is that, in times of turbulence, the least busy directors swing the most weight. He or she has time. Others don't. Least busy may not be the best criteria for leadership, but that's how it happens on boards if you haven't nailed down your own agenda. There's also this other thing that happens: When a director is "between opportunities" he or she will give your business far more attention than it requires, positioning themselves for a spot when you trip. And they'll sprinkle banana peels before you.

Adams succeeded in putting in a crony of his as interim; the same guy who previously approached us about a merger. His crony posed as uninterested in the job, but posted it on his web site before he started and forgot that he had sent me his resume earlier. A collection of CEO candidate resumes I had collected, forty-four in all, disappeared from the email files, somehow, the day after I left.

Scotland Yard couldn't have figured out who deleted those resumes, because the day I left, I sent the executive staff my passwords for phone messages and email. Adams' crony met with the executive staff and they agreed the CFO would scan my email and voice messages daily, decide which were company and which were personal, and pass them on appropriately.

A reasonable thing.

Adams' crony, however, after leading that meeting, slithered down into the operations cubicles, talked to a low-ranking worker and had him divert all emails to himself before the CFO saw them, and suggested it was unnecessary to mention this to anybody.

A less reasonable thing, I would posit, unless the business was questionable or had hints of fraud, and a touch embarrassing if everybody found out. And everybody found out. The interim, Adams' crony, noticeably less bright than a rusty nail, began answering some of my emails, which of course uncovered his covert activity on day one.

Remember, this happened under the direction of my handpicked board, a truly world-class bunch. It goes to show you how badly I failed by allowing this one ethically challenged director to remain lurking. It shows how a group of new directors, lured by stock options for a company about to go public, turn off their brains four seconds after the IPO is withdrawn.

You can't blame them. They were joining for a different ride and some gains on their options before the market tanked. That's reasonable motivation for talented folks to join a board. Anybody who's eager to join your board in other circumstances will be a lousy director, because there's such little rational reason for joining any board. Signing up then proves they're dumb. The status is hollow and the liabilities real, and if you do it right you don't control much, so why would you join?

I told a couple directors, far too late, about a couple of Mike Adams' misdeeds. Adams resigned but his crony ran the search. A chaotic search for the permanent CEO, if there is such a thing, was completed.

How's he? Time will tell. The committee didn't check references. Sigh. They let the recruiter do that. Sort of like asking your barber if you need a haircut; the answer's reasonably predictable.

I was gone. But I couldn't resist and checked a reference. Don't ask. Well, okay, have you ever had a publicly held company tell you, in writing, to not hire an ex-employee of theirs? And divulge that his sales claims were for clients that didn't exist? In writing?

Well, that's what I got with calls.

Euphoric, I guess—with all the cash raised, the board decided to spend faster, so the new CEO's salary more than tripled my highest rate. That's aggressive. They paid his utility bills. Go figure. They leased a house for him, I kid you not. And while prior practice allowed no company cars, the board leased a luxury model for him with expenses to burn. I never knew other contract details, but just to build respect among the executives, he announced that his contract required such hefty cancellation clauses that the board couldn't afford to ever remove him.

That inspired the troops. In his tenure, the fellow had trouble getting to work by 9:00 A.M. and couldn't stay beyond 6:00 P.M., but assigned a staffer to turn off his office lights and lock his doors a couple hours later for appearance's sake. That fooled everybody.

In this descent into madness, Adams' crony was put on the board in Adams' place. And a cynic might suggest he was positioning himself to step back in should the new leader stumble, which seemed a fairly safe bet. Adams announced that his crony was joining his firm, which, given the size of their fund, would have only mildly overstaffed it, but that made him seem less interested in what he was interested in.

Adams, his crony, and the other holdover director, who had time on his hands, had set the perks and salary high enough to make it a plum for salary-suckers, and the pile of cash I raised still pushed up the ceiling tiles, but began to shrink.

Let me say one more time that every director, except Adams, had graduate degrees from prestigious schools. Every director had experience creating or sitting on public company boards. Every director except Adams had two commas on their W-2s, and more wealth from stocks they created than from mere paychecks.

Anyway, one of the company's executives seemed to arise above the others in this turmoil. Mike Adams and his crony instantly tried to recruit him for another business.

Right. You guessed it. Mike Adams' firm was a dominant investor in that other business. A cynic might suggest they're both stealing any talent they see from a company in which they have little equity for a company they have more ownership of, and, in the process, making it easier to move back into my alma mater where there was more money. But I'm not a cynic, so I would never say that.

Please remember that this whole comedy stemmed from my failure to squeeze out or isolate an ethically challenged director. And the director who moved in to chair the business had just transitioned out of his investment partnership, so was looking for something to do and psychologically needed an office, which he got. Even though he and Mike Adams despised each other, they teamed up in this restructuring, gave Adams' crony the job he lusted for until he shot himself in the foot with abuses, and together they then recruited a CEO with bad references and overpaid him.

Let's be fair. Maybe all this is my sour grapes. We've all seen many CEOs without the grace to wish their successors well. All I can say is that I had more personal money invested in this deal than anybody, that my net worth was well below that of the other directors and investors on average, and so I, more than anybody, wanted it to work.

But that doesn't guarantee my rationality. So perhaps the new CEO would show us a different facet with his leadership.

Let's examine his first hire. After hearing the announcement of this new CEO's first draft, I did what the employees suggested and entered this new officer's name as a key word in a Web search and found him.

There was a posting of him as an officer at his prior employer's web site.

There was an article from the March 6 *Herald* quoting him. "The Dallas County Sheriff's officers arrived without warning," the newspaper reported, "on a warm spring morning six weeks ago at the headquarters . . ." and goes on to describe the shutdown of a fraudulent business.

"The news came like a thunderbolt to the company's chief financial officer," and they name our new hire, "who had gone on holiday just two days before with no inkling that there was a financial crisis pending. 'I knew nothing of that judgment,' he said, 'I now realize that there was a lot of information that was kept from me . . . I am very angry about this.' "

Hmm. Do you suppose the next banker might do a Web search before financing our business?

Why lay this soap opera on you? It's important you understand how disastrous mismanaging a board can be, and it's an entirely different style. It's also good therapy to vent.

I didn't mention the news article to anybody, there was no need, everybody knew about it. I did mention the comments I got on the new CEO which caused a momentary stir with the chairman, but it's unclear whether he told the rest of the board. The CEO did have the lawyers send me a letter, saying any attempt to check his references would be an invasion of his privacy.

Right.

And the only reason I so easily got references on his nonperformance at a prior employer, a place where he claimed to have been vice president of a group that didn't exist, was simple. One of my better friends from college was the founder, and it turns out he'd never heard of the guy. Call me a troublemaker.

I couldn't make this stuff up. And hang on, I'm not just trying to weave an interesting story; there are some points to be made out of all this. They follow.

This board was made up of people who had private planes, sat on many other boards that were far larger, which may be another part of the problem, by the way, and every last one except possibly Adams were magnitudes wealthier than I from noninherited accomplishments and inarguably better educated. And, gulp, every one was younger than I.

Oh, that Mike Adams acronym? Made it up myself. **M**y **I**nstincts **K**ill **E**quity. That's where I got **MIKE**. Hey! Can you allow me to be childish just this once? Mike Adams bruised a business within one year, a business with a nice supply of cash. And he didn't do that alone; it required help from his crony, then from the worst executive search process done in the history of western civilization, abetted by another director with spare time and no operating experience.

Always **D**ivert **A**ny **M**oney **S**omehow. And there's **ADAMS**.

My tone here is a tacit admission of embarrassment at mishandling these boards, and the painful results show. It's a skill I have not mastered nor even been introduced to. For companies to excel, the CEO must be able to deal professionally with the board. Fortunately for more socially challenged CEOs like myself, turnarounds offer some refuge from that practice.

In our last case, Mike Adams had proclaimed the business to be worth $500 million in my last stormy board meeting, when he killed my attempt to sell at a starting point of $350 million.

The company still exists, and nothing would delight me more than to see the business explode with success, making every implication of this chapter wrong in the longer term.

It's a pleasure to report the new CEO was fired within five months, and the board members who recruited him resigned. It's frustrating that so much time was lost, and the fault was more mine than anybody's.

The company still has lots of cash at this writing, and a new executive team that I introduced to the board. This lame duck shareholder had one quack left.

Boards need coddling in normal times. If you don't, the company wobbles. That's the way it is. They're ill-prepared to manage, only to advise.

Boards are only there for the big moments. You guide them and they know they're being guided. When things go awry, they'll make the big moves and change the CEO.

You must remove schizoid and underemployed directors. The smaller their world, the more time they have to disrupt in turbulent times.

You must work the directors individually outside of board meetings, so that any votes are predetermined. If they're busy, and pray that they are, they appreciate advance preparation. They're big boys (and girls) and understand exactly what you're doing and can cope with that just fine.

But you see this is board management in normal times. And what they are used to.

In a turnaround, you simply don't have time to handhold directors. They won't want involvement until the business starts to revive anyway, when you'll see several of them volunteering to pile on.

What you must do in a turnaround is diagnose the business first. Then you'll know if you even want to take it on, and have a generalized idea of how you'll try to fix it. This is key. The best heart surgeons know how to pick patients, and their percentages just keep getting better.

But it's also critical for the directors. Your diagnosis gives them your roadmap. They must have that before you start. They were there when things went wrong, so they're not quite heroes, but since you're invited to look, they are doing the heroic thing now and hopefully in time.

I hereby give you the right to Xerox this chapter, free from copyright violations. (This chapter only, c'mon, give me and Wiley Publishing a break; you'll spend too much time copying other chapters anyway. Buy more copies.)

If it helps, hand a copy of this expert advice to the directors as part of your reasoning for requiring abnormally strong independence during the turnaround. Your replacement will bring back the normal interaction with the board, once cash flow is restored.

Sign a contract that allows for a weekly meeting of an hour or two for the first month, casual, no preparation, no more contact than that. Go to monthly meetings of two hours for months two through six. If the board is comfortable, ask them to assign a single point of contact. Make your contract specific on those terms.

Don't change the board. They're responsible and a few will leave out of fear. But they do have some history, and you certainly don't understand enough yet to explain the business to a gaggle of new directors. And anybody who would join now is not likely to have an IQ stretching much above room temperature.

My first turnaround contract required the controlling owner to leave the building and never come back without asking permission. He never asked. Board meetings were to be held only if and when I called them. I never did, we just had the lawyers create minutes for the single, legally required annual meeting.

Those owners saw the first money they'd ever experienced from this company, and lots of it.

My second turnaround specified one phone call per week of an hour or less, going to one visit per month after the first. That turnaround went so well they tried to extend my contract. I agreed to, but only if we could drop my pay by 50% per month for the first added month, then double it every month after. That gave them plenty of incentive to get serious about the CEO search that was under way, without abuse.

Should you end up running a conventional business, with profits and cash flows and all those lovelies, remember to work the house. Talk to board members individually. Make sure every vote is predetermined. That's part of the theater, and a good play it can be.

Understand the difference between new directors and old. In the situation just described, a group of normally, historically, and generally professional directors turned into the Keystone Kops. Take another exceptional group of directors, recruit them with options, have the market tank, the CEO bail out, and marketing agreements fail to produce, and guess what? History repeats.

I failed to tutor my new board. I was distracted by the pending IPO and a bit woozy from the pills. If you're good at turnarounds, you probably don't have the patience for the proper care and feeding of a board.

That's why the central theme of this book is a management change for the turnaround, and a second management change after the Six-Month Fix. Different styles. Different leaders.

(A note for you geezer CEOs: High blood pressure is a thing to watch for, and beatable. Humor the doctor and let them put you on pills. But quit your job, work out harder, and lose some weight. When the action described above took place, I was put on 20 mg of Lotensin which was stepped up to 40 mg with little effect, and had readings as high as 170/120. One year later, after leaving, dropping twenty pounds, and competing in a triathlon, the medication was cut in half and the numbers hit 105/80 and dropping. In that time I joined five boards, wrote this, plus a novel, and started a company, so the change wasn't total. You've got to take charge and do this before your doctor will believe you—too many patients don't—and then you can be weaned from the drugs, which is a good thing.)

CHAPTER 67

SHAREHOLDERS ONLY

Well-intentioned fuzz-brains are confusing corporations. You see this in diversity creeping into annual reports and mission statements.

"Consolidated Widgets' mission is to provide superior products at fair prices to our customers, support the communities we operate in as a good citizen, and provide challenging work to our employees while delivering great returns to our shareholders."

Bunk.

And by trying to put a chip on every square, there's no chance of gain, let alone having anyone remember what the message was.

You exist for one thing. You exist to provide superior returns to the shareholders.

Say so. Don't quibble. Make your employees all shareholders so you get rid of any possible conflict there. Realize that no business which delivers bad product serves its shareholders well. At least not for long. And the communities do just fine when you make profits so you can pay taxes and make some donations to local charities.

Ever notice who the best corporate citizens are? Right. The utilities and phone companies, at least they were prior to deregulation. They gave $100,000 to the local symphony each year and passed along $200,000 to you in their monthly bills, sending part of the markup to the politicians, insuring that no nasty things like competitive pricing came along. Don't get confused about this.

You use roads, you're protected by the military (we hope), and while public schools are sinking into a black hole, in some places you can still use them. Make a profit. That way you pay taxes to cover these things and the cops who work hard for less respect than they deserve and the firefighters who don't have anything to do anymore with better construction materials, so they have time to lobby for bigger budgets and create calendars and cookbooks, but that's a different subject about how things work. And it dilutes my point.

Make a profit for the shareholders. Employees benefit. Customers must as well, or you die. Communities are covered by the occasional donation, some time off for workers who want to help, and the taxes you then pay.

And every time someone arches their nose while telling you they work for a not-for-profit organization tell them you're proud to be paying for their share of the tax burden.

If you've read this book in the proper sequence, you're approaching profits now and there's a temptation to get stupid. Don't lose your direction already. The only purpose of your business, now that you've passed survival, is to generate even more profits. Period. Absent that, all those other warm and fuzzy thoughts go empty, so keep stressing profits without shame.

CHAPTER 68

AUTHOR'S TRACK RECORD

I t's time to let you in on a nasty little secret. You paid more for this book than the ink, glue, and paper cost. Much more.

C'mon, now, you wouldn't respect me or the theme of this book if we didn't hustle you for a buck, would you? But under the assumption that there's some value in the ideas conveyed, we early on suggested you should know a bit about the author before accepting the ideas.

What I'll give here is every measured result for the twenty years prior to writing *The Six-Month Fix*. I had sixteen years of pretty noneventful chores prior to the twenty years documented, with two exceptions. One was championing the development of autofocus for Honeywell, a concept few would support. That cost $100K to develop and, as one of our chapters shows, yielded $500 million in royalties in 1993 alone.

Good idea. How much of that was great marketing and aggressive lawyering after my birthing, is a valid challenge to my claimed contribution.

The other worthwhile effort was being Marketing VP of Montron, a toy startup that was eventually acquired by Fisher-Price. The product innovations there were greater than the financial returns, but a guy's got to learn somehow.

So here's what I did, all of it, between 1980 and 2000. If you find stories in the book that don't seem to fit in here, and about half don't, that's because I've disguised many industries and locations to avoid embarrassment to some folks who are decent people but miscast in their business roles.

The following briefs have more detail on the web site, including CPA partners' names to document or SEC filings that support the outrageous claims.

1980–1986, CEO, US Press: 78% annually compounded operating profits via acquisition. 31% annually compounded operating profits internally. Erratic, however, due to leverage. Sold for 32× projected earnings. Revenue growth from $8 million to $90 million. Net earnings always above industry average but pulled down by interest expense. Infinite return since cash flows paid off all acquisition expense in the period.

1986–1989, CEO, Checks To-Go: Ten prior years of losses, became profitable in my first quarter and sold business to Rocky Mountain Banknote in eighteen months.

1989–1990, CEO, Smiley Industries: Reversed first year loss of 35% to a profit, barely, in the second quarter and sold to Precision Aerotech in the second year.

1990–1996, CEO, Knight Protective Industries: Delivered a 53× cash return to shareholders.

1996–2000, CEO, SkyDesk: Boosted valuation in five financings from $1.3 million at start to $240 million in 2000.

Those are the full-time CEO positions I held in the last twenty years. More detail is available at www.sixmonthfix.com. In that same period I held four part-time positions.

First was CEO of PopAD, a doomed retail advertising business in Hawaii. All I did here was extend the life of a bad idea.

Next was consulting to ALTO Waste, a garbage-hauling business, where my contributions were less than light.

Third was cofounder of Teledesic, and part-time ramrod for five years. This business went from an idea to a $3 billion dollar valuation within the decade, under money from AT&T, Bill Gates, Boeing, Craig McCaw, Motorola, the Crown Prince of Saudi Arabia, and others. Jury's still out.

Fourth was a director and ultimately chairman of Kelsey-Jenney Business College, a turnaround that worked well, going from 125 to 980 students, but I was never CEO.

CHAPTER 69

THE 31 STEPS THAT CONVERT BLEEDERS INTO WINNERS

Forgive me. I've resisted pleas for a magic formula, knowing none exist. But you've finally worn me down, so here are thirty-one steps to transform a money loser into a cash generator.

It'll never happen quite this way. No two are the same.

And until you've stared down bankruptcies, missed a few payrolls, kept your cool and prevailed, you cannot simply apply these rules. You need the presence of mind to know when to skip a step, change the sequence, push one that matters over another with less promise.

But being forced by never-ending requests for the checklist, here goes:

1. Survey the situation.

   As an outsider, you bring in a fresh perspective. Do this in one week, talking to trade editors, customers, employees, executives, and owners. Give the board your report the following week. If salvageable, give them a contract offer for the turnaround with your report.
2. If they buy it, you're a team. Now you can execute without the distraction of explaining every move to the board. If they don't buy it, better you part ways with only a week's time lost.

   Some businesses are terminal. If that's your feeling, the board has received the favor of this outside opinion. Anything they manage after that will feel like an accomplishment.

   With your proposal, if you see hope, give the board less than a week to discuss and sign your contract. If they take longer, they don't feel enough pain yet, or are dysfunctional. If you were brought in by a creditor, take your fat fees. If by a shareholder, split the payments between fees and equity.

If the board signs your contract, delay announcing it for several days. Use those days to meet with creditors and solicit their support before publicly committing. Let only the incumbent CEO know.

3. Renegotiate credit. Do this the first week. Make offers with short deadlines. Offer some warrants for debt reduction.

4. Meet with the executive staff. Calculate with them the approximate date that the doors will shut, given the current cost and revenue situation. Make sure every officer is involved in this meeting, push it into the evening. Help everyone believe that change, big change, is the only option.

Figure out that night how to let all employees and vendors know, and do it the next day.

If you're a charismatic type, also use this moment to renew commitment.

Here's how Shakespeare believed King Henry V spoke to his troops on the evening before the battle of Agincourt. The fight would begin on St. Crispin's Day, an English holiday. Henry's troops were on French soil, hungry, ill-equipped, and tired. The French numbered 60,000 to the English 12,000. Henry heard his cousin wishing for 10,000 more troops. He replied, with my translation, to all his commanders:

"Who wishes so?

"My cousin Westmoreland. No, my fair cousin.

"If we are marked to die, we are enough to do our country's loss. If to live, the fewer the men, the greater each share of honor.

"God's will, I pray, ask for not one man more.

"I care not who takes my gold for pay, or armor for battle.

"Such outward things dwell not in my desires.

"But if it's a sin to covet honor, then I am the most offensive soul alive.

"No, faith my cousin, wish not another man from England.

"God knows I would not lose so little an honor as one more arriving troop would take from me. For the best hope I have, oh, do not wish for one more.

"Rather proclaim it, Westmoreland, that he who has no stomach for this fight, depart. We will put coins in his purse and arrange his passage home.

"We would not die in that man's company . . . he who fears to die with us.

"The day is the Feast of Crispin.

"He who lives this day and comes safe home will stand on tip-toe, aroused, when the holiday is remembered. He will live to old age and yearly strip his sleeves on the Feast of Crispin to show the neighbors his scars.

"Old men forget. But he'll remember always his feats of this day. And our names shall be familiar forever to his mouth, Harry the King, Bedford and Exeter, Warwick and Talbot, Salisbury and Glouchester.

"All shall be remembered in their flowing cups.

"This story shall the good father teach his son. And the Feast of Crispin will never go by, from this day to the end of the world, but we in this battle shall be honored.

"We few, we happy few, we band of brothers . . . for he who sheds his blood here with me shall be my brother. This day shall enoble his status, and gentlemen now asleep in England shall think themselves cursed that they were not here. They shall lower their eyes while anyone speaks who fought here with us on the Feast of Crispin day."

10,000 French perished in the battle that followed while 520 English died. Now if you've never heard spontaneous applause while giving a presentation, this approach, or anything like it, is probably a bit over the top for you.

So, spend a few hours with the staff, going through your plan, changing it on the spot where they convince you, put it down in writing and ask everyone to sign it. Save that document for a celebration when cash flow reappears.

Plot the date for the return of cash flow. Explain to all that cash, nothing else, matters until the date that sustainable, positive cash flow returns. Look each in the eye, and explain not everybody will survive to enjoy that moment, but that your hopes are that everybody will try to stay for the fight.

5. Meet with creditors and explain the plan. Unions too, if there are any. Announce times for employees who want to hear more, after hours, in the lunchroom or your office or a conference room.

6. Take over the checkbook and sign checks for a few hours every week. You'll be amazed at what you see. This also keeps you angry enough to keep cutting costs.

7. Blow out all inventory. Sell everything at any price you can, without plugging distribution completely. Now you know what it was really worth.

8. Factor your accounts receivable. Push the collections group to knock several days off your receivables every month. Start by knocking a day off the first week. Then factor after the first two months of tighter collections.

9. Find where the gross margin is. If the books reveal that, terrific. But don't trust them. Listen to customer service activity, sales effort, and returns or cancels. Find out which services or products generate more than their fair share of overhead. Sit down then with accounting and show them where the margin is, and see if they don't agree.

10. Lay off people involved in the lower-margin areas. Lease or sell space and equipment related to those efforts. Allow 20% of the best employees in these spaces to transfer into the remaining areas, but terminate 20% in the businesses you'll keep, to make room without boosting expenses.

11. Renegotiate the union contracts and leases. Now's the best time.

12. Show the new cost basis to vendors, and get better terms.

13. Cut purchases. Stand on the loading dock door and see what's coming in. Force purchasing to squeeze pricing by a targeted amount each month, and have weekly meetings to insure they're on target.

14. Boost sales commissions and drop base salaries.

15. Give someone, somewhere, a raise for notable effort. Publicize their accomplishment (not the raise) in the company newsletter.

16. Tinker with a remaining, but marginal, product or service. Raise its price 10% and see what happens. If that fails, cut price by 20% but watch it very closely, and kill it if volume doesn't jump to recover margin.

17. Eliminate two development programs. Stretch the remaining effort.

18. Now start the CEO search. Six weeks have already passed, you understand the business a bit, so it's time.

19. Make one more cutback. Go deep enough that this will be the last.

20. Change your credit policy. Either tighten or loosen it. Make pricing and commission adjustments simultaneously, so internal effects are minimal.

21. Eliminate several problem customers.

22. Go back to the key creditors and try to renegotiate terms again.

23. Eliminate a problem territory.

24. Spend two weeks out of the second month making customer calls.

25. Adjust prices and volume discounts.

26. If cash is returning, offer to pay off a key vendor or creditor ahead of schedule, in exchange for a discount. Let other vendors and creditors

know. Don't ask them to do the same. One or two will approach you. Deal with them.

27. Launch internal competitions for best customer service and best cost savings. Personally make weekly awards of dinners or weekend trips with a plaque and photo in the company newsletter.

28. Have a company picnic. Spend time cooking the burgers or being the clown in the dunk tank or competing in the three-legged race.

29. Select a department or service to outsource. Do it.

30. Hire the new CEO.

31. Disappear. Leave the new CEO your phone number, just in case.

INDEX